Contributions to Management Science

The series *Contributions to Management Science* contains research publications in all fields of business and management science. These publications are primarily monographs and multiple author works containing new research results, and also feature selected conference-based publications are also considered. The focus of the series lies in presenting the development of latest theoretical and empirical research across different viewpoints.

This book series is indexed in Scopus.

More information about this series at http://www.springer.com/series/1505

Hannah Ulbrich • Marco Wedel •
Hans-Liudger Dienel
Editors

Internal Crowdsourcing in Companies

Theoretical Foundations and Practical Applications

Springer

Editors
Hannah Ulbrich
Institute for Vocational Education and Work Studies Department Work, Technology and Participation
Technische Universität Berlin
Berlin, Germany

Marco Wedel
Institute for Vocational Education and Work Studies Department Work, Technology and Participation
Technische Universität Berlin
Berlin, Germany

Hans-Liudger Dienel
Institute for Vocational Education and Work Studies Department Work, Technology and Participation
Technische Universität Berlin
Berlin, Germany

ISSN 1431-1941 ISSN 2197-716X (electronic)
Contributions to Management Science
ISBN 978-3-030-52880-5 ISBN 978-3-030-52881-2 (eBook)
https://doi.org/10.1007/978-3-030-52881-2

We acknowledge support by the Open Access Publication Fund of TU. Berlin
This book is an open access publication.

This Springer imprint is published by the registered company Springer Nature Switzerland AG.
The registered company address is: Gewerbestrasse 11, 6330 Cham, Switzerland

Acknowledgement

This publication has been enabled in affiliation with Technische Universität Berlin. We acknowledge the support of the Open Access Publication Fund of TU Berlin.

The underlying research and development project was funded by the German Federal Ministry of Education and Research (BMBF) and the European Social Fund (ESF) under the 'Future of Work' programme and implemented by the Project Management Agency Karlsruhe (PTKA). The authors are responsible for the content of this publication.

Contents

Introduction to Internal Crowdsourcing: Theoretical Foundations and Practical Applications

Hannah Ulbrich, Marco Wedel, and Hans-Liudger Dienel

The research landscape in the area of forecasting and assessing working conditions has become increasingly difficult to understand. There are plenty of identified reasons, drivers and catchwords to describe a systemic transformation. Individual- and subject-specific approaches to describe and understand the changes to work are being developed in almost every scientific discipline, as well as by (economic) associations and actors in the sociopolitical spheres. Despite all complexity and contradictions, 'digitalization' seems to be one focal point when it comes to identifying independent variables to explain the 'future of work'. The corresponding discussions, analyses, recommendations and scenarios can be found under the well-known headings 'Work 4.0', 'Industry 4.0', 'Education 4.0', 'Society 4.0', etc. In addition to systemic descriptions, oftentimes dominated by economics and business management approaches, there are changing individual, subject-inherent perceptual understandings indicating a change in social values with regard to work and its function. Ultimately, for the majority of the population and the (welfare) state, work remains the necessary prerequisite for financially securing their livelihoods.

This brief contextualization shows the burdensome complexity of the overall research field. Bearing this complexity in mind, when seeking to approach the topic in a constructive way, it is neither meaningful nor possible to choose research foci that try to understand *the* digitalization of work. To avoid banality and generalizations, it is important to differentiate within the overall subject matter and arrive at concise and manageable research subjects.

H. Ulbrich (✉) · M. Wedel
Technische Universität Berlin, Institute for Vocational Education and Work Studies, Berlin, Germany
e-mail: hannah.ulbrich@tu-berlin.de; marco.wedel@tu-berlin.de

H.-L. Dienel
Technische Universität Berlin, Center for Technology and Society, Berlin, Germany
e-mail: dienel@ztg.tu-berlin.de

H. Ulbrich et al. (eds.), *Internal Crowdsourcing in Companies*, Contributions to Management Science, https://doi.org/10.1007/978-3-030-52881-2_1

Such an approach has been instigated by the German Federal Ministry of Education and Research (Bundesministerium für Bildung und Forschung—BMBF). At the beginning of 2015, the Ministry announced guidelines for funding measures with the research focus 'work in the digitalized world' within the framework of the R&D programme 'the Future of Work' as part of the umbrella programme 'Innovations for Tomorrow's Production, Services and Work'. The initially broad aim has been to explore the possibilities of digital technologies and to develop and disseminate solutions for working in the digital world. The resulting research programme 'Transformation of Work Through Digitalization' (TransWork) declared that its central goal would be to examine the effects of digital technologies on employment and labour markets, health protection and business organization and to develop and disseminate approaches to solutions for working in the digital world. Respective research projects where expected with the aim of analysing and evaluating current research fields in the design of work (competence development, mastering complexity, productivity management and the design and regulation of work) and changes brought about by digitization while disseminating examples of designs for 'good work' for specific target groups (BMBF 2015; TransWork 2017).

To narrow down this still broad approach, five focus groups consisting of individual research projects have been created: 'Assistance Systems and Competence Development', 'Project and Team Work in the Digitalized Working World', 'Productivity Management', 'Work Design in the Process of Digital Change' and 'Designing Work-Networks and Flexibility' (TransWork 2017).

The research project 'Internal Crowdsourcing in Companies' (**I**nternes **C**rowdsourcing in **U**nternehmen—ICU) has been selected as part of the latter focus group. Its overall goal is to research approaches as to how good humane work can succeed under the changed conditions of network-bound, temporally and locally flexible work. The phenomenon of Internal Crowdsourcing in that context represents a concise and manageable research subject to inform reliable hypotheses on the digitalization of work with respect to the social component of sociotechnical systems (human-machine interaction is not the focus; machine-machine interaction is not meant). While the role and influence of Internal Crowdsourcing in the context of the digitalization of working environments is neither empirically nor theoretically well understood, ICU has been designed to lay down some initial theoretical foundations and foster an understanding of practical applications for an ongoing discussion.

1 About the Research Project 'Internal Crowdsourcing in Companies' (ICU)

> Internal Crowdsourcing refers to the firm extending its problem-solving to a large and diverse group of self-selected contributors beyond the formal internal boundaries of a large firm; across business divisions, bridging geographic locations, levelling hierarchical structures. (Elin Byrèn 2013, p. 4)

The basic idea of Internal Crowdsourcing is to mobilize and strengthen the internal exchange of knowledge and interaction within the company. The process is intended to directly promote problem-solving capacities through cross-departmental and interdisciplinary thinking and collaborative action skills for cooperation between employees and between management and employees. Existing knowledge, both explicit, but above all also person-related implicit technical and experiential knowledge, the so-called sticky knowledge, can be quickly accessed within the company through the application of Internal Crowdsourcing and used to develop solutions, processes and decisions. By testing new communication and collaboration possibilities at low thresholds, in particular, Internal Crowdsourcing can make an important contribution towards an employee-friendly and more agile corporate culture for the digitalized working world. It touches upon aspects such as growing demands for participation by and of employees, the desire for flatter hierarchies including cross-company and cross-divisional communication channels, agile and modern working methods and organization, demands for the stronger democratization of companies as well as a basic corporate capability to survive in the working world of the twenty-first century (Industry 4.0, Work 4.0, Economy 4.0, etc.). Since IC changes or supplements the cross-company and cross-divisional communication possibilities, it creates new work and interaction spaces and enables the digital integration of employees while opening up space for design and experimentation with respect to the future organization of work.

While the above clearly hints at one potential for Internal Crowdsourcing to serve as a catalyst for establishing a digital working culture, it is astonishing that IC, both in research and in practice, has almost exclusively been treated as yet another tool for innovation management (Keinz 2015; Zhu et al. 2014, 2016; Zuchowski et al. 2016). Within the framework of the research project 'Internal Crowdsourcing in Companies' (ICU), that lens has been broadened for the first time by arriving at the well-founded assumption that the method has further potential for use beyond its innovation-generating character, namely, for employee participation on the one hand and for employee qualification on the other.

1.1 Employee Participation

As an instrument for digital employee participation, Internal Crowdsourcing can give employees the opportunity to participate at different levels of the company. They are given the opportunity to contribute their personal experience and knowledge in the form of suggestions and ideas with regard to company processes and to help shape the working environment in a constructive manner. Through the technical mediation of the process, Internal Crowdsourcing achieves a high reach with little effort and opens up a fast and direct channel of communication within the company. In principle, employee participation, among other factors, contributes to a working atmosphere based on appreciation and recognition for all involved.

1.2 Employee Qualification

In order to prepare employees for the new requirements presented by the ongoing digitalization in everyday work and to qualify them for new activities that arise in this context, companies must find new ways and measures to open up internal career development opportunities. Particularly since the introduction of the 'European Qualifications Framework' in 2008, there has been a recognizable shift in the academic and practice-relevant specialist debates from the 'hard' facts of qualifications certificates to the 'soft' indicators of abilities, skills and knowledge, i.e. competences. Although qualifications have of course lost none of their importance as a necessary indication of existing vocational skills, it is clear that they do not represent a guarantee that these skills will be implemented in practice. The competence approach has also been adapted in corporate practice, e.g. in connection with procedures for filling vacancies internally. In order to assess the actual 'skills' of employees who have already been hired, formal qualifications are usually of secondary importance, with an employee's competence profile being more meaningful. Furthermore, assessing competence in the company can also pursue the goal of determining the need for further training or of evaluating the learning situation as a prerequisite for independent/self-organized learning processes and for the necessary learning support (Metzger 2016, p. 10; Wegerich 2015; Melzer et al. 2019, p. 11).

Of course, the potential for product, service or process innovation through IC remains very high and should not be neglected as an important part of Internal Crowdsourcing.

1.3 Project Objectives and Methodical Approach

Against this background, the goal of the ICU research project has been to develop a cross-industry model in a multistage, iterative process that would serve as a reference case for good practice that is useful for future crowdsourcing activities. This so-called ICU model is composed of a process designed specifically for Internal Crowdsourcing, which, in addition to innovation management, strategically addresses the dimensions of employee participation and employee qualification, a process management system and an IC platform.

Based on analyses of operational IC implementations, scientific research and practical experience, a basic model was first designed and implemented as a pilot at the company collaboration partner within the project, the energy service provider GASAG AG (first iteration). This model has since then been optimized and transformed into the GASAG good practice example (second iteration). A cross-industry reference model has been developed based on the good practice example, the main features of which will be presented in this book.

The focus in the development process has been the employee-oriented design of the application of Internal Crowdsourcing. In order to take into account the different demands involved, we have applied a participatory approach to develop the ICU model together with all relevant stakeholders (employees/management and works council) and with the active support of the union to ensure proper consideration of the legal and political framework for the process. Furthermore, the guidelines for good digital work of the Enquete Commission Internet and Digital Society (2013) and the guidelines for good digital work of the DGB (2014) were also taken into account. By maintaining legal and social working standards, the aim has been to create a future-oriented and sustainable working environment as well as a better quality of work in the digitalized world.

The ICU model has been designed to primarily address companies that need orientation in their individual transformation process and are interested in using digital processes to mobilize their potential internal knowledgebase as well as existing competencies. Therefore, the practical experiences of digital champions, large RD&D avers corporations and agile start-ups did not serve as a benchmark for the project but merely as an aspiration during the development process. According to a study on innovation in German companies (Pohlisch 2019) conducted as part of the project, the industry partner GASAG AG very much represents this cross-section of German SMEs in view of the challenges for competitiveness in the context of digitalization. With regard to innovation activities, though energy providers have below-average quotas, they are nonetheless exposed to strong adaptational pressure against the backdrop of the far-reaching upheavals taking place within the German and European energy system (Pohlisch 2019; Wedel 2016). Thus, the GASAG AG qualifies as a valid example with regard to the necessity of implementing innovation-facilitating procedures to ensure success and competitiveness and represents the ideal application case for the project objectives.

1.4 Project Partners

Technical University of Berlin: Department of Vocational Education/Technology and Participation/Institute of Vocational Education and Work Studies (Fachgebiet Arbeitslehre/Technik und Partizipation/Institut für Berufliche Bildung und Arbeitslehre)

The Institute of Vocational Education and Work Studies at the Technical University of Berlin has existed since the year 2000 and is composed of the Department of Technical Didactics of the Vocational Disciplines and Work Studies, the Department of Vocational Education/Technology and Participation and the Department of Economic Education and Sustainable Consumption. The Department of Vocational Education/Technology and Participation has three main areas of research:

- In the field 'technology and participation', participative methods that involve school pupils, customers and citizens in the process to develop new technological products and services are being evolved. This participative product development is still in its infancy. New methods of political citizens' participation in the development of technology are being translated.

- In the field 'technology and education', definitions and images of technology are being developed, knowledge and abilities are being compared, and new understandings of technology are being applied in WAT lessons as well as more generally to technological education.
- In the field 'future of technology', historic and present visions of technology are being compared, and sustainable scenarios and models are being developed, in order to contribute these to future applied academic research.

Technical University of Berlin: Quality and Usability Lab/ Institute of Software Engineering and Theoretical Computer Science (Quality and Usability Lab: Institut für Softwaretechnik und Theoretische Informatik)

The Quality and Usability Lab offers courses on three layers: technology, interaction design and user. In the Quality and Usability Lab, students in electrical engineering, information technology and computer science learn to estimate the effects of the systems they develop on the user and are excellently prepared for interdisciplinary cooperation. Our long-term goals are to develop methods for measuring the quality and usability of information and communication technology, to establish a relationship between quality and usability and the technical characteristics of the systems and services, to derive guidelines for system and service design on that basis, to predict quality and usability-based system characteristics and to implement the described methods in the cycle of specification, planning, design, implementation, optimization and monitoring of new systems and services. We apply these principles, for example, to systems for transmitting speech, audio and video signals (telephony, voice-over-IP, radio, IP-based-television, telephone conferences, etc.), multimodal human-machine interaction (spoken dialogue systems, web-based services, multimodal dialogue systems, etc.), as well as—in a broader sense—all systems enabling multimodal interaction between humans, machines and the environment (virtual environments, augmented environments, context-sensitive systems, etc.).

Technical University of Berlin: Department of Innovation Economics, Institute for Technology and Management (Fachgebiet Innovationsökonomik: Institut für Technologie und Management)

The Department of Innovation Economics at the Institute for Technology and Management in the Faculty of Economics and Management at the Technical University Berlin has been headed by Prof. Knut Blind since 2006. Prof. Blind is also responsible for the innovation and regulation business unit at the Fraunhofer Institute for Systems and Innovation Research. In our teaching, we focus on the field of tension between theoretical models of innovation economics and their empirical application, alternating between prospects of economics and business studies. Our research covers a broad range of questions, especially relating to the influence that different institutional frameworks have on various forms of innovation. More specifically, our work includes the fields of standardization, intellectual property rights, regulation (e.g. concerning environmental, labour market or public procurement issues), open innovation, peer innovation and open source. Our mission is to foster responsible innovation research towards the achievement of the Sustainable Development Goals. The Department's research is spread within the global scientific community among policymakers, business representatives and civil society. The Department is an open platform connecting international researchers, students and practitioners.

Institute for Future Studies and Technology Assessment (Institut für Zukunftsstudien und Technologiebewertung)

The Institute for Future Studies and Technology Assessment is an interdisciplinary research and consulting institute. Future-oriented studies with long-term social significance and providing support to decision-makers in the areas of business, politics and society by contributing practical knowledge are the goals of the institute. In doing so, the Institute for Future Studies and Technology Assessment is committed to the principle of sustainable development. Future research and scenario building, the analysis and promotion of new technologies as well as the assessment and evaluation of their economic, political, ecological and social consequences are the main focuses of the Institute for Future Studies and Technology Assessment's work. Last but not least, the Institute for Future Studies and Technology Assessment stands for inter- and transdisciplinary future research as well as implementation orientation, participation and stakeholder integration.

GASAG Group

Founded in 1847 in Berlin/Germany, the GASAG Group today is a modern, nationwide energy service provider whose range of services has long since expanded beyond electricity and natural gas. The group of companies is intensively engaged in innovative technologies and is driving the expansion of renewable energy. It demonstrates this commitment with products such as the 'EcoPool' virtual power plant, energy solutions for entire neighbourhoods and comprehensive energy consulting. In contracting and bio-natural gas solutions, the GASAG Group is the market leader in the capital region and continues to provide impetus for the energy revolution along the entire energy process chain. For several years, the GASAG Group has been producing eco-electricity and biomethane in its own plants, the number of which it expanded for the first time in 2016 with a wind farm in Brandenburg.

Social Technology Design Forum at the German Trade Union Confederation (DGB) in the District of Baden-Württemberg (Forum Soziale Technikgestaltung beim DGB Baden-Württemberg)

The Social Technology Design Forum at the German Trade Union Confederation (DGB) in the Federal State of Baden-Württemberg was founded on 7 October 1991 in Stuttgart as a consultative network within the DGB for the Federal State of Baden-Württemberg and closely linked to various trade unions—in particular IG Metall, ver.di, IG BCE, GEW and DGB. The Social Technology Design Forum is an open network of more than 2900 men and women from works and staff councils, colleagues, shop stewards, employees, self-employed, freelancers and job seekers and young and old. The participants bring in expert knowledge and experience from companies and administrations, science and technology, trade unions and professional associations, universities and research institutions, industry and services, crafts and municipalities, educational institutions and social institutions and online communities and crowds and from the areas of art and culture. It sees itself as a building block that facilitates the transfer of knowledge and provides experience in the mediation of knowledge. In moderated processes, the Social Technology Design Forum wants to 'translate' complex technical expertise into the living world of working people and, conversely, to confidently transfer experience-based design requirements from the working world into science, research and development.

2 Structure of This Book

As mentioned above, this anthology on the subject of Internal Crowdsourcing in companies is the result of a research project of the same name. As such, it addresses the overall research theme 'Work in the Digitalized Work' by applying a concise research focus within the framework of network-bound, temporally and locally flexible work, in this case, the subject of Internal Crowdsourcing. In its entirety, and since the goal of the ICU Research Project has been to develop a cross-industry model that would serve as a reference case for good practice in future crowdsourcing activities, the anthology represents an employee-oriented, cross-industry reference model for good practice in Internal Crowdsourcing.

As has been clear from the very beginning, Internal Crowdsourcing is neither empirically nor theoretically well understood yet. Therefore, the research presented in this book is roughly divided into two major parts: one part that is mainly dedicated to theoretical foundations and the other that is mainly dedicated to practical applications. The theory part includes this chapter, "An Introduction to Internal Crowdsourcing", "Managing the Crowd: A Literature Review of Empirical Studies on Internal Crowdsourcing" and "Systematization Approach for the Development and Description of an Internal Crowdsourcing System" by Pohlisch, Ulbrich and Wedel, which introduce, discuss and present theoretical foundations for Internal Crowdsourcing in order to foster an understanding of it for the ongoing scientific debate and to design practical applications. In chapters "Design of a Process and Role Model for Internal Crowdsourcing" and "An Empirical Analysis of an Internal Crowdsourcing Platform: IT Implications for Improving Employee Participation", the authors Iskender, Polzehl and Schröter bridge the gap between theory and application by referring to empirical results from the research project (here with respect to IT implications) and extensive work experience (here with respect to 4600 women and men from works councils and staff councils, union representative bodies and the workforce) in order to derive general implications for IC applications in both theory and praxis. Finally, in chapters "Proposals for the Future of Internal Crowdsourcing: A Trade-Union-Based Approach", "Good Practice at GASAG-

Group: Recommendations for the Application of Internal Crowdsourcing from a Business Perspective" and "The Living Group Works Council Agreement as Social Innovation: Internal Crowdsourcing in the GASAG Group", Porth, Schröter, Uhl and Göll compile practical insights derived during the application of Internal Crowdsourcing in a company by including management perspectives as well as trade union perspectives and by focusing on qualification and competence development in organizations. The book finishes by looking beyond the horizon of the research project. In chapter "The Use of Internal Crowdsourcing for Qualification and Competence Development in Organizations", Zinke-Wehlmann, Friedrich and Römer discuss how the theoretical foundations and practical applications presented in this book can be applied to the concept of social business. The articles in detail are:

An Introduction to Internal Crowdsourcing
Jakob Pohlisch
This chapter aims to provide the reader with an introduction to crowdsourcing in general and Internal Crowdsourcing in particular. First of all, the elementary principles of crowdsourcing are introduced, finishing with a definition that constitutes the basis for this book. Secondly, different crowdsourcing typologies are described to inform the reader about classifications of the phenomenon in the academic literature. Thirdly, the crowdsourcing process is outlined in order to clarify the general procedure of this new kind of work organization. Lastly, the concept is transferred to the intra-organizational context, providing a description and definition of the concept of Internal Crowdsourcing that represents the main topic of this book.

Managing the Crowd: A Literature Review of Empirical Studies on Internal Crowdsourcing
Jakob Pohlisch
The phenomenon of crowdsourcing is increasingly being addressed within academic literature. Companies utilize crowdsourcing to search outside of the companies' boundaries for solutions to internal problems, thus accessing the vast and diverse knowledge and creativity of people all over the world. More recently, a growing interest has emerged, which concentrates on the intra-organizational application of this phenomenon—Internal Crowdsourcing. While conventional internal innovation activities have mostly been concentrated within a few dedicated departments, this new approach helps companies to open up their innovation process to all employees. Internal Crowdsourcing can help companies bridge geographical distances, integrate new employees, predict the market success of products and create ideas for new businesses.

This chapter aims to provide a comprehensive overview of the existing empirical findings regarding the management of Internal Crowdsourcing. In this review, 28 papers covering more than 100 companies are analysed. They are based on more than 800 interviews, participant observations, action design research, surveys and datasets of internal innovation contests. The results of this review will help practitioners to design the management of Internal Crowdsourcing, based on existing implementations and lessons learned, helping them to unleash the full innovation potential of their employees, creating a valuable competitive advantage.

Systematization Approach for the Development and Description of an Internal Crowdsourcing System

Marco Wedel and Hannah Ulbrich

There is a need for both a scientific foundation and theoretical fundamentals to describe Internal Crowdsourcing systems with binding, consensus-based terminologies and descriptions. (How) Can the already described subcategories and aspects of an IC system be meaningfully referenced and placed in an orderly overall relationship? What must be added, if necessary and possible, to system descriptions? The present article concentrates on identifying existing descriptions *and* definitions in connection with systematization approaches for the development of an Internal Crowdsourcing system. Since the phenomenon itself eludes allocation to an exclusively dedicated scientific discipline, it seems appropriate to choose interdisciplinary approaches and to build on existing theoretical and terminological approaches from related sciences.

Design of a Process and Role Model for Internal Crowdsourcing

Hannah Ulbrich and Marco Wedel

The successful implementation of Internal Crowdsourcing (IC) in a company requires a precise description and definition of the personnel responsibilities for the various process levels and process components within each process phase of IC. As part of the research project 'ICU—Internal Crowdsourcing in Companies', we have developed a new role model for Internal Crowdsourcing based on the practical application of IC in the company GASAG AG, an energy provider located in Berlin/ Germany. The aim of this article is to present the main features of this role model. It is based on the roles of the agile Scrum model, because partial aspects of the Internal Crowdsourcing process and certain process-steering tasks have similarities with the procedure and task descriptions of Scrum. Scrum, as a mature and practice-proven set of rules with role descriptions, rules, events and artefacts, provides helpful implications for the design of an Internal Crowdsourcing role model as we will demonstrate in further detail.

An Empirical Analysis of an Internal Crowdsourcing Platform: IT Implications for Improving Employee Participation

Neslihan Iskender and Tim Polzehl

Crowdsourcing has become one of the main resources for working on so-called 'micro-tasks' that require human intelligence to solve tasks that computers cannot yet solve and for connecting to external knowledge and expertise. Instead of using external crowds, several organizations have increasingly been using their employees as a crowd, to exploit employee's potentials, to mobilize unused technical and personal experience and to include personal skills for innovation or product enhancement. However, understanding the dynamics of this new way of digital co-working from the technical point of view plays a vital role in the success of Internal Crowdsourcing, and, to our knowledge, no study has yet investigated the relationship between the technical features and participation in Internal Crowdsourcing in empirical terms. This paper therefore aims to provide a guideline for organizations and employers from the perspective of the technical design of Internal Crowdsourcing, specifically regarding issues of data protection, privacy and security concerns as well as task type, design, duration and participation time based on the empirical findings of an Internal Crowdsourcing platform.

Proposals for the Future of Internal Crowdsourcing: A Trade Union-Based Approach

Welf Schröter

The 'FST' personnel network 'Forum Soziale Technikgestaltung' (Forum for Social Forms of Technology) from the German Trade Union Confederation (DGB) of Baden-Württemberg has been examining the subjects of informatization of work and digitalization since 1991. More than 4600 women and men from works councils and staff councils, union representative bodies and the workforce and from large companies and small- and medium-sized enterprises, the manual trades as well as self-employed people have been involved in an exchange about their experiences in production and services and in administrations. Against this background, and drawing on the accumulated knowledge gained from experience, the following proposals for the future of Internal Crowdsourcing have been derived. The proposals represent a trade union-based approach.

Good Practices at GASAG Group: Recommendations for the Application of Internal Crowdsourcing from a Business Perspective

Florian Porth

Innovative and marketable products and services as well as maintaining innovation capacity are basic conditions for a company's economic success, and these present implicit challenges in adapting to twenty-first century needs. These success factors are endangered by silo mentalities, insufficiently pronounced or cross-departmental knowledge transfers. The GASAG Group, which has an organizational layout typical for medium-sized enterprises in Germany, has been and still is confronted with these challenges as well. In order to cope with them, the GASAG Group decided to work on company culture as well as develop an open and innovative mindset, leading it to join the research project ICU in 2017.

The aim of the article is to describe the approach taken by ICU from the practical, company perspective of the GASAG Group and to map out identified success factors as well to provide general recommendations for the implementation of Internal Crowdsourcing in a business environment.

The Living Group Works Council Agreement as Social Innovation: Internal Crowdsourcing in the GASAG Group

Andreas Otte, Welf Schröter, Ingo Breite, Frank Gerth, Sylvia Laur, Volker Ost, Can Sekertekin, Andreas Tabor, Marco Wedel and Hannah Ulbrich

Shortly after the formal launch of the ICU project in the summer of 2017, representatives from the group works council of the GASAG group sat down with the trade union network Forum for the Social Forms of Technology, the FST, to start up an independent practical initiative to examine the topic of Internal Crowdsourcing to be implemented soon after. In 2018, a model works council agreement between the group workers' council and the management was agreed, henceforth providing a framework for the IC procedure in the GASAG Group. The aim of the agreement was to serve as a template for the introduction of Internal Crowdsourcing in other companies and industries. A special feature of the agreement is the so-called 'living' group works council agreement. The following article analyses its significance and provides a translation by reproducing wording of the agreement.

The Use of Internal Crowdsourcing for Qualification and Competence Development in Organizations

André Uhl and Edgar Göll

This article deals with the question of how Internal Crowdsourcing can be used as a tool to support the development of employee qualification and competence in organizations. In the first chapter, the current state of the competence research is examined. A paradigm shift from 'qualification and professional development' towards 'competences' and the implications of this for the concept are described. Chapter "An Introduction to Internal Crowdsourcing" deals with the analyses and work on the subject of competence acquisition and development, including considering the results of two interview series and two workshops. In chapter "Managing the Crowd: A Literature Review of Empirical Studies on Internal Crowdsourcing", the authors present a combined and practical approach to support competence development through Internal Crowdsourcing in organizations. Finally, the last chapter sums up main results and perspectives for competence development through a combination of virtual and face-to-face working processes.

Power to the Network: The Concept of Social Business and its Relevance for IC

Christian Zinke-Wehlmann, Julia Friedrich, Vanita Römer

The concept of IC places a focus on the employees, in their potential role as crowdsourcees, campaign owners or initiators. This reflects the emancipatory and participatory principle that goes hand in hand with the concept of social business. The basic idea of social business is not to link the business success of a company exclusively to its management capabilities or its business plan but to understand and value the individual stakeholder as part of a successful enterprise network. For social business, value is not exclusively understood as business value; rather, the perspective is expanded to include social added value, in the sense that the value of the work for the employee, society or the environment is considered as an indirect corporate goal. Thus, social business is defined as a framework or strategy that uses digital social networks (enterprise social networks) with the primary goal of generating social, ecological and economic benefits. This article introduces the social business reference model, which supports the adoption and implementation of the outlined strategy and contrasts it to the IC model in order to identify the strengths as well as the weaknesses of both models.

Acknowledgements The goal of this book is to advance the state of Internal Crowdsourcing theory and its application knowledge. We invite the reader to examine the deductions presented here and to reflect upon their strengths and limitations. Since it is the ideal of science to be self-consciously error seeking and thus self-correcting (Sabatier 2007, p. 5), we hope that this contribution acts as an impulse to set in motion a constructive scientific discourse. We are sure that it is a helpful contribution towards the good application of IC in companies. To enable the best possible transfer of knowledge, we are very happy to present this volume as an open access publication. This is only possible due to the generous financial support of the Open Access Publication Fund of TU Berlin. Thank you to Elena Di Rosa and Dagmar Schobert of the Publication Fund of the University Library of TU Berlin. We would also like to thank the authors of this book, without whose contributions the production of the anthology would have been impossible. In the end, we wish the reader an insightful and interesting read and look forward to further exciting debates and discoveries.

References

Bundesministerium für Bildung und Forschung (BMBF) (2015) Bekanntmachung. https://www.bmbf.de/foerderungen/bekanntmachung-1017.html

Byrèn E (2013) Internal crowdsourcing for innovation development - how multi-national companies can obtain the advantages of crowdsourcing utilising internal resources. Sweden: Department of Technology Management and Economics. http://publications.lib.chalmers.se/records/fulltext/181969/181969.pdf

DGB Bundeskongress (2014) Leitlinien guter digitaler Arbeit. https://innovation-gute-arbeit.verdi.de/++file++53db58e16f684449d10003e0/download/Antrag%20Gute%20Digitale%20Dienstleistungsarbeit%202014.pdf

Enquete-Kommission Internet und digitale Gesellschaft (2013) Leitlinien für eine gute digitale Arbeit. In: Achter Zwischenbericht, Wirtschaft, Arbeit: Green IT, 13.03.2013, http://webarchiv.bundestag.de/cgi/show.php?fileToLoad=2944&id=1223

Keinz P (2015) Auf den Schultern von ... Vielen! Crowdsourcing als neue Methode in der Neuproduktentwicklung. Schmalenbachs Zeitschrift für betriebswirtschaftliche Forschung 67 (1):35–69. https://doi.org/10.1007/BF03372915

Melzer A, Heim Y, Sanders T, Bullinger-Hoffmann AC (2019) Zur Zukunft des Kompetenzmanagements. In: Bullinger-Hoffmann AC (ed) Zukunftstechnologien und Kompetenzbedarfe. Kompetenzentwicklung in der Arbeitswelt 4.0. Springer Nature, Berlin, pp 11–26

Metzger M (2016) Organisationsentwicklungsmaßnahmen in der strategischen Personalplanung von Schlüsselkompetenzen. Igel Verlag RWS, Hamburg

Pohlisch J (2019) Bericht – Innovationsaktivitäten Deutscher Unternehmen. Technische Universität Berlin, Fachgebiet Innovation Economics, Berlin. https://tubcloud.tu-berlin.de/s/2m2BzwNyR3T9s8a#pdfviewer. Zugegriffen am 10.10.2019

Sabatier PA (ed) (2007) Theories of the policy process, 2nd edn. Westview Press, Boulder, Colo

TransWork (2017) Förderschwerpunkt. https://www.transwork.de/index.php/foerderschwerpunkt/

Wedel M (2016) The European integration of RES-E promotion: the case of Germany and Poland. Springer Fachmedien Wiesbaden, Wiesbaden

Wegerich C (2015) Strategische Personalentwicklung in der Praxis. Instrumente, Erfolgsmodelle, Checklisten, Praxisbeispiele, 3rd edn. Springer, Berlin. https://doi.org/10.1007/978-3-662-43699-8

Zhu H, Djurjagina K, Leker J (2014) Innovative behaviour types and their influence on individual crowdsourcing performances. Int J Innov Manag 18(06):1–18. https://doi.org/10.1142/S1363919614400155

Zhu H, Sick N, Leker J (2016) How to use crowdsourcing for innovation?: A comparative case study of internal and external idea sourcing in the chemical industry. In: Kocaoglu DF (ed) Technology management for social innovation: PICMET'16: Portland international conference on management of engineering and technology: Proceedings. IEEE, Piscataway, NJ
Zuchowski O, Posegga O, Schlagwein D, Fischbach K (2016) Internal crowdsourcing: conceptual framework, structured review, and research agenda. J Inf Technol 31(2):166–184. https://doi.org/10.1057/jit.2016.14

Hannah Ulbrich holds a Degree in Sociology (Dipl. Soz.—Bielefeld/Berlin) and is a Senior Researcher at the Department of Vocational Education/Technology and Participation at the Technical University of Berlin. There, she is the project leader of the BMBF- and ESF-funded research project 'ICU—Internal Crowdsourcing in Companies'. In addition to her work as a project manager, she is a scholarship holder of the Berlin Professional School of Economics and Law where she is currently completing a part-time MBA programme. Her research focus is on Entrepreneurship and Innovation, New Work and Agility and Digital Transformation and Leadership.

Dr. Marco Wedel is a Political Scientist (Dipl.rer.pol., Dr. phil.) and Senior Researcher at the Department of Vocational Education/Technology and Participation at the Technical University of Berlin. In addition to study visits in Boston, Constance and Berlin, he has worked in the Energy Sector (BASF) and in Science Management (Falling Walls Foundation), among others. His current research activities focus on the topics 'Future of Work', Entrepreneurship, Digitalization and Media Competence. His long-term research focuses on European Integration, Democratic Competence and Sustainable Development. Marco Wedel is co-editor of the science journal 'Innovation: The European Journal of Social Science Research'.

Prof. Dr. Hans-Liudger Dienel is a professor for Vocational Education/Technology and Participation at the Technical University of Berlin. He is Dean of the School of Education, Head of a Masters' Programme in Science Management and of an MBA in Sustainable Mobility Management. Prof. Dienel is the Managing Director of the nexus Institut für Kooperationsmanagement GmbH, which designs participation processes in politics and business. After studying Mechanical Engineering (Dipl.-Ing.), History, Philosophy and Sociology (M.A., Dr.phil.) in Hanover, Washington and Munich, Prof. Dienel worked at the Research Institute of the Deutsches Museum in Munich before he became Head of the Center for Technology and Society at the TU Berlin. Prof. Dienel conducts research on participation processes and is a member of the VDI Advisory Board for Society and Technology, the Steering Committee of the Citizen Participation Network and the Steering Committee of the international Democracy R&D network.

An Introduction to Internal Crowdsourcing

Jakob Pohlisch

Abstract This chapter aims to provide the reader with an introduction to crowdsourcing in general and internal crowdsourcing in particular. First, the elementary principles of crowdsourcing will be introduced, completed by a definition that will constitute the basis for this book. Second, different crowdsourcing typologies will be described to inform the reader about classifications of the phenomenon in scientific literature. Third, the crowdsourcing process is outlined to clarify the general procedure of this new kind of work organization. Lastly, the concept will be transferred to the intraorganizational context, describing and defining the concept of internal crowdsourcing which represents the main topic of this book.

Keywords Crowdsourcing · Crowdsourcing typologies · Crowdsourcing process · Internal crowdsourcing

1 Definitions of Crowdsourcing

The term crowdsourcing can be traced back to Jeff Howe's article "The Rise of Crowdsourcing" in Wired Magazine in 2006 (Howe 2006b). Howe defines crowdsourcing as "the act of a company or institution taking a function once performed by employees and outsourcing it to an undefined (and generally large) network of people in the form of an open call" (Howe 2006a). The word crowdsourcing is a neologism created by combining the terms "outsourcing" and "crowd" (Hirth et al. 2011). While outsourcing refers to the outsourcing of internal activities using bilateral relationships (Grossman and Helpman 2005), crowdsourcing refers to outsourcing using an undefined group of individuals called the crowd (Leimeister 2012). Since the publication of Howe, the topic has garnered tremendous interest in both business and science. In order to create a common

J. Pohlisch (✉)
Technische Universität Berlin, Chair of Innovation Economics, Berlin, Germany
e-mail: Jakob.Pohlisch@tu-berlin.de

H. Ulbrich et al. (eds.), *Internal Crowdsourcing in Companies*, Contributions to Management Science, https://doi.org/10.1007/978-3-030-52881-2_2

understanding of crowdsourcing for the remainder of this book, this first chapter will provide a definition of crowdsourcing.

The academic literature contains a wide variety of attempts to create a definition for crowdsourcing. While most of these have many common features, some of them address different phenomena to some extent. For example, Bücheler et al. (2010) and Huberman et al. (2009) classify Wikipedia and YouTube as examples of crowdsourcing, while other authors explicitly exclude these platforms (Kleemann et al. 2008; Brabham 2012). Perhaps the most notable attempt to resolve the problem of arriving at a generally accepted definition was undertaken by Estellés-Arolas and González-Ladrón-de-Guevara (2012). By conducting a literature review, they identified 209 articles containing 40 different definitions of crowdsourcing. From this they have derived an exhaustive and consistent definition:

> Crowdsourcing is a type of participative online activity in which an individual, an institution, a non-profit organization, or company proposes to a group of individuals of varying knowledge, heterogeneity, and number, via a flexible open call, the voluntary undertaking of a task. The undertaking of the task, of variable complexity and modularity, and in which the crowd should participate bringing their work, money, knowledge and/or experience, always entails mutual benefit. The user will receive the satisfaction of a given type of need, be it economic, social recognition, self-esteem, or the development of individual skills, while the crowdsourcer will obtain and utilize to their advantage what the user has brought to the venture, whose form will depend on the type of activity undertaken. (Estellés-Arolas and González-Ladrón-de-Guevara 2012, p. 197).

In a recent article, Kietzmann (2017) argues that several technological developments and their rapid diffusion over the last few years have led to the fact that knowledge can nowadays be accessed much more quickly, easily, and efficiently. From these changes and the progress of research in the field of crowdsourcing, he derives implications that require a broader definition of crowdsourcing. However, most of his points are already included in the definition by Estellés-Arolas and González-Ladrón-de-Guevara (2012) and, therefore, do not need to be discussed again. Nevertheless, the essential distinction is that Kietzmann (2017) assumes that the task does not necessarily have to be performed by humans but that a combination of humans and machines can also serve as a crowd.

Crowdsourcing is based on the principle of the wisdom of the crowds (Surowiecki 2004). This principle, in turn, is based on the idea of collective intelligence (Lévy 1997), which describes the intelligence of a group of people created by the interaction of its peers. Surowiecki (2004) argues that, under certain conditions, a group of individuals can produce better decisions and results than individuals, even if the latter are in principle better qualified to carry out the respective task. Crowdsourcing can therefore be used as a mechanism to access the wisdom of the crowd in order to solve a given problem.

Crowdsourcing platforms constitute so-called information systems. Alter (2008, p. 451) defines these information systems as a "system in which human participants and/or machines perform work (processes and activities) using information, technology, and other resources to produce informational products and/or services for internal or external custom."

Based on this definition Geiger and Schader (2014, p. 4) define crowdsourcing-specific information systems as "socio-technical systems that provide informational products and services by harnessing the potential of large groups of people via the Web."

The parties involved in crowdsourcing can principally be divided into the two roles of the crowdsourcer or content owner and the crowd. The content owner is the principal who searches for a solution to a given problem, while the crowd consists of the agents solving it (Leimeister et al. 2015). The crowdsourcing process itself takes place on an IT-enabled crowdsourcing platform. This allows content owners to create and share tasks and allows the crowd to solve them collaboratively or individually and to submit solutions. If an intermediary operates this platform, a third role is created that of the crowdsourcing intermediary (Leimeister et al. 2015).

In assuming an intraorganizational perspective, additional roles have to be considered in describing the information system of internal crowdsourcing. Ulbrich and Wedel (see chapter "Systematization Approach for the Development and Description of an Internal Crowdsourcing System" of this book) build a complex model describing the primary, secondary, and tertiary roles necessary for a successful implementation of internal crowdsourcing. In total, they describe eight different roles: (1) crowd master, (2) campaign owner, (3) crowd technology master, (4) content owner, (5) secondary counterpart, (6) crowd, (7) executive board, and (8) employee union representation. For a more detailed description of the role model for internal crowdsourcing and the corresponding descriptions of the roles, see chapter "Systematization Approach for the Development and Description of an Internal Crowdsourcing System" in this book.

2 Crowdsourcing Typologies

Over the years different typologies for crowdsourcing have emerged that are intended to help categorize different types of crowdsourcing. Afuah and Tucci (2012), for example, differentiate between tournament-based and collaboration-based crowdsourcing, depending on how results are generated within the crowd. In tournament-based crowdsourcing, each participant submits an independently developed solution, and the content owner ultimately selects the best solution. In collaboration-based crowdsourcing, on the other hand, a joint solution is developed by the entire crowd. Similarly, Boudreau and Lakhani (2013) classify crowdsourcing according to whether the participants work independently or collaboratively on the solution of the task.

Leimeister (2012) additionally distinguishes between crowdfunding, crowdvoting, and crowdcreation, according to the type of task the crowd performs. In crowdfunding, the participants from the crowd are used to achieve a particular financing goal. In crowdvoting, each participant from the crowd provides a ranking of options given the context of a specific question. This can be, for example, the evaluation of a product or a vote on a new product name. Within the scope of crowdcreation, the crowd participants have to invest significantly more work effort, as this involves the generation of ideas, designs, prototypes, or entirely new business models. The work of the crowd is therefore characterized by significantly higher expenses and production costs.

Geiger and Schader (2014) differentiate crowdsourcing initiatives using two dimensions—the homogeneity and aggregation of contributions from the crowd. Accordingly, contributions can be very similar (homogeneous) or very individual (heterogeneous) in their characteristics. Homogeneous contributions are mostly the result of clearly structured and standardized tasks, while heterogeneous contributions are most often a consequence of unstructured and open tasks (Blohm et al. 2017). The aggregation of the contributions is based on whether the added value of crowdsourcing can be derived selectively from individual contributions or integratively from the entirety of contributions (Blohm et al. 2017). This classification of integrative and selective crowdsourcing can also be found in Schenk and Guittard (2011). From the two described dimensions, Geiger and Schader (2014) derive four types of crowdsourcing information systems (see Fig. 1):

1. Crowd rating: This type of crowdsourcing is based on many homogeneous contributions whose value is not derived from the individual contributions but from their aggregate (e.g., TripAdvisor rating).
2. Crowd creation: The value of this crowdsourcing approach results from the aggregation of many heterogeneous contributions. The contributions are complementary and achieve a comprehensive body of work when aggregated (e.g., Wikipedia).
3. Crowd processing: This type of crowdsourcing is based on a large number of contributions that exhibit a high degree of homogeneity (e.g., reCAPTCHA).
4. Crowd solving: In this case, a heterogeneous set of contributions is submitted, each of which represents an individual and different solution to a given problem. The solutions can be complements or substitutes.

Geiger and Schader (2014) describe these types of crowdsourcing as archetypes and state that mixed forms are mostly observed in real-life settings.

Similarly, Prpić et al. (2015) categorize different types of crowdsourcing. Like Geiger and Schader (2014), they identify two dimensions from which four different types of crowdsourcing are derived. The first dimension is based on the nature of the contributions, while the way in which the contributions are used to derive the solution is the foundation for the second dimension. The latter dimension is quite similar to the aggregation dimension of Geiger and Schader (2014). However, the former dimension differs from the classification based on the homogeneity of contributions. Instead, the focus lies on whether the crowd submissions are objective or subjective in nature. Objective contributions represent facts that can be researched and compiled by the crowd, while subjective contributions are, for example, opinions, beliefs, or assessments.

Finally, a distinction between internal and external crowdsourcing can be made based on the location of the crowd. In internal crowdsourcing, the company's employees form the crowd and can submit solutions, while in external

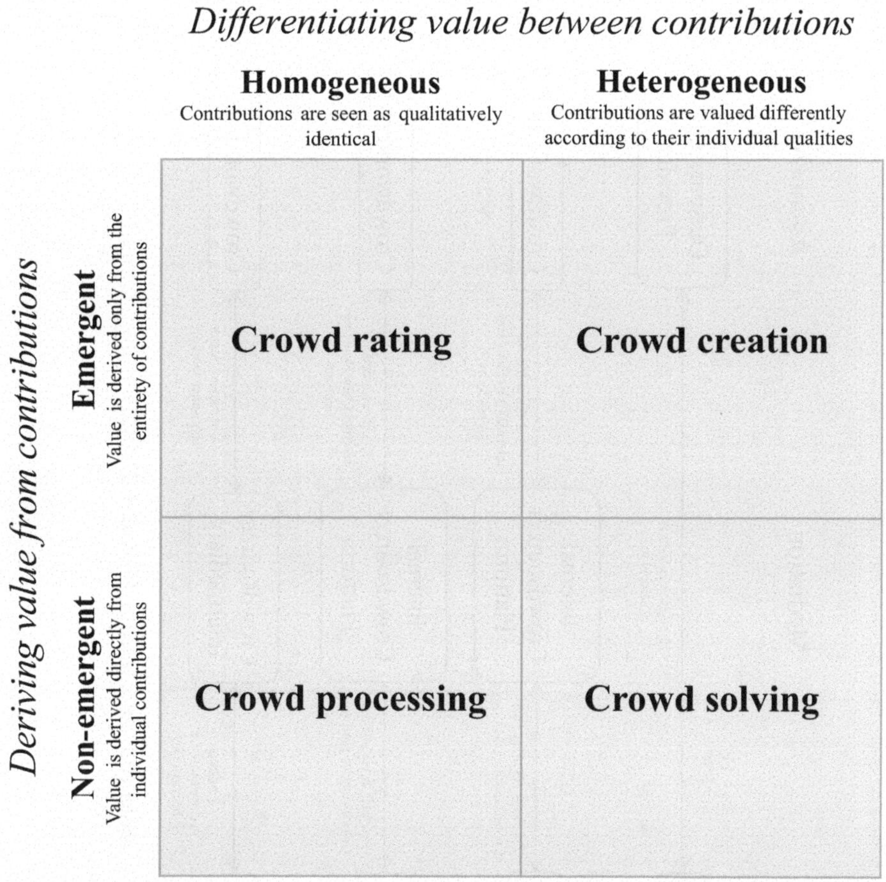

Fig. 1 Typology of crowdsourcing platforms (reproduced from Geiger and Schader 2014)

crowdsourcing, the crowd is formed by an undefined number of individuals outside the company (Leimeister et al. 2015). Crowdsourcing can be classified as a coordination model between market and hierarchy due to the possibility of assigning tasks both internally and externally (Leimeister 2012). An illustration of the roles and the location of the crowd can be found in Fig. 2. A more detailed description of internal crowdsourcing is provided in Sect. 4.

3 The Crowdsourcing Process

As with the definition and typology of crowdsourcing, various descriptions of the crowdsourcing process exist (Lopez et al. 2010; Pedersen et al. 2013; Zhu et al. 2016). However, Geiger and Schader (2014) argue that these are merely variations of

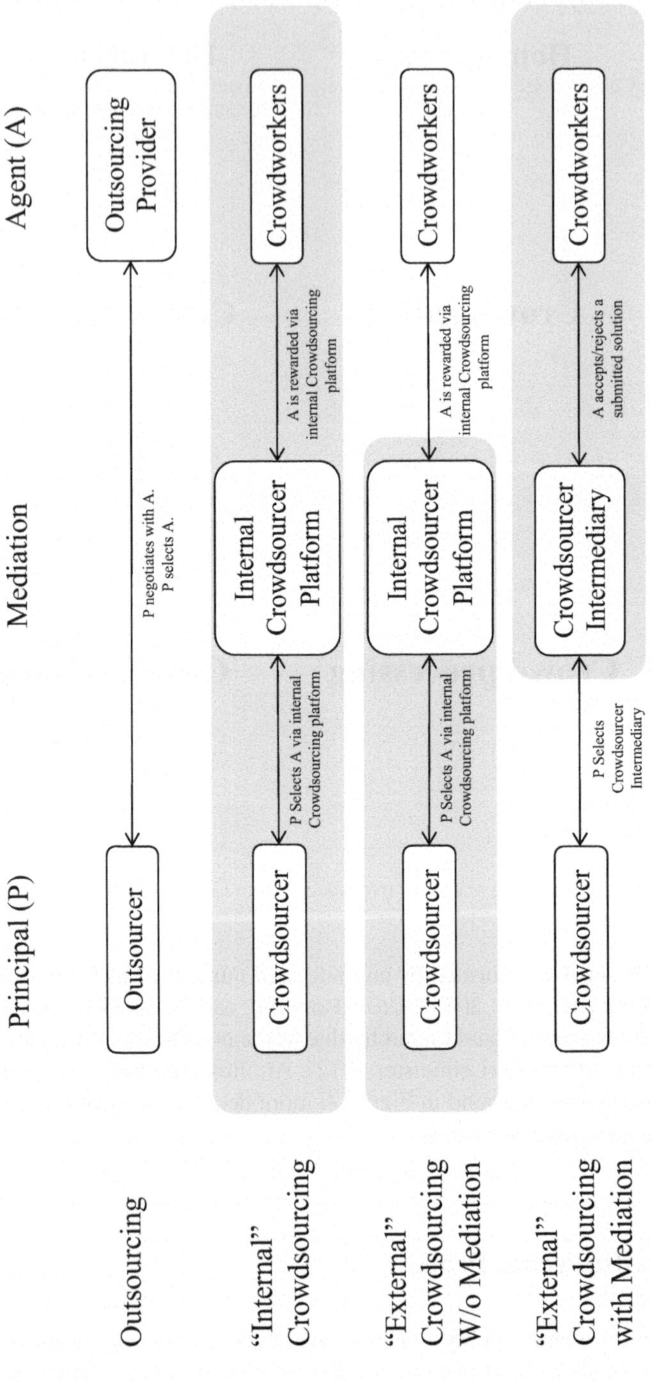

Fig. 2 Roles and location of the crowd (reproduced from Leimeister et al. 2015, based on Hoßfeld et al. 2012)

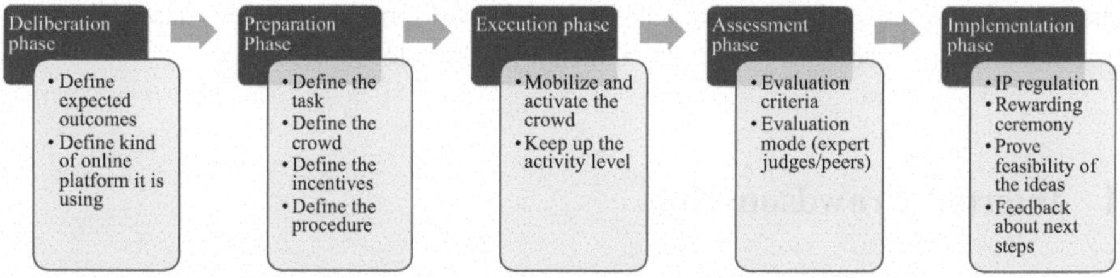

Fig. 3 Process phases and their design criteria (reproduced from Zhu et al. 2016)

a relatively generic process. An agent publishes a task utilizing an open call to an undefined crowd, whose individuals then decide freely whether they want to engage with and contribute to this task. Afterward, the best solution is selected from all submissions. Pedersen et al. (2013, p. 581) summarize this generic process as follows:

> A process is a set of actions undertaken by all actors in a crowdsourcing project to achieve a particular outcome or solve a particular problem. In this context, the process refers to the design of a step-by-step plan of action for solving a crowdsourcing problem.

With the help of a comprehensive literature search, Zuchowski et al. (2016) define four elemental steps within the internal crowdsourcing process: (1) preparation, (2) execution, (3) evaluation/aggregation, and (4) resolution. The preparatory phase includes tasks such as the description of the actual assignment, the prerequisites, expectations, evaluation criteria, the selection criteria for the crowd, and ultimately of the incentive structure. The act of crowdsourcing takes place during the execution phase, in which the task is published and the crowd submits their solution proposals. In the third step, the evaluation and aggregation of the submissions from the crowd take place. Either all solutions that meet a certain quality standard (integration) or only the best solution (selection) can be selected (Geiger et al. 2011). During the final phase, the chosen solution is finally implemented, and the submitter of the solution is rewarded. Zhu et al. (2016) as well as Muhdi et al. (2011) add a fifth step to the crowdsourcing process, which precedes the four steps introduced by Zuchowski et al. (2016)—the deliberation phase. Although this phase overlaps conceptually with the preparation phase, another critical aspect is taken into account here. During the deliberation phase, the agent decides whether crowdsourcing can be considered at all as a solution strategy for the particular problem at hand (Fig. 3).

But even this conceptualization might be seen as too broad, especially for the complex system of internal crowdsourcing. More recently, Ulbrich and Wedel (see chapter "Systematization Approach for the Development and Description of an Internal Crowdsourcing System" of this book) developed a more granular description of the internal crowdsourcing process. They differentiate between (1) impetus, (2) decision, (3) conceptualization, (4) execution, (5) assessment, (6) exploitation, and (7) feedback. In part, these processual steps can be parallelized or aggregated in less individual steps. For a more detailed discussion of the different phases, see chapter "Systematization Approach for the Development and Description of an Internal Crowdsourcing System" by Ulbrich and Wedel in this book.

4 Internal Crowdsourcing

Recently, one type of crowdsourcing in particular—internal crowdsourcing—has attracted considerable interest and initiated a first wave of research (Benbya and Leidner 2018; Smith et al. 2017; Zuchowski et al. 2016). Benbya and van Alstyne (2011) were among the first to highlight the potential of internal knowledge markets to improve the flow of information within companies and to find solutions to problems internally. Internal crowdsourcing can be particularly advantageous for large companies with many geographically dispersed employees that possess diverse backgrounds. Successful implementations of internal crowdsourcing have already been reported in several case studies, including world-renowned companies like Siemens, McKinsey & Co, Eli Lilly (Benbya and van Alstyne 2011), Allianz (Benbya and Leidner 2018), Deltares (Leung et al. 2014), Deutsche Telekom (Rohrbeck et al. 2015), IBM (Bjelland and Wood 2008), Microsoft (Bailey and Horvitz 2010), and NASA (Davis et al. 2015).

As internal crowdsourcing takes place within a company, resources in terms of the size of the crowd are naturally limited. Hence, the general concept of crowdsourcing is now analyzed within the intraorganizational context. It is no longer about tapping into the knowledge of an undefined but about tapping into the knowledge of a defined crowd of people—the employees of the company. These employees often possess comprehensive knowledge, especially implicit knowledge about customers, products, and services (Henttonen et al. 2017). Thus, internal crowdsourcing opens up the innovation process by enabling the development of ideas and innovations not only by employees of the research and development department but by all employees of the company (Simula and Ahola 2014).

One of the first descriptions of internal crowdsourcing can be found in Villarroel and Reis (2010, p. 2), who define internal crowdsourcing as a "distributed organizational model used by the firm to extend problem-solving to a large and diverse pool of self-selected contributors beyond the formal internal boundaries of a multi-business firm [. . .]."

This definition clearly states that internal crowdsourcing helps to solve problems by overcoming intraorganizational boundaries. However, this definition does not include further information on how the problems are broadcasted, how individuals in the crowd interact, and how problems are solved. An even broader definition can be found at Simula and Vuori (2012), who describe internal crowdsourcing as the introduction of open innovation principles at the intraorganizational level. The most comprehensive definition of internal crowdsourcing to date is provided by Zuchowski et al. (2016). Based on a structured literature review, they propose to define internal crowdsourcing as an "IT-enabled group activity based on an open call for participation in an enterprise" (Zuchowski et al. 2016, p. 168).

Following Zuchowski et al. (2016), internal crowdsourcing is therefore first and foremost a phenomenon that is fundamentally made possible by (social) information and telecommunications technologies. Secondly, internal crowdsourcing is a group activity in which collaborative or competitive approaches are possible as mentioned above. Thirdly, internal crowdsourcing is based on an open call, which can be explicit (e.g., an explicit call) or implicit (e.g., through an open technology such as an Enterprise Social Network, which permanently invites participation). In contrast to external crowdsourcing, however, the crowd addressed here is known—the employees of the focal firm. This definition will serve as a basis for the remainder of this book.

For a typology of internal crowdsourcing and an elaborate description of its process, the reader is referred to chapter "Systematization Approach for the Development and Description of an Internal Crowdsourcing System" of this book.

5 Conclusion

In summary, the potential of internal crowdsourcing lies in developing new ideas and innovations, finding effective solutions to problems, reducing costs, and shortening product development cycles (Brabham 2008; Simula and Vuori 2012; Vukovic 2009) and can thus make a valuable contribution to existing innovation activities within a firm (Leung et al. 2014).

Compared to external crowdsourcing, internal crowdsourcing has advantages as well as disadvantages. With internal crowdsourcing, the parameters for idea competitions can be set more broadly. Employees can, for example, develop new business areas or develop incremental innovations (Leung et al. 2014). This observation is again based on the implicit knowledge of the employees mentioned above, in particular about customers, products, and services (Henttonen et al. 2017). Malhotra et al. (2017) call this "local knowledge" and emphasize that the solutions of employees are often better oriented toward the requirements of customers and are feasible given the possibilities of the focal firm. This could further facilitate a faster and better implementation of the proposed solutions. On the other hand, restriction to the internal crowd naturally implies a smaller and therefore more homogeneous number of participants, which can lead to a reduction in the likelihood of radical innovation (Malhotra et al. 2017).

An enterprise may also use internal idea competitions in order to promote unity and to encourage creativity and entrepreneurial skills among employees (Leung et al. 2014). Internal crowdsourcing enables employees to make their ideas and innovative solutions more visible and accessible. It also encourages employees by giving them the feeling that their ideas are valued and taken seriously by the company (Malhotra et al. 2017) and that anyone can submit and implement an idea (Rao 2016). These characteristics of internal crowdsourcing can ultimately lead to more committed employees (Rao 2016; Malhotra et al. 2017). The degree of support for innovative activities has a positive influence on the innovation behavior of employees (Scott and Bruce 1994), and companies with more committed employees exhibit higher productivity, higher quality of work, and higher revenues (Baldoni 2013). Moreover, Jette et al. (2015) show that the satisfaction and productivity of employees increase when they are entrusted with meaningful and creative tasks. While, in the case of external crowdsourcing, the agent must decide strategically how to handle intellectual property rights in order to capture the optimum benefit from the submitted solutions (Mazzola et al. 2018), this usually only plays a minor role in internal crowdsourcing (Simula and Vuori 2012). Finally, internal crowdsourcing is a good solution for problems for which secrecy and competitive pressures would render external crowdsourcing inappropriate (Zuchowski et al. 2016; Simula and Vuori 2012).

References

Afuah A, Tucci CL (2012) Crowdsourcing as a solution to distant search. Acad Manag Rev 37 (3):355–375

Alter S (2008) Defining information systems as work systems: implications for the IS field. Eur J Inform Syst 17(5):448–469

Bailey BP, Horvitz E (2010) What's your idea? A case study of a grassroots innovation pipeline within a large software company. In: Proceedings of the 28th international conference on human factors in computing systems, pp 2065–2074

Baldoni J (2013) Employee engagement does more than boost productivity. Harv Bus Rev

Benbya H, Leidner D (2018) How Allianz UK used an idea management platform to harness employee innovation. MIS Q Exec 17(2):139–155

Benbya H, van Alstyne MW (2011) How to find answers within your company. MIT Sloan Manag Rev 52(2):65–76

Bjelland O, Wood RC (2008) An inside view of IBM's 'innovation jam'. MIT Sloan Manag Rev 50 (1):32–40

Blohm I, Zogaj S, Bretschneider U, Leimeister JM (2017) How to manage crowdsourcing platforms effectively? Calif Manag Rev 60(2):122–149

Boudreau KJ, Lakhani KR (2013) Using the crowd as an innovation partner. Harv Bus Rev 91 (4):60–69

Brabham DC (2008) Crowdsourcing as a model for problem solving. Convergence Int J Res New Media Technol 14(1):75–90

Brabham DC (2012) A model for leveraging online communities. In: Delwiche A, Henderson J (eds) The participatory cultures. Routledge, New York, pp 120–129

Bücheler T, Sieg JH, Füchslin RM, Pfeifer R (2010) Crowdsourcing, open innovation and collective intelligence in the scientific method—a research agenda and operational framework. In Artificial life XII. Proceedings of the twelfth international conference on the synthesis and simulation of living systems, Odense, Denmark, 19–23 Aug 2010, pp 679–686

Davis JR, Richard EE, Keeton KE (2015) Open innovation at NASA: a new business model for advancing human health and performance innovations. Res Technol Manag 58(3):52–58

Estellés-Arolas E, González-Ladrón-de-Guevara F (2012) Towards an integrated crowdsourcing definition. J Inform Sci 38(2):189–200

Geiger D, Schader M (2014) Personalized task recommendation in crowdsourcing information systems—current state of the art. Decis Supp Syst 65:3–16

Geiger D, Seedorf S, Schulze T, Nickerson RC, Schader M (2011) Managing the crowd: towards a taxonomy of crowdsourcing processes. In: Proceedings of the seventeenth Americas conference on information systems, Detroit, MI, USA, 4–7 August

Grossman GM, Helpman E (2005) Outsourcing in a global economy. Rev Econ Stud 72 (1):135–159

Henttonen K, Rissanen T, Eriksson P, Hallikas J (2017) Cultivating the wisdom of personnel through internal crowdsourcing. Int J Innovat Technol Manag (IJITM) 16(2):117–132

Hirth M, Hoßfeld T, Tran-Gia P (2011) Anatomy of a crowdsourcing platform—using the example of Microworkers.com. In: Fifth international conference on innovative mobile and internet services in ubiquitous computing, pp 322–329.

Hoßfeld T, Hirth M, Tran-Gia P (2012) Aktuelles Schlagwort: crowdsourcing. Informatik Spektrum 35(3):204–208

Howe J (2006a) Crowdsourcing: a definition: wired blog network: crowdsourcing

Howe J (2006b) The rise of crowdsourcing. Wired Mag 14(6):1–4

Huberman BA, Romero DM, Wu F (2009) Crowdsourcing, attention and productivity. J Inform Sci 35(6):758–765

Jette A, Breck A, Johns R (2015) Integrating balanced scorecard performance management with crowdsourced strategic planning. In Proceedings of the transportation research board annual meeting, Washington, DC

Kietzmann JH (2017) Crowdsourcing: a revised definition and introduction to new research. Bus Horiz 60(2):151–153

Kleemann F, Voß GG, Rieder K (2008) Un(der)paid innovators: The commercial utilization of consumer work through crowdsourcing. Sci Technol Innovat Stud 4(1):5–26

Leimeister JM (2012) Crowdsourcing: crowdfunding, crowdvoting, crowdcreation. Zeitschrift für Controlling und Management 56(6):388–392

Leimeister JM, Zogaj S, Durward D (2015) New forms of employment and IT—crowdsourcing. In 4th conference of the regulating for decent work network, Genf, Schweiz

Leung N, van Rooij A, van Deen J (2014) Eureka!: lessons learned from an evaluation of the idea contest at Deltares. Res Technol Manag 57(4):44–50

Lévy P (1997) Collective intelligence: Mankind's emerging world in cyberspace. Perseus, Cambridge, MA

Lopez M, Vukovic M, Laredo J (2010) PeopleCloud service for enterprise crowdsourcing. In: Proceedings of the IEEE international conference on services computing, Miami, FL, USA, pp 538–545

Malhotra A, Majchrzak A, Kesebi L, Looram S (2017) Developing innovative solutions through internal crowdsourcing. MIT Sloan Manag Rev 58(4):73–79

Mazzola E, Acur N, Piazza M, Perrone G (2018) "To own or not to own?" A study on the determinants and consequences of alternative intellectual property rights arrangements in crowdsourcing for innovation contests. J Prod Innovat Manag 35(6):908–929

Muhdi L, Daiber M, Friesike S, Boutellier R (2011) The crowdsourcing process: An intermediary mediated idea generation approach in the early phase of innovation. Int J Entrepren Innovat Manag 14(4):315–332

Pedersen J, Kocsis D, Tripathi A, Tarrell A, Weerakoon A, Tahmasbi N, Xiong J, Deng W, Oh O, de Vreede G-J (2013) Conceptual foundations of crowdsourcing: a review of IS research. In 2013 46th Hawaii international conference on system sciences (HICSS 2013): Wailea, [Maui], HI, USA, 7–10 January 2013. IEEE, Piscataway, NJ, pp 579–588

Prpić J, Shukla PP, Kietzmann JH, McCarthy IP (2015) How to work a crowd: Developing crowd capital through crowdsourcing. Bus Horiz 58(1):77–85

Rao D (2016) Enterprise crowdsourcing to sustain culture of innovation. http://www.cio.in/opinions/enterprise-crowdsourcing-sustain-culture-innovation. Accessed 21 Nov 2018

Rohrbeck R, Thom N, Arnold H (2015) IT tools for foresight: IT tools for foresight: The integrated insight and response system of Deutsche Telekom Innovation Laboratories. Technol Forecast Soc Change 97:115–126

Schenk E, Guittard C (2011) Towards a characterization of crowdsourcing practices. J Innovat Econ Manag 7(1):93–107
Scott SG, Bruce RA (1994) Determinants of innovative behavior: a path model of individual innovation in the workplace. Acad Manag J 37(3):580–607
Simula H, Ahola T (2014) A network perspective on idea and innovation crowdsourcing in industrial firms. Ind Market Manag 43(3):400–408
Simula H, Vuori M (2012) Benefits and barriers of crowdsourcing in B2B firms: generating ideas with internal and external crowds. Int J Innovat Manag 16(06):1240011
Smith C, Fixson SK, Paniagua-Ferrari C, Parise S (2017) The evolution of an innovation capability. Res Technol Manag 60(2):26–35
Surowiecki J (2004) The wisdom of crowds: Why the many are smarter than the few and how collective wisdom shapes business, economies, societies, and nations. Doubleday, New York
Villarroel AJ, Reis F (2010) Intra-corporate crowdsourcing (ICC): leveraging upon rank and site marginality for innovation. In: CrowdConf, San Francisco, CA, USA, 4 October
Vukovic M (2009) Crowdsourcing for enterprises. In: Proceedings of the 2009 congress on services, Washington, DC, USA. IEEE, pp 686–692
Zhu H, Sick N, Leker J (2016) How to use crowdsourcing for innovation? A comparative case study of internal and external idea sourcing in the chemical industry. In: Proceedings of the IEEE management of engineering and technology (PICMET), Honolulu, HI, USA, 4–8 September. IEEE, Portland, OR, pp 887–901
Zuchowski O, Posegga O, Schlagwein D, Fischbach K (2016) Internal crowdsourcing: Conceptual framework, structured review, and research agenda. J Inf Technol 31(2):166–184

Jakob Pohlisch has been working at the Chair of Innovation Economics at the Technical University of Berlin since 2015. He is currently working on the project “Peer Innovation—Sustainable Household Sector Innovation in Collaborative Networks,” funded by the Federal Ministry of Education and Research. Prior to that, he worked on the project “Internal Crowdsourcing in Companies.” His research focuses on open innovation, crowdsourcing, and user innovation. He has published articles in high-ranking international journals such as *Research Policy*, *International Journal of Production Economics*, and *The Journal of Technology Transfer*. Jakob holds a master’s degree in Statistics from Humboldt University Berlin and is currently pursuing his PhD.

Managing the Crowd: A Literature Review of Empirical Studies on Internal Crowdsourcing

Jakob Pohlisch

Abstract The phenomenon of crowdsourcing is increasingly being addressed in academic literature. Companies utilize crowdsourcing to search for solutions to internal problems outside of the companies' boundaries, accessing the vast and diverse knowledge and creativity of people all over the world. More recently, a growing interest has emerged that concentrates on the intra-organizational application of this phenomenon—internal crowdsourcing. While conventional internal innovation activities are mostly concentrated within a few dedicated departments, this new approach helps companies to open up their innovation process to all employees. Internal crowdsourcing can help companies bridge geographical distances, integrate new employees, predict the market success of products, and create ideas for new businesses.

This chapter aims to provide a comprehensive overview of the existing empirical findings regarding the management of internal crowdsourcing. In this review, 27 papers, covering more than 100 companies, are analysed. They are based on more than 800 interviews, participant observations, action design research, surveys, and datasets of internal innovation contests. The results of this review will help practitioners to design the management of internal crowdsourcing based on existing implementations and lessons learned, helping them to unleash the full innovation potential of their employees, creating a valuable competitive advantage.

Keywords Crowdsourcing · Internal crowdsourcing · Corporate crowdsourcing · Governance · Management · Innovation · Knowledge · Literature review

---

J. Pohlisch (✉)
Technische Universität Berlin, Chair of Innovation Economics, Berlin, Germany
e-mail: Jakob.Pohlisch@tu-berlin.de

H. Ulbrich et al. (eds.), *Internal Crowdsourcing in Companies*, Contributions to Management Science, https://doi.org/10.1007/978-3-030-52881-2_3

1 Introduction

To ensure long-term competitiveness and withstand increasing global competition, strategic innovation activities are becoming increasingly important. In their search for innovative ideas, companies are relying more and more on the principle of crowd wisdom (Surowiecki 2004). If internal company problems are solved by an undefined external crowd of people via the Internet, this is referred to as crowdsourcing (Howe 2006). The idea is to use an Internet platform to bring together internal problems and external knowledge in order to generate new solutions.

In the recent past, this approach has been internalized by firms and has received considerable academic interest (Erickson et al. 2012; Zuchowski et al. 2016; Benbya and Leidner 2018). Several well-known companies like Siemens, McKinsey & Co., Eli Lilly (Benbya and van Alstyne 2011), Allianz (Benbya and Leidner 2018), Deltares (Leung et al. 2014), Deutsche Telekom (Rohrbeck et al. 2015), IBM (Bjelland and Wood 2008), Microsoft (Bailey and Horvitz 2010), and NASA (Davis et al. 2015) have already been reported as having implemented internal crowdsourcing. Companies use internal crowdsourcing to access the knowledge of the entire workforce, identifying solutions to problems and accessing innovative ideas that might not have arisen within a traditional R&D department (Simula and Ahola 2014). Multinational corporations with a large number of geographically dispersed employees in particular can use this technology to overcome information silos, using the full potential of the company crowd more effectively and efficiently (Malhotra et al. 2017; Majchrzak et al. 2009; Dimitrova and Scarso 2017). Supported by an intranet- or Internet-based platform, employees from various company divisions can connect, share ideas, and work collaboratively. The most comprehensive definition of internal crowdsourcing to date can be found in Zuchowski et al. (2016). Based on a structured literature review, a consistent definition was created, relying on 74 academic articles on internal crowdsourcing. As a result, internal crowdsourcing is defined as an 'IT-enabled group activity based on an open call for participation in an enterprise' (Zuchowski et al. 2016, p. 168).

Compared to external crowdsourcing, internal crowdsourcing has some important advantages. It allows the parameters of idea competitions to be set in a comparatively broad manner (Leung et al. 2014). Further, employees often have implicit knowledge, in particular about customers, products, and services that are not inherent in external crowds (Henttonen et al. 2017; Malhotra et al. 2017). Internal crowdsourcing can be used to encourage entrepreneurial skills (Leung et al. 2014) and can help employees to gain a broader awareness for their ideas within the company (Malhotra et al. 2017), potentially leading to more committed employees (Rao 2016; Malhotra et al. 2017). Hence, it helps to create a more open innovation culture, allowing for more collaboration and participation (Scupola and Nicolajsen 2014). It also potentially helps huge companies to connect their existing employees with one another and to integrate new ones (Majchrzak et al. 2009). Further, Rohrbeck et al. (2015) found that it positively impacts knowledge management.

Stieger et al. (2012) show that internal crowdsourcing can be used to support employee involvement in strategy dialogues.

To fully leverage the positive impacts and potential competitive advantages of internal crowdsourcing, it is of paramount importance to understand, coordinate, and optimally implement its governance tasks (Pedersen et al. 2013; Zuchowski et al. 2016; Smith et al. 2017). Governance tasks in this context are understood as the totality of all activities and strategies to control the internal crowd as well as the entire crowdsourcing process (Zuchowski et al. 2016). However, Wedel and Ulbrich (see this chapter) argue that governance, due to its prior utilization in the sphere of political science, might be a slightly misleading terminology. Instead, they propose the use of 'management of crowdsourcing'. We follow their argumentation and will refer to management instead of governance in the following. For more information, see this chapter.

Although quite extensive literature on external crowdsourcing exists, internal crowdsourcing is much less researched (Zuchowski et al. 2016; Zhu et al. 2016). Due to the inherent structural differences between the two concepts, one can, unfortunately, not readily draw from existing knowledge on external crowdsourcing (Knop et al. 2017). As an example, this has been confirmed for the perceived importance of different rewards for participation in crowdsourcing in external and internal crowdsourcing scenarios (Muhdi and Boutellier 2011).

This study aims to provide a comprehensive overview of the existing empirical findings regarding the management of internal crowdsourcing. To do so, the recently published governance framework for internal crowdsourcing by Zuchowski et al. (2016), which relies on previous work by Pedersen et al. (2013) and Zogaj and Bretschneider (2014), is used to structure this review. Based on a structured literature review, the authors developed a conceptual framework that will help us to meaningfully describe the management tasks of internal crowdsourcing. The proposed framework consists of six different components:

1. Corporate culture and change management
2. Incentive design
3. Task definition and decomposition
4. Quality assurance
5. Community management
6. Regulations and legal implications

This study relies only on empirical academic papers that are based on primary information sources. Hence, theoretical deliberations and derivatives of other forms of internal idea markets that could be relevant for this study are not used here. In total, 27 papers that reported empirical findings and contained relevant information on at least one of the six dimensions of the chosen framework were found and analysed. These contributions cover more than 100 companies and are based on more than 800 interviews, participant observations, actions design research, surveys, and the datasets of internal idea contests.

Based on the management tasks introduced above and the analysed literature, the present chapter provides insights into the following research question: how do the observed companies optimally design their management to implement internal crowdsourcing successfully? As internal crowdsourcing is not yet a widely adopted approach to source knowledge and ideas from employees (Stieger et al. 2012; Zhu et al. 2016, 2019), the findings of this chapter contribute to understanding the determinants of successful internal crowdsourcing implementations. This will provide a resource that companies willing to incorporate internal crowdsourcing can use to adequately transform their management. Consequently, this chapter will help companies to unleash the full innovation potential of their employees, creating a valuable competitive advantage.

This study is structured as follows. First, the methodology applied in this study is described. Following that, the synthesis of the existing empirical academic literature is presented. Finally, a summary of the most critical aspects is provided.

2 Methodology

As described above, the management tasks introduced in Zuchowski et al. (2016) are used as a categorization scheme to structure the literature review. The methodology is following the approach towards conducting a literature review as described by Webster and Watson (2002).

For the literature review at hand, the ScienceDirect, Scopus, EBSCO Business Host, SpringerLink, Web of Science, and Google Scholar databases were accessed and searched. The keywords chosen covered different synonyms for internal crowdsourcing (corporate crowdsourcing, intra-organizational crowdsourcing, internal collaboration innovation, employee idea platform, enterprise crowdsourcing, internal crowdsourcing, crowdsourcing company, employee crowdsourcing). Additionally, backward and forward reference searching was conducted to identify additional relevant studies.

The inclusion decision process was as follows: First, after deleting duplicates, articles not published in peer-reviewed journals or conference proceedings were excluded. Second, articles that do not explicitly or implicitly deal with the concept of internal crowdsourcing were excluded. Third, articles were rejected if they do not address at least one component related to the management of internal crowdsourcing (see above). Lastly, to be included, the articles must contain a contribution on how to manage internal crowdsourcing based on the empirical analysis of primary data.

Of all articles, 27 relevant contributions have been identified and included in the present analysis. Table 1 contains a list of the 27 papers, their authors, and titles, as well as the primary data they are based on, if available. Their individual relevance to the discussion of each of the management tasks is depicted in Table 2. The selected articles cover more than 100 firms and are based on more than 800 interviews, participant observation, actions design research, surveys, and datasets of idea contests. Thus, the present study relies on various implementations of internal crowdsourcing in a variety of contextual settings—including sector, company size, company age, employee composition, etc. As a result, the description of the

Table 1 Overview of the included empirical studies on internal crowdsourcing

Author (Year)	Title	Case companies	Data	Published in
Arena et al. (2017)	How to Catalyse Innovation in Your Organization	At least 20 well-known organizations	More than 560 interviews	MIT Sloan Management Review
Bailey and Horvitz (2010)	What's Your Idea? A Case Study of a Grassroots Innovation Pipeline within a Large Software Company	Microsoft Corporation	32 semi-structured interviews; data analyses of content, interaction data, and user participation within the platform	Proceedings of the 28th International Conference on Human Factors in Computing Systems
Benbya and Leidner (2018)	How Allianz UK Used an Idea Management Platform to Harness Employee Innovation	Allianz UK	35 semi-structured interviews	MIS Quarterly Executive
Benbya and van Alstyne (2011)	How to Find Answers Within Your Company	At least 23 companies that implemented internal knowledge markets	Interviews, in-depth case studies, analyses of 20 internal knowledge markets, prototype development and testing in three companies	MIT Sloan Management Review
Bjelland and Wood (2008)	An Inside View of IBM's 'Innovation Jam'	IBM	Participant observations, review of Jam Web pages, more than 20 interviews	MIT Sloan Management Review
Davis et al. (2015)	Open Innovation at NASA: A New Business Model for Advancing Human Health and Performance Innovations	Human Health and Performance Directorate (HH&P), NASA	Participant observations	Research-Technology Management
Dimitrova and Scarso (2017)	The Impact of Crowdsourcing on the Evolution of Knowledge Management: Insights from a Case Study	Bombardier Transportation	3 semi-structured interviews	Knowledge and Process Management

(continued)

Table 1 (continued)

Author (Year)	Title	Case companies	Data	Published in
Elerud-Tryde and Hooge (2014)	Beyond the Generation of Ideas: Virtual Idea Campaigns to Spur Creativity and Innovation	Volvo Cars and Renault	25 semi-structured interviews, direct observation and action research	Creativity and Innovation Management
Knop and Blohm (2018)	Leveraging the Internal Work Force through Crowdtesting Crowdsourcing in Banking	Bank of Switzerland	N/A, most likely participant observation	ICIS 2018 Proceedings
Knop et al. (2017)	How to Design an Internal Crowdsourcing System	Schweizer Bank	Action design research project, 2 interviews	ICIS 2017 Proceedings
Leung et al. (2014)	Eureka!: Lessons Learned from an Evaluation of the Idea Contest at Deltares	Deltares	16 in-depth interviews	Research-Technology Management
Majchrzak et al. (2009)	Harnessing the Power of the Crowds with Corporate Social Networking Tools: How IBM Does It	IBM	N/A	MIS Quarterly Executive
Malhotra et al. (2017)	Developing Innovative Solutions Through Internal Crowdsourcing	Three large organizations (one in health care, one in telecommunications, and one in retail) and seven other companies (distribution, telecommunications company, telecommunications infrastructure, data storage and analytics, graphics design, industrial products, e-commerce platform provider)	Multi-method research project, interviews (number not explicitly mentioned)	MIT Sloan Management Review

(continued)

Table 1 (continued)

Author (Year)	Title	Case companies	Data	Published in
Muhdi and Boutellier (2011)	Motivational Factors Affecting Participation and Contribution of Members in Two Different Swiss Innovation Communities	PostFinance	Survey with 69 responses	International Journal of Innovation Management
Muller et al. (2013)	Crowdfunding Inside the Enterprise: Employee Initiatives for Innovation and Collaboration	IBM	Data logs of events, 24 interviews, email survey	Proceedings of the SIGCHI Conference on Human Factors in Computing Systems
Pohlisch (2019)	Crowdsourcing at SAP	SAP	10 in-depth interviews	Proceedings of the 14th European Conference on Innovation and Entrepreneurship
Rando et al. (2011)	Open Collaboration: A Problem-Solving Strategy That Is Redefining NASA's Innovative Spirit	NASA	Interviews (number of interviews not mentioned) and survey among solvers with 50 responses	Proceedings of the 62nd IAC Conference
Riemer et al. (2012b)	Powercrowd: Enterprise Social Networking in Professional Service Work: A Case Study of Yammer at Deloitte Australia	Deloitte (Yammer Platform)	Dataset of 44,589 messages from an enterprise social networking	Business Information Systems Working Paper Series
Rohrbeck et al. (2015)	IT Tools for Foresight: The Integrated Insight and Response System of Deutsche Telekom Innovation Laboratories	Deutsche Telekom	N/A, most likely participant observation	Technological Forecasting and Social Change

(continued)

Table 1 (continued)

Author (Year)	Title	Case companies	Data	Published in
Scupola and Nicolajsen (2014)	The Impact of Social Media Enterprise Crowdsourcing on Company Innovation Culture: The Case of an Engineering Consultancy	Engineering consultancy in Denmark	24 semi-structured interviews	Nordic Contributions in IS Research
Simula and Vuori (2012)	Benefits and Barriers of Crowdsourcing in B2B Firms: Generating Ideas with Internal and External Crowds	5 large Finnish industrial B2B companies	8 interviews	International Journal of Innovation Management
Smith et al. (2017)	The Evolution of an Innovation Capability	EMC	N/A, most likely participant observation	Research-Technology Management
Stephens et al. (2016)	Bubbling Up the Good Ideas: A Two-Mode Network Analysis of an Intra-organizational Idea Challenge	Global IT	Dataset from one idea challenge, bipartite network of 768 employees and 640 ideas	Journal of Computer-Mediated Communication
Stieger et al. (2012)	Democratizing Strategy: How Crowdsourcing Can Be Used for Strategy Dialogues	Austrian automation supplier	Participant observation; 10 semi-structured interviews	California Management Review
Wendelken et al. (2014)	Innovation Without Me: Why Employees Do (Not) Participate in Organizational Innovation Communities	Habermaaß GmbH	Participant observation; 30 semi-structured interviews	R&D Management
Zhu et al. (2016)	How to Use Crowdsourcing for Innovation?: A Comparative Case Study of Internal and External Idea Sourcing in the Chemical Industry	Evonik Industries AG	Participant observation	Portland International Conference on Management of Engineering and Technology

(continued)

Table 1 (continued)

Author (Year)	Title	Case companies	Data	Published in
Zhu et al. (2019)	How Does Online Interaction Affect Idea Quality? The Effect of Feedback in Firm-Internal Idea Competitions	Global, multiunit specialty chemicals company headquartered in Germany	Dataset of 351 active participants that contributed 598 comments across 160 ideas	Journal of Product Innovation Management

phenomenon is based on a range of different settings that allow contradictions and consensuses between the analysed case studies to be revealed. In the next section, the findings of all case studies with respect to the six management components will be reported.

3 Synthesis of the Literature

3.1 Corporate Culture and Change Management

Managing corporate culture and the changes that can be triggered by internal crowdsourcing is a significant challenge that does not exist in external crowdsourcing (Denyer et al. 2011). This involves creating an open and collaborative corporate culture in which internal crowdsourcing can function optimally (Simula and Vuori 2012; Steinhuser et al. 2011; Stocker et al. 2012). Internal crowdsourcing can help to break down hierarchical structures in companies and enable communication on equal terms (Riemer et al. 2015; Scupola and Nicolajsen 2014). However, not only hierarchical structures are questioned, but also well-established project-based innovation processes, since such platforms tackle innovation within a company in a much more open and informal manner, which is particularly important and challenging for larger companies (Scupola and Nicolajsen 2014). Internal crowdsourcing calls for a move towards open and transparent structures, which can only be achieved through active change management (Abu El-Ella et al. 2013; Riemer et al. 2012a).

Steinhuser et al. (2011) define specific requirements for 'Enterprise 2.0 Readiness': open communication culture, availability of resources, willingness to share knowledge, extroversion, education, and responsibility. A lack of openness to ideas from other departments could lead, for example, to employees not recognizing ideas from other departments—the not-invented-here syndrome (Lüttgens et al. 2014). Arena et al. (2017) call this environment an adaptive space. Within this space, ideas, people, and information can move freely across the organization. Employees' ideas must be accepted and valued, which can be communicated, for example, through

Table 2 Relevance of studies to the respective management task

Author (year)	Corporate culture and change management	Incentive Design	Task definition and decomposition	Quality assurance	Crowd selection	Regulations and legal implications
Arena et al. (2017)	x	–	–	(x)	(x)	–
Bailey and Horvitz (2010)	(x)	x	–	x	(x)	–
Benbya and Leidner (2018)	x	x	x	(x)	(x)	(x)
Benbya and van Alstyne (2011)	x	x	–	–	–	x
Bjelland and Wood (2008)	–	–	–	x	–	–
Davis et al. (2015)	x	x	x	–	–	–
Dimitrova and Scarso (2017)	(x)	–	–	–	(x)	–
Elerud-Tryde and Hooge (2014)	x	–	–	(x)	x	–
Knop and Blohm (2018)	x	–	–	–	(x)	(x)
Knop et al. (2017)	–	(x)	–	–	(x)	–
Leung et al. (2014)	x	x	–	x	–	–
Majchrzak et al. (2009)	x	–	–	(x)	–	–
Malhotra et al. (2017)	x	x	(x)	x	x	x
Muhdi and Boutellier (2011)	–	x	–	–	–	–
Muller et al. (2013)	–	–	–	(x)	(x)	–
Pohlisch (2019)	x	x	–	x	–	(x)
Rando et al. (2011)	–	x	x	–	–	–
Riemer et al. (2012b)	–	–	(x)	–	(x)	–

Rohrbeck et al. (2015)	(x)	–	x	(x)	–	x
Scupola and Nicolajsen (2014)	x	x	–	(x)	x	–
Simula and Vuori (2012)	x	–	(x)	(x)	–	–
Smith et al. (2017)	x	x	x	x	–	–
Stephens et al. (2016)	–	–	–	x	–	–
Stieger et al. (2012)	x	(x)	–	x	x	x
Wendelken et al. (2014)	(x)	x	–	–	x	–
Zhu et al. (2016)	x	(x)	x	–	x	(x)
Zhu et al. (2019)	–	–	–	x	(x)	–

Importance is determined as follows:
–: The article either does or does not relevantly address the respective management aspect
(x): The article addresses the respective management aspect; relevant findings are presented
x: The article delivers key insights into the respective management aspect

timely feedback (Boudreau et al. 2011; Henttonen et al. 2017; Simula and Vuori 2012). Support and buy-in from top management are seen as particularly important (Lüttgens et al. 2014; Benbya and Leidner 2018; Pohlisch 2019). Management should utilize a proactive leadership style, promote participation in crowdsourcing, create incentive structures, and ensure a sufficient provision of resources (Erickson et al. 2012). This does not simply mean that management approves the project plan and the budget for the implementation of a crowdsourcing project. Instead, in addition to approving investments, it is vital to obtain general support from various business units that should have the capacity and ability to subsequently adopt and integrate the results (Ooms et al. 2015; Pohlisch 2019). Additionally, it seems that internal crowdsourcing approaches that were initiated bottom-up received high recognition and acceptance, hinting that top management should be aware of and support such endeavours (Pohlisch 2019).

Furthermore, executive leadership should concentrate on setting policy, promoting flexibility, and ensuring liquidity inside the internal crowdsourcing system (Benbya and van Alstyne 2011). In line with this argument, Stieger et al. (2012) report that, while active communication of management with idea owners (e.g., by commenting) increased participation, this form of engagement can easily distract management from other tasks. Nevertheless, sufficient resources seem to be the prevailing bottleneck, which has been reported as being particularly important for non-product-carrying units, as they usually have smaller R&D budgets to begin with (Smith et al. 2017). To overcome the problem of reaching a critical mass, management could seed the market with ideas and subsidize the creation of key knowledge (Benbya and van Alstyne 2011).

To sustain the capabilities of internal crowdsourcing, one idea would be to install a dedicated team, responsible for promoting and adjusting the system (Benbya and Leidner 2018; Elerud-Tryde and Hooge 2014; Stieger et al. 2012). Benbya and Leidner (2018) describe how an innovation champion can promote internal crowdsourcing practices in their working environment as well as with senior management and provide coaching and mentoring for participating colleagues. Ulbrich and Wedel (see chapter 'Systematization Approach for the Development and Description of an Internal Crowdsourcing System' of this book) argue that additional roles must be considered to manage internal crowdsourcing successfully. In building their model, they introduce primary, secondary, and tertiary roles which employees can take on. In total, they describe eight different roles with specific duties and functions: (1) Crowd Master, (2) Campaign Owner, (3) Crowd Technology Master, (4) Content Owner, (5) Secondary Counterpart, (6) Crowd, (7) Executive Board, and (8) Employee Union Representation. This framework can help companies to unam biguously attribute necessary functions to suitable employees, reducing the risk of overlapping competencies and preventing potential conflicts. For a more detailed description of the role model for internal crowdsourcing and the corresponding descriptions of the roles, see Ulbrich and Wedel (see chapter 'Systematization Approach for the Development and Description of an Internal Crowdsourcing System' of this book).

To raise awareness for such a system, it is vital to communicate its advantages and opportunities throughout the company. In order to achieve this, the management could use newsletters, workshops, and lecture series with internal and external speakers (Davis et al. 2015). Stieger et al. (2012) further report the use of introduction videos, posters, flyers, and particularly on-site presentations to increase awareness. Direct superiors in particular should be encouraged to inform employees about the possibilities to participate. Employees often do not even know what crowdsourcing initiatives and opportunities to participate in the innovation process are on offer, even if they are already engaged in one of them (Pohlisch 2019). Pohlisch (2019) concludes that more awareness about the different initiatives could raise positive externalities and create synergies between them.

Building a community in which true collaboration is fostered is critical. The internal crowdsourcing platform should help employees connect and actively share knowledge and ideas instead of only providing solutions to given problems (Malhotra et al. 2017; Simula and Vuori 2012). The network aspect should be much more than just employees being active in generating ideas. The firm should furthermore identify and support experts (e.g., human resources, finance, marketing, etc.) who could support the idea of development process with their knowledge and networks (Smith et al. 2017). This approach can also help integrate internal crowdsourcing into the innovation process and promote its acceptance by the crowd (Zhu et al. 2016).

Managers must have realistic expectations concerning the failure rates of internal crowdsourcing activities (Bailey and Horvitz 2010; Stieger et al. 2012; Pohlisch 2019). They need to be aware of the different paths along with which ideas can create value. Financial returns might be expected to be higher in some business areas than in others. Nevertheless, ideas can also be related to brand image, customer satisfaction, and employee engagement (Benbya and Leidner 2018). Often enough, internal crowdsourcing is not primarily undertaken to generate innovations and revenue streams or to reduce costs but to increase each employee's innovation efforts and to create a more entrepreneurial and collaborative culture (Elerud-Tryde and Hooge 2014; Leung et al. 2014). The commitment, attitude, and mentality of those directly responsible must also be considered (Leung et al. 2014). Managers who can decide on budgets and activities within the research and innovation departments can be named as key stakeholders here (Benbya and Leidner 2018; Zhu et al. 2016). Their buy-in across the organization was found to be critical for success (Benbya and Leidner 2018; Leung et al. 2014; Zhu et al. 2016). These direct supervisors are often more reluctant to accept the additional task of crowdsourcing (Leung et al. 2014) as they fear it might keep their staff from working on their regular jobs (Knop and Blohm 2018).

From the employee's point of view, it is particularly important that existing work obligations are recognized and taken into account (Wagenknecht et al. 2017). Building on this, internal crowdsourcing must not be created as an additional task (Prpić et al. 2015). Benbya and Leidner (2018) report that weekly idea meetings can help incorporate internal crowdsourcing into the work routine, therefore making it feel more like part of the regular day job. What is more, the platform needs to be seamlessly integrated into the workflow of employees and easily accessible from everywhere at all times in order to mitigate entry barriers (Rohrbeck et al. 2015). The time invested by employees must be seen as time well spent and not as a waste of resources (Leung et al. 2014; Elerud-Tryde and Hooge 2014; Knop and Blohm 2018; Majchrzak et al. 2009; Pohlisch 2019), and innovation activities must be legitimized (Elerud-Tryde and Hooge 2014; Pohlisch 2019). However, too many tasks and the associated excessive demands can cause the creativity and innovativeness of employees to drop (Arena et al. 2017).

Notwithstanding this, it should be clear that specific time resources need to be allocated towards innovative activities in general and work on the crowdsourcing platform specifically (Malhotra et al. 2017; Simula and Vuori 2012; Wendelken et al. 2014). Stieger et al. (2012) argue that the amount of time allocated should be communicated unambiguously by management in order to prevent employees who participate heavily from being wrongly accused of not working to capacity. This also helps employees assess the amount of time they have to commit (Wendelken et al. 2014). The cultivation of relationships with one's employees must have a high priority and be planned for the long term, as the crowd is much more static than in external crowdsourcing (Prpić et al. 2015). To increase the number of ideas generated, participants should also be encouraged to freely explore ideas without restrictions, like risk management and cost considerations (Elerud-Tryde and Hooge 2014). The focus should be not so much on monitoring and controlling employees as on creating confidence that time and manpower will be used by employees in a meaningful way (Majchrzak et al. 2009). Management should rely on openness, transparency, and social control mechanisms (Zuchowski et al. 2016).

3.2 Incentive Design

In the academic debate concerning the correct design of the incentive structures of IC, no uniform opinion has emerged so far. However, a strategic examination of the topic is of immense importance in order to ensure a high level of crowd participation. In some of the articles examined, it is assumed that a specific incentive structure is not necessary, as participation should be sufficiently reflected by salaries and bonus payments (Lopez et al. 2010; Skopik et al. 2012). However, most studies advocate specific incentive structures to ensure long-term employee commitment. If an organization decides in favour of concrete incentive structures, material and immaterial incentives are generally possible.

Material incentives include monetary remuneration or non-cash prizes like gift cards and vouchers (Benbya and van Alstyne 2011; Dimitrova and Scarso 2017; Malhotra et al. 2017; Stieger et al. 2012). One possibility to incorporate this would be to introduce a new measurement of innovation performance into the employee appraisal process that takes crowdsourcing activities into account (Benbya and Leidner 2018). In addition to cash prizes for solving a challenge, money could also be awarded to idea owners in order to further develop ideas (Majchrzak et al.

2009), combining material incentives with the intangible incentive of receiving an opportunity to implement one's idea.

Intangible incentives include, for example, recognition by colleagues (Muhdi and Boutellier 2011; Simula and Vuori 2012; Dimitrova and Scarso 2017; Knop and Blohm 2018; Leung et al. 2014; Scupola and Nicolajsen 2014; Zhu et al. 2016), fun and games (Muhdi and Boutellier 2011; Leung et al. 2014), learning entrepreneurial skills (Dos Santos and Spann 2011; Leung et al. 2014), learning and discovering new things (Muhdi and Boutellier 2011), doing something with purpose (Knop and Blohm 2018), building networks within the organization (Dahl et al. 2011), creating visibility for own ideas (Muhdi and Boutellier 2011; Bailey and Horvitz 2010), and seeing them implemented (Bailey and Horvitz 2010) or employees implementing them themselves (Leung et al. 2014; Malhotra et al. 2017; Zhu et al. 2016). In addition, the commitment of top management is cited as an incentive to participate (Leung et al. 2014). Analysing an internal crowdsourcing community, Muhdi and Boutellier (2011) show that participants value education, broaden their horizons, find like-minded peers, and link for collaboration as most important. Rando et al. (2011) find that helping others, collaboration, problem-solving, curiosity, and dealing with something outside of daily routines were significant motivating factors. Muller et al. (2013) note the ability to make changes in the immediate work environment as a critical motivational factor. In line with the above-mentioned motivational aspects, Scupola and Nicolajsen (2014) find that intangible incentives were more important than material ones. An important aspect reported by Wendelken et al. (2014) is that altruism was not observed to bring a motivational factor in internal innovation communities, although it is an essential aspect of their external counterparts.

However, companies should not rely exclusively on material or immaterial incentives when designing their incentive structures, but rather combine both to optimally promote employee motivation (Benbya and van Alstyne 2011; Smith et al. 2017). Wendelken et al. (2014) find that refraining from monetary rewards will result in a crowd that is smaller, yet more interested in the specific topic and with high intrinsic motivation while turning to monetary rewards tends to increase community size. The incentives should also be tailored to the crowd within the company, since motivational structures can also differ between individual departments of a company (Benbya and Leidner 2018). Taking this idea a step further, Davis et al. (2015) report that, at NASA, employees were asked to submit and vote on ideas on how to remunerate participants. Hence, NASA basically crowdsourced the design of the incentive system to its employees.

Benbya and van Alstyne (2011) recommend using absolute rather than relative incentives to encourage information sharing among employees and to promote an open corporate culture. The idea is that, in this way, not only the relative position in a ranking is relevant for the reward. Instead, all submissions that meet a certain quality standard are rewarded. Relative rewards, however, should be preferred when solutions are substitutes and need to be solved quickly. Furthermore, Benbya and van Alstyne (2011) advocate using variable rewards—for example, by introducing virtual currencies. The underlying problem is that fixed rewards lead to an over- or undersupply of ideas if the reward level is not chosen perfectly. If the reward is too low, ideas with a higher value or ideas that require significant effort will not be submitted. On the other hand, if the reward is too high, employees neglect other important tasks, and there is an oversupply of ideas. Blohm et al. 2010 propose reward team performance instead of individual performance in order to encourage collaboration within and competition between teams. If, however, not individual but collective performance is rewarded, this can lead to a free-riding mentality. Stieger et al. (2012) therefore recommend awarding rewards on an individual basis.

Perhaps one of the strongest motivations for employees to contribute to internal crowdsourcing initiatives is to create ownership in their ideas. As the employee is more strongly linked to the outcome of the initiative (positive and negative), this might increase commitment, which can in turn increase self-satisfaction and a higher identification with the company's goals (Pohlisch 2019).

In addition to rewards for selected and particularly good ideas, incentive structures should also provide rewards for unfinished ideas to motivate and address as many employees as possible (Malhotra et al. 2017). Ideas from all submitters should always be appreciated in order to signalize to employees that their submissions have value for the company, even if they are not ultimately selected or implemented (Boudreau et al. 2011). To create incentives to comment on other employees' ideas, Benbya and van Alstyne (2011) and Malhotra et al. (2017) also propose rewarding helpful comments, as well as flagging obsolete and organizing dispersed content. In line with these findings, Scupola and Nicolajsen (2014) find that rewarding these different roles—instead of just the idea contributor—can help to raise awareness of the miscellaneous efforts necessary for a successful internal crowdsourcing process. Pohlisch (2019) finds that giving campaigns a less competitive character and incorporating commenting into the incentive structure could foster the collaborative development of ideas.

One way to present awards could be an event that takes place at a prestigious location. The tremendous visibility of such an event can amplify the incentives provided and deliver significant social recognition (Benbya and Leidner 2018; Smith et al. 2017). Next to physical events, success stories can also be published in the intranet or on a company blog to increase social recognition (Rando et al. 2011).

3.3 Task Definition and Decomposition

The definition, modularization, and distribution of tasks are an integral part of the management of internal crowdsourcing activities and have a significant influence on their success probability (Blohm et al. 2017; Zogaj et al. 2015; Stocker et al. 2012; Simula and Vuori 2012). Defining tasks in a way that they can be solved by individual participants is of great importance to ensure that the solutions can be reintegrated later into complex structures (Zuchowski et al. 2016). More significant tasks need to be processed and edited in such a way that single employees in the crowd can complete them (Knop and Blohm 2018). To increase the likelihood of the emergence of excellent ideas, Benbya and Leidner (2018) recommend formulating problems that address a business need in a very specific and targeted manner. Summarizing, they find that 'the best approach is to define the scope, provide context, identify constraints and clear goals, and remove as many assumptions as possible' (Benbya and Leidner 2018, p. 148). Smith et al. (2017) describe the same phenomenon by stating that the problem may potentially be formulated either too broadly or too narrowly. If too broad, the ideas might not be relevant, while the other extreme might hamper more radical ideas. In line with Benbya and Leidner (2018), they argue that ideas should align with the strategic goals of the company. As one potential solution, they propose that challenges can be tied to certain business units. Malhotra et al. (2017) follow this line of argument, stating that how the questions is framed is crucial and influences the employees' decision whether to participate in internal crowdsourcing or not.

Furthermore, internal crowdsourcing should be used for problems that impact the company in the long-term and not for short-term improvements (Malhotra et al. 2017). In contrast, Riemer et al. (2012b) report that internal crowdsourcing could also be used as a form of ad hoc idea-generation tool comparable to an online brainstorming session, in which an employee starts a conversation with the aim of sourcing spontaneous ideas. However, all things aside, providing assistance to the problem owner so that the particular internal crowdsourcing can be adequately formulated seems of vital importance (Benbya and Leidner 2018; Rando et al. 2011).

Davis et al. (2015) point out another crucial aspect, namely, the knowledge of employees about when to use which open innovation tool for what kind of problem. The idea is that employees need to be educated with respect to the possibilities but also potential problems and pitfalls of internal crowdsourcing so that they are able to use the tool for adequate problems. Hence, in their study Davis et al. (2015) describe how a knowledge management and decision analysis tool was implemented at NASA to help employees decide which of the various innovative tools at hand would be appropriate for their problem.

One last aspect is referring to how time management in setting up a crowdsourcing campaign is related to the specificity of the task. Zhu et al. (2016) propose allocating more time to highly specific tasks, so that participants can develop highly sophisticated solutions, while less time should be allocated to less specific tasks, in order to spur participants to come up with more creative and spontaneous ideas.

3.4 Quality Assurance

Quality assurance within internal crowdsourcing refers to all activities related to ensuring the quality of submissions and final results (Zuchowski et al. 2016). Besides defining tasks, quality assurance has the most significant influence on the success of crowdsourcing campaigns (Zogaj et al. 2015). Ensuring high-quality results is essential to increase the usefulness and credibility of IC campaigns and to avoid employees associating crowdsourcing with low-quality results (Bailey and Horvitz 2010). Crowdsourcing campaigns often generate a plethora of ideas—not all of them are useful. Hence, quality assurance is crucial for the success of crowdsourcing campaigns (Erickson 2012; Pedersen et al. 2013; Vukovic and Naik 2011).

The ideas can be evaluated either by the crowd itself (Bailey and Horvitz 2010; Leimeister et al. 2009; Vukovic and Naik 2011) or with criteria defined a priori (Benbya and Leidner 2018).

The so-called crowdvoting is generally used to generate an initial evaluation of the ideas, while expert evaluation usually takes place according to defined criteria before solutions are actually implemented (Bailey and Horvitz 2010; Benbya and Leidner 2018). Stephens et al. (2016) have shown that crowdvoting is well suited to selecting ideas from a large mass of ideas. At the same time, however, they point out that there is a high degree of centrality with regard to participants and ideas, i.e., a small number of employees are responsible for a large proportion of the activity, which in turn concentrates on a small number of ideas. Thus, popular ideas are usually upvoted more strongly, resulting in a Matthew effect. They have also found evidence of a shared affiliation effect, meaning that employees tend to upvote ideas of their direct peers more often. To solve these problems, they advocate pushing the visibility of less endorsed ideas as well as ideas from outside the employees' cluster of peers. The results of the work done by Bailey and Horvitz (2010) confirm this and show that the outcome of crowdvotings can reflect the status and network of an employee instead of the quality of the idea. However, they also acknowledge the importance of voting and commenting as a source of input for the author in further developing an idea. To suppress the tendency of users to vote for popular, well-marketed ideas, they recommend letting employees vote on relevant business dimensions instead of merely 'liking' ideas. Next to merely voting and rating, the amount of comments on an idea and how in-depth they are can be a significant predictor of idea quality as shown by Elerud-Tryde and Hooge (2014). Comments by peers also help increase the quality of submissions by filtering requests that have no added value to the company (Majchrzak et al. 2009). However, even the amount of comments and votes together might not be a good measure of the impact of a submission. Stieger et al. (2012) find that the higher the entry barrier to engaging meaningfully in a discussion, e.g., because highly specific knowledge is required, the lower the participation rates. However, this might bear no correlation at all to the potential of individual submissions. As an alternative to voting mechanisms, Scupola and Nicolajsen (2014) propose trading fictitious shares of an idea among employees. Muller et al. (2013) reported about one case at an IBM Research organization where every employee was given $100 to invest in idea proposals.

Ransbotham and Westerman (2016) state in their study that internal crowd valuations are distorted by popularity and social aspects and expert valuations are often more closely aligned with the company's objectives. Correspondingly, Bjelland and Wood (2008) found high-level analysts and managers to be best at selecting the most promising ideas. Leung et al. (2014) report that safe environments for employees can be created if companies rely solely on internal experts in the early stages of the selection process. Further incorporating external experts later on can add a valuable market perspective to the evaluation process. Experts often rank ideas on several different dimensions like innovativeness, feasibility, market potential, and team composition. In a study on internal crowdsourcing processes at SAP, Pohlisch (2019) found that employees sometimes tend to vote strategically and might not possess the often very specific knowledge to adequately evaluate ideas. One massive problem with regard to evaluations by a selected group of experts is that such experts often represent a rare resource and are thus relatively expensive. In addition, identifying experts is a complex and time-consuming process (Lüttgens et al. 2014). Another aspect worth mentioning is that participants might consider the expertise of the judging experts as being insufficient to validate their ideas, especially if they consider themselves to be the expert in a particular field (Leung et al. 2014).

In order to avoid a situation where the evaluation process is not accepted, the evaluation process must be as open and transparent as possible (Leung et al. 2014; Simula and Vuori 2012; Malhotra et al. 2017). Ultimately, feedback to the participants in crowdsourcing initiatives should be as direct as possible. Zhu et al. (2019) were able to show that feedback in internal idea competitions leads to a significantly higher quality of ideas. Furthermore, the feedback should be detailed and should contain constructive proposals on how to improve the ideas, especially if ideas are rejected (Leung et al. 2014; Malhotra et al. 2017). While feedback is normally provided by problem owners and management, the platform should allow for all employees to provide feedback on ideas, possibly leading to a coevolution of ideas (Malhotra et al. 2017). Another approach would be to let senior executives write responses to the most important contributions (Stieger et al. 2012).

To ensure long-lasting participation as well as the best use of the provided solutions, it is vital to integrate the internal crowdsourcing process into a company's commercialization infrastructure (Leung et al. 2014; Malhotra et al. 2017; Rohrbeck et al. 2015; Pohlisch 2019). This means that there should be a dedicated follow-up process in place for winning as well as for losing ideas. Alternative avenues towards pursuing an idea that was not selected as well as a clear commercialization path for selected ideas should be provided (Leung et al. 2014). Smith et al. (2017) describe one such process at EMC, where a stage-gate process was introduced to ensure that ideas are moved efficiently from concept to implementation. This way, the success rate of ideas could be substantially increased and the process times decreased. Solutions that are not selected should be allowed to be resubmitted at a later stage (Malhotra et al. 2017) and screened for potential other avenues of development (Smith et al. 2017).

3.5 *Crowd Selection*

With community management, Zuchowski et al. (2016) introduce another component of their governance framework but mainly describe aspects related to selecting the appropriate crowd. Since community management can be understood as a more comprehensive term (Young 2013), this aspect is going to be named 'crowd selection'. Furthermore, there is a differentiation between the community, which is defined as the entirety of the employees of the company, and the crowd, which refers to the fraction of employees who eventually engage in the internal crowdsourcing activities (Ulbrich and Wedel, see chapter 'Systematization Approach for the Development and Description of an Internal Crowdsourcing System' of this book).

Crowd selection is about defining the openness of IC. Usually, IC should be entirely open to all employees of the company. Opening up the process increases the number and diversity of participants and therefore serendipity (Leung et al. 2014; Stieger et al. 2012; Zhu et al. 2016, 2019). What is more, the openness of the platform sends a signal that the contributions of all employees—regardless of hierarchies and organizational affiliation—are welcome, which in turn can lead to increased motivation among participants (Muhdi and Boutellier 2011; Scupola and Nicolajsen 2014; Elerud-Tryde and Hooge 2014). Diversity in the participants leads to a greater variety of solutions, which in turn potentially leads to creative rebound effects (Elerud-Tryde and Hooge 2014). In fact, Arena et al. (2017, p. 4) observed that the majority of winning projects were actually submitted by employees 'below the radar or working in remote offices'. Not only ideas created by experts are valuable, and smaller, fuzzy ideas often turn out to be very valuable as well (Scupola and Nicolajsen 2014).

Furthermore, Bailey and Horvitz (2010) report that the primary motivation for creating an internal crowdsourcing system at Microsoft was to develop a channel for ideas that were not related to employees' daily work routines. In line with the previous findings, Muller et al. (2013) do not find significantly different participation rates between managers and non-managers or between different hierarchical levels. Also, the very nature of the idea challenges makes internal crowdsourcing and, along with it, innovation as a normal activity much more present for all employees (Elerud-Tryde and Hooge 2014). In this way, internal crowdsourcing can be seen as creating more equality and opening up the innovation process to all employees regardless of their hierarchical position, area of expertise, or organizational affiliation, potentially leading to a sense of empowerment among employees (Scupola and Nicolajsen 2014).

One problem in opening up the crowdsourcing innovation process to all employees within a company is that not all employees might have access to computers. One way to solve this problem could be to set up terminals in production environments that employees can use to post their ideas, although this entry barrier also poses a hurdle most employees are not willing to take on (Stieger et al. 2012). Allowing employees to submit ideas in the name of colleagues while giving credit to the original idea owner could be another way (Dimitrova and Scarso 2017). Aside from purely access issues, differences in IT competences between employees can introduce biassed participation. To address this, the company could provide 'a training process to lift the IT and workflow competences of employees in the crowd to a minimum level' (Knop and Blohm 2018, p. 11).

On the other hand, it is possible to restrict the crowd to a selected circle of employees. Selection is usually based on specific skills and knowledge or context-based criteria, such as membership in a particular organizational unit (Geiger et al. 2011; Simula and Vuori 2012; Knop et al. 2017). Although this reduces the level of diversity among participants, it can lead to a higher degree of professionalism in the contributions (Simula and Ahola 2014). Benbya and Leidner (2018) argue that it is necessary to select participants depending on the properties of the specific task at hand. Experts should be favoured for specialized problems, while less specialized problems benefit from access to miscellaneous knowledge normally distributed throughout the company. Zhu et al. (2016), instead, base their argument on the distinction between process and product innovation. A specified crowd with specific knowledge is to be favoured when process innovations are pursued, while unspecified crowds with diverse knowledge are better suited for product innovations.

In contrast to the idea of including experts in the crowd, Malhotra et al. (2017) propose limiting the influence of these experts, because other participants might be deterred from submitting their ideas by the fact that experts are part of the crowd. They suggest that experts should be used as moderators and motivators. To further increase the number of participants, early adopters can be used to create a critical mass and encourage other employees to participate (Benbya and Leidner 2018; Simula and Vuori 2012; Stocker et al. 2012). Following the same line of argument, Wendelken et al. (2014) report about the strategy of one German toy manufacturer that took this aspect to the extreme. By specifically deciding not to address R&D employees, design staff, lead users, and others who one would expect to be asked, they purposefully engaged employees who were normally excluded from the innovation process. Rando et al. (2011) distinguish between theoretical and technical challenges. While the former benefit from the broad participation of employees with various backgrounds, the latter often require in-depth domain knowledge by experts. While preselecting the crowd might be beneficial in some cases, addressing only R&D employees, for example, might lead to a decrease in the participation of other employees (Riemer et al. 2012b), which in turn could potentially lead to a significant loss in serendipity, negatively influencing the diversity and even radicalness of outcomes.

3.6 Regulations and Legal Implications

An analysis of the literature reveals that this part of managing internal crowdsourcing is heavily under-researched. Only seven of the identified studies mention relevant aspects of this topic at all, and only four of those contribute to the discussion to a significant extent. Their findings can be summarized by three key elements: (1) transparency, (2) anonymity, and (3) protection of information.

First, transparency in this context means that the conditions of participation are clear and that the internal crowdsourcing process is presented as clearly and transparently as possible—from the launch to the process to select a solution (Benbya and

Leidner 2018; Pohlisch 2019). Not only being transparent about the design but also allowing participants to ask for changes or additional features could make the system more attractive to employees (Benbya and van Alstyne 2011). Complete transparency concerning the crowdsourcing process can also help reduce objections about any 'potential exploitation of employees as well as a deterioration in working conditions' (Knop and Blohm 2018, p. 11) that the works council might have and which in turn could impede the introduction of such a tool within the company (Rohrbeck et al. 2015; Knop and Blohm 2018). Furthermore, barrier-free access needs to be established so that disabled employees (Rohrbeck et al. 2015), employees who do not have access to computers during their daily work routines (Dimitrova and Scarso 2017), or employees who are not physically present on the company site, like salespeople, are not excluded (Stieger et al. 2012). Personal information collected about employees needs to be regulated (Rohrbeck et al. 2015) and should be transparent as well.

Second, anonymity or the option for employees to anonymously participate in the crowdsourcing process is advised repeatedly (Benbya and van Alstyne 2011; Malhotra et al. 2017; Stieger et al. 2012). The idea is that employees might be afraid to admit what they do not know and that protected spaces or the option of anonymity could allow for an environment where controversial information is shared much more readily and freely (Benbya and van Alstyne 2011). Another aspect of this is the fact that anonymity can free employees from their organizational role, hierarchical position, or departmental affiliation, allowing them to more freely share and advocate ideas (Malhotra et al. 2017). However, it is worth mentioning that anonymity within such systems is technically impossible, as postings can always be traced back to their author. The fear that management could theoretically be tracing posts might once again potentially lead to controversial thoughts not being published (Stieger et al. 2012). Stieger et al. (2012) also point out that anonymity would reduce anxiety and apprehensions that could result from being evaluated by peers within the company.

The last aspect mentioned in the reviewed papers is the protection of information. Benbya and van Alstyne (2011) specifically warn about the 'risk of competitive disclosure'. However, it is generally assumed that intellectual property issues hardly play any role at all in internal crowdsourcing, because all participants from the crowd are contractually bound to the company (Simula and Vuori 2012) and this employment contract usually takes property rights into account (Vukovic and Bartolini 2010). Furthermore, confidentiality agreements or general laws on employee inventions often apply (Zhu et al. 2016). In Germany, for example, the Act on Employee Inventions applies, under which the employee is entitled to remuneration, but the ownership rights to the invention are transferred to the employer if the invention has been developed as part of an employee's official work duties (Bundesministerium der Justiz und für Verbraucherschutz 2009). Internal crowdsourcing is thus a way of accessing the distributed knowledge of the crowd without risking the same problems concerning intellectual property rights that could occur in external crowdsourcing (Villarroel and Reis 2010).

4 Conclusion

The purpose of this literature review is to summarize the empirical literature on the management of internal crowdsourcing. The findings presented provide a well-structured source of information that can be used by companies to design their internal crowdsourcing implementations. This might allow them to access the innovation potential of their employees, thereby creating a valuable competitive advantage.

The review above shows that certain aspects of the management of internal crowdsourcing are better understood and much more researched than others. While most studies covered aspects of corporate culture and incentive design, only a few studies contributed to an understanding of task definition and decomposition or regulations and legal considerations. Hence, these two management tasks represent a promising avenue for future research. The works council aspect in particular seems to have been somewhat neglected in the literature. This is astounding, considering that the works council has a right of co-determination for tools like internal crowdsourcing—at least in Germany. Furthermore, endorsement by the works council for the implementation of such tools will most likely increase participation and acceptance among employees.

However, this does not necessarily mean that areas that are more researched are far better understood. As it becomes evident when looking at incentive structures, more work is required concerning the impact of contextual factors (e.g., industry, the goal of crowdsourcing, hierarchy structures, etc.) on the motivations of employees. It is also worth noting that most studies in the analysed sample discuss internal crowdsourcing implementations at large multinational corporations within complex industries, limiting the generalizability of the findings. Hence, future research should also consider investigating the potential of internal crowdsourcing for low-technology industries and small- and medium-sized enterprises.

References

Abu El-Ella N, Stoetzel M, Bessant J, Pinkwart A (2013) Accelerating high involvement: The role of new technologies in enabling employee participation in innovation. Int J Innovat Manag 17 (06):1340020

Arena M, Cross R, Sims J, Uhl-Bien M (2017) How to catalyze innovation in your organization. MIT Sloan Manag Rev 58(4):38–48

Bailey BP, Horvitz E (2010) What's your idea? A case study of a grassroots innovation pipeline within a large software company. In: Proceedings of the 28th international conference on human factors in computing systems, pp 2065–2074

Benbya H, Leidner D (2018) How Allianz UK Used an idea management platform to harness employee innovation. MIS Q Exec 17(2):139–155

Benbya H, van Alstyne MW (2011) How to find answers within your company. MIT Sloan Manag Rev 52(2):65–76

Bjelland O, Wood RC (2008) An inside view of IBM's 'innovation jam'. MIT Sloan Manag Rev 50 (1):32–40
Blohm I, Bretschneider U, Leimeister JM, Krcmar H (2010) Does collaboration among participants lead to better ideas in IT-based idea competitions? An empirical investigation. In: Proceedings of the 43rd Hawaii international conference on system sciences, Koloa, Kauai, HI, USA, 5–8 January
Blohm I, Zogaj S, Bretschneider U, Leimeister JM (2017) How to manage crowdsourcing platforms effectively? Calif Manag Rev 60(2):122–149
Boudreau KJ, Lacetera N, Lakhani KR (2011) Incentives and problem uncertainty in innovation contests: an empirical analysis. Manag Sci 57(5):843–863
Bundesministerium der Justiz und für Verbraucherschutz (2009) Gesetz über Arbeitnehmererfindungen: ArbnErfG
Dahl A, Lawrence J, Pierce J (2011) Building an innovation community. Res Technol Manag 54 (5):19–27
Davis JR, Richard EE, Keeton KE (2015) Open innovation at NASA: a new business model for advancing human health and performance innovations. Res Technol Manag 58(3):52–58
Denyer D, Parry E, Flowers P (2011) "Social", "open" and "participative"? Exploring personal experiences and organisational effects of Enterprise2.0 use. Soc Softw Strat Technol Community 44(5):375–396
Dimitrova S, Scarso E (2017) The impact of crowdsourcing on the evolution of knowledge management: Insights from a case study. Knowl Process Manag 24(4):287–295
Dos Santos R, Spann M (2011) Collective entrepreneurship at Qualcomm: combining collective and entrepreneurial practices to turn employee ideas into action. R&D Manag 41(5):443–456
Elerud-Tryde A, Hooge S (2014) Beyond the generation of ideas: virtual idea campaigns to spur creativity and innovation. Creativ Innovat Manag 23(3):290–302
Erickson LB (2012) Leveraging the crowd as a source of innovation: does crowdsourcing represent a new model for product and service innovation? In Proceedings of the 50th annual conference on computers and people research, Milwaukee, WI, USA, May, pp 91–96
Erickson LB, Trauth EM, Petrick I (2012) Getting inside your employees' heads: Navigating barriers to internal-crowdsourcing for product and service innovation. In ICIS 2012 proceedings
Geiger D, Seedorf S, Schulze T, Nickerson RC, Schader M (2011) Managing the crowd: towards a taxonomy of crowdsourcing processes. In: Proceedings of the seventeenth Americas conference on information systems, Detroit, MI, USA, 4–7 August
Henttonen K, Rissanen T, Eriksson P, Hallikas J (2017) Cultivating the wisdom of personnel through internal crowdsourcing. Int J Innovat Technol Manag (IJITM) 16(2):117–132
Howe J (2006) The rise of crowdsourcing. Wired Mag 14(6):1–4
Knop N, Blohm I (2018) Leveraging the internal work force through crowdtesting: crowdsourcing in banking. In: ICIS 2018 proceedings, San Francisco, USA
Knop N, Durward D, Blohm I (2017) How to design an internal crowdsourcing system. In: ICIS 2017 proceedings
Leimeister JM, Huber M, Bretschneider U, Krcmar H (2009) Leveraging crowdsourcing: activation-supporting components for IT-based ideas competition. J Manag Inform Syst 26 (1):197–224
Leung N, van Rooij A, van Deen J (2014) Eureka!: lessons learned from an evaluation of the idea contest at Deltares. Res Technol Manag 57(4):44–50
Lopez M, Vukovic M, Laredo J (2010) PeopleCloud service for enterprise crowdsourcing. In: Proceedings of the IEEE international conference on services computing, Miami, Florida, USA, pp 538–545
Lüttgens D, Pollok P, Antons D, Piller F (2014) Wisdom of the crowd and capabilities of a few: internal success factors of crowdsourcing for innovation. J Bus Econ 84(3):339–374
Majchrzak A, Cherbakov L, Ives B (2009) Harnessing the power of the crowds with corporate social networking tools: how IBM does it. MIS Q Exec 8(2)

Malhotra A, Majchrzak A, Kesebi L, Looram S (2017) Developing innovative solutions through internal crowdsourcing. MIT Sloan Manag Rev 58(4):73–79

Muhdi L, Boutellier R (2011) Motivational factors affecting participation and contribution of members in two different Swiss innovation communities. Int J Innovat Manag 15(03):543–562

Muller M, Geyer W, Soule T, Daniels S, Cheng L-T (2013) Crowdfunding inside the enterprise: employee-initiatives for innovation and collaboration. In: Proceedings of the SIGCHI conference on human factors in computing systems, pp 503–512

Ooms W, Bell J, Kok RAW (2015) Use of social media in inbound open innovation: building capabilities for absorptive capacity. Creativ Innovat Manag 24(1):136–150

Pedersen J, Kocsis D, Tripathi A, Tarrell A, Weerakoon A, Tahmasbi N, Xiong J, Deng W, Oh O, de Vreede G-J (2013) Conceptual foundations of crowdsourcing: a review of IS research. In: 46th Hawaii international conference on system sciences (HICSS 2013): Wailea, [Maui], HI, USA, 7–10 Jan 2013

Pohlisch J (2019) Internal crowdsourcing at SAP. In: Proceedings of the 14th European conference on innovation and entrepreneurship (ECIE), Kalamata, Greece, 19–20 September, pp 1201–1209

Prpić J, Shukla PP, Kietzmann JH, McCarthy IP (2015) How to work a crowd: Developing crowd capital through crowdsourcing. Bus Horiz 58(1):77–85

Rando CM, Fogarty JA, Richard EE, Davis JR (2011) Open collaboration: a problem solving strategy that is redefining NASA's innovative spirit. In: 62nd international astronautical congress

Ransbotham S, Westerman GF (2016) Agency conflict in internal corporate innovation contests

Rao D (2016) Enterprise crowdsourcing to sustain culture of innovation. http://www.cio.in/opinions/enterprise-crowdsourcing-sustain-culture-innovation. Accessed 21 Nov 2018

Riemer K, Overfeld P, Scifleet P, Richter A (2012a) Oh, SNEP! The dynamics of social network emergence—the case of Capgemini Yammer. Business information systems working paper series

Riemer K, Scifleet P, Reddig R (2012b) Powercrowd: enterprise social networking in professional service work: a case study of Yammer at Deloitte Australia. Business information systems working paper series

Riemer K, Stieglitz S, Meske C (2015) From top to bottom—investigating the changing role of hierarchy in enterprise social networks. Bus Inform Syst Eng 57(3):197–212

Rohrbeck R, Thom N, Arnold H (2015) IT tools for foresight: IT tools for foresight: The integrated insight and response system of Deutsche Telekom Innovation Laboratories. Technol Forecast Soc Change 97:115–126

Scupola A, Nicolajsen HW (2014) The impact of enterprise crowdsourcing on company innovation culture: the case of an engineering consultancy. In: Commisso TH, Nørbjerg J, Pries-Heje J (eds) Nordic contributions in IS research. Springer, Cham

Simula H, Ahola T (2014) A network perspective on idea and innovation crowdsourcing in industrial firms. Ind Market Manag 43(3):400–408

Simula H, Vuori M (2012) Benefits and barriers of crowdsourcing in B2B firms: generating ideas with internal and external crowds. Int J Innovat Manag 16(06):1240011

Skopik F, Schall D, Dustdar S (2012) Discovering and managing social compositions in collaborative enterprise crowdsourcing systems. Int J Cooper Inform Syst 21(04):297–341

Smith C, Fixson SK, Paniagua-Ferrari C, Parise S (2017) The evolution of an innovation capability. Res Technol Manag 60(2):26–35

Steinhuser M, Smolnik S, Hoppe U (2011) Towards a measurement model of corporate social software success—evidences from an exploratory multiple case study. In 2011 44th Hawaii international conference on system sciences (HICSS), 4–7 Jan 2011, Koloa, Kauai, HI, pp 1–10

Stephens B, Chen W, Butler JS (2016) Bubbling up the good ideas: a two-mode network analysis of an intra-organizational idea challenge. J Comput Mediated Commun 21(3):210–229

Stieger D, Matzler K, Chatterjee S, Ladstaetter-Fussenegger F (2012) Democratizing strategy: how crowdsourcing can be used for strategy dialogues. Calif Manag Rev 54(4):44–68

Stocker A, Richter A, Hoefler P, Tochtermann K (2012) Exploring appropriation of enterprise wikis. Comput Support Cooper Work (CSCW) 21(2-3):317–356
Surowiecki J (2004) The wisdom of crowds: Why the many are smarter than the few and how collective wisdom shapes business, economies, societies, and nations. Doubleday, New York
Villarroel AJ, Reis F (2010) Intra-corporate crowdsourcing (ICC): leveraging upon rank and site marginality for innovation. In: CrowdConf, San Francisco, CA, USA, 4 October
Vukovic M, Bartolini C (2010) Towards a research agenda for enterprise crowdsourcing. Leveraging applications of formal methods, verification, and validation. In 4th international symposium on leveraging applications, Heraklion, Crete, Greece, 18–21 October. Springer, Berlin pp 425–434
Vukovic M, Naik VK (2011) Managing enterprise IT systems using online communities. In: 2011 IEEE international conference on services computing (SCC), Washington, DC, USA, 4–9 July. IEEE, pp 552–559
Wagenknecht T, Levina O, Weinhardt C (2017) Crowdsourcing in a public organization: transformation and culture. In: AMCIS 2017 proceedings
Webster J, Watson RT (2002) Analyzing the past to prepare for the future: writing a literature review. MIS Q 26(2):xiii–xxiii
Wendelken A, Danzinger F, Rau C, Moeslein KM (2014) Innovation without me: why employees do (not) participate in organizational innovation communities. R&D Manag 44(2):217–236
Young C (2013) Community management that works: how to build and sustain a thriving online health community. J Med Internet Res 15(6):e119
Zhu H, Sick N, Leker J (2016) How to use crowdsourcing for innovation? A comparative case study of internal and external idea sourcing in the chemical industry. In: Proceedings of the IEEE management of engineering and technology (PICMET), Honolulu, HI, USA, 4–8 September, Portland, OR, USA. IEEE, pp 887–901
Zhu H, Kock A, Wentker M, Leker J (2019) How does online interaction affect idea quality? The effect of feedback in firm-internal idea competitions. J Prod Innovat Manag 36(1):24–40
Zogaj S,Bretschneider U (2014) Analyzing governance mechanisms for crowdsourcing information systems: a multiple case analysis. In: ECIS 2014 proceedings
Zogaj S, Leicht N, Blohm I, Bretschneider U (2015) Towards successful crowdsourcing projects: evaluating the implementation of governance mechanisms. In: ICIS 2015 proceedings
Zuchowski O, Posegga O, Schlagwein D, Fischbach K (2016) Internal crowdsourcing: conceptual framework, structured review, and research agenda. J Inform Technol 31(2):166–184

Jakob Pohlisch has been working at the Chair of Innovation Economics at the Technical University of Berlin since 2015. He is currently working on the project 'Peer Innovation—Sustainable Household Sector Innovation in Collaborative Networks', funded by the Federal Ministry of Education and Research. Prior to that, he worked on the project 'Internal Crowdsourcing in Companies'. His research focusses on open innovation, crowdsourcing, and user innovation. He has published articles in high-ranking international journals such as *Research Policy*, *International Journal of Production Economics*, and *The Journal of Technology Transfer*. Jakob holds a master's degree in Statistics from Humboldt University Berlin and is currently pursuing his PhD.

Systematization Approach for the Development and Description of an Internal Crowdsourcing System

Marco Wedel and Hannah Ulbrich

Abstract There is a need for a scientific and theoretical foundation in the description of internal crowdsourcing systems with binding, consensus-based terminologies and descriptions. (How) Can the already described subcategories and aspects of an IC System be meaningfully described and placed in an orderly overall relationship? What needs to be added to existing system descriptions, if at all? The present article concentrates on identifying existing descriptions *and* definitions in connection with approaches to systematize the development of an internal crowdsourcing system (Some aspects of this article will also be published in German. Please be referred to: Daum, M.; Wedel, M.; Zinke-Wehlmann, C.; Ulbrich, H. (ed.) (2020): Gestaltung vernetzt-flexibler Arbeit. Beiträge aus Theorie und Praxis für die digitale Arbeitswelt. Berlin: Springer Vieweg). Since the phenomenon itself eludes allocation to an exclusively dedicated academic discipline, it seems appropriate to choose interdisciplinary approaches and to build on existing theoretical and terminological approaches from related sciences.

Keywords Crowdsourcing · Internal crowdsourcing · Corporate crowdsourcing · Governance · Management · IC System · Crowdsourcing frameworks · Theory frameworks · Crowdsourcing theory

1 Introduction to the Present Status of Crowdsourcing Theory

Based on what Sabatier (2007, p. 323) and Schlager (1995) stated for theories pertaining to the policy process, one could characterize the current state of crowdsourcing theory, including internal crowdsourcing (IC), as mountain islands

M. Wedel (✉) · H. Ulbrich
Institute for Vocational Education and Work Studies, Technische Universität Berlin, Berlin, Germany
e-mail: marco.wedel@tu-berlin.de; hannah.ulbrich@tu-berlin.de

H. Ulbrich et al. (eds.), *Internal Crowdsourcing in Companies*, Contributions to Management Science, https://doi.org/10.1007/978-3-030-52881-2_4

of empirical work, intermingled with, and occasionally attached together by foothills of shared methods and concepts, merely hinting at distant theoretical ideas (see also Wedel 2016, p. 13). The lack of theoretical foundations becomes clear in the terminological vagueness to be found in the existing empirical and descriptive works on IC.

As will be shown here, the reason for this is that, on the one hand, various independently applied terminologies supposedly refer to the same phenomena, and, on the other hand, certain applied vocabulary neglects its ascribed meaning. Consequently, the occupation with fundamental research questions regarding, e.g. regulating crowdsourcing by way of academic discourse is impeded, because respective contributions stand as isolated, non-related inputs rather than further augmentations to and of an ongoing scientific discussion.

Given this heterogeneity and fuzziness of—first and foremost—the applied terminologies in the context of IC, and the confusion it creates, there is a need for a scientific foundation, that is, theoretical fundamentals that can be applied to arrive at a description of an IC System with binding, consensus-based categories. Of course, the lack of definitional clarity is not surprising given the relatively recent nature of the IC phenomenon. Due to its growing (scientific) popularity, however, it is necessary to start a discourse on system-defining theoretical foundations for IC in order to avoid a nonbinding, in the worst case self-referential, coexistence of a rapidly growing stock of research. Since the phenomenon itself eludes allocation to an exclusively dedicated scientific discipline, it seems appropriate to choose interdisciplinary approaches and—without having to reinvent the wheel—to build on existing theoretical and terminological approaches from related academic fields.

Building on Pohlisch (here), a reasonable first starting point to identify theoretical cornerstones for a system-description-to-be is provided by recently published governance frameworks *and* by identifying the terminological range and clarity within the existing descriptions of steering activities in connection with crowdsourcing (crowdsourcing management). The following example illustrates the nature of the problem within the referred-to discourse: terms such as 'governance' and 'process management' are applied interchangeably, while approaches, such as sociotechnical systems theory (STS), are introduced on top of that (Blohm et al. 2018; Knop et al. 2017). And, terms like 'control' and 'governance' are used synonymously to describe such different things as role, task, structure and technology descriptions, framework conditions, general mechanisms or task assignments, furthermore also task definitions, task types, evaluation mechanisms, qualification and incentivization mechanisms as well as general regulations and agreements (Alam and Campbell 2013; Blohm et al. 2018; Knop et al. 2017; Zogaj and Bretschneider 2014; Zuchowski et al. 2016).

Although a binding system description for IC should address, reference and explain all these subareas, the individual sub-dimensions in and of themselves cannot, however, become the sufficient descriptive feature of the whole, in this case an IC System. For a future, target-oriented (academic) discourse, the subcategories and aspects of an IC System need to be meaningfully described and placed in an orderly overall relationship.

The overarching question is therefore: (How) Can the already described subcategories and aspects of an IC System be meaningfully described and placed in an orderly overall relationship? What needs to be added to the existing system descriptions, if at all?

The present article concentrates on identifying existing descriptions *and* definitions in connection with approaches towards a systematization of the development of an internal crowdsourcing system.

2 Discussion

2.1 Description Approaches and Control Principles of Crowdsourcing

Approaches towards describing systemic structures usually find their starting point in the analysis of identifiable framework conditions which, as such, provide a first indication of phenomenon-immanent characteristics. Pedersen et al. (2013) identified the elements 'problem', 'people', 'governance', 'process', 'technology' and 'outcome' as relevant categories for the academic description and analysis of crowdsourcing with regard to initial conceptual foundations. Based on a structured analysis of the literature on internal crowdsourcing, Zuchowski et al. (2016, 168 f.) adopt this six-component logic and describe respective framework conditions. Accordingly, the *problems component*, *governance component*, *people component*, *IT component*, *process component* and *outcome component* become the descriptive characteristics deemed to be sufficient for a basic IC Framework (Zuchowski et al. 2016, ibid.).

In brief, the 'problems component' addresses the dimension of problems which can be solved by crowdsourcing including considerations with respect to the degrees of complexity and differentiation that can be taken up, considered and dealt with in a crowdsourcing procedure. The 'governance component' according to Pedersen et al. (2013, p. 582) is based on steering considerations under the premise of achieving a desired goal. According to the Zuchowski et al. (2016, p. 169), governance describes general management tasks. Pedersen et al. (2013, p. 581) subsume under 'process' a series of measures that must be realized by parties involved in a crowdsourcing project in order to solve a specific problem or achieve a specific goal. Following Zuchowski et al. (2016, p. 169), process can be divided into the phases 'preparation', 'implementation', 'evaluation' and 'solution/decision'. The element 'people' addresses roles and role models and social conditions for the implementation of crowdsourcing activities. The heading 'Technology' or 'IT' deals with information technology conditions for crowdsourcing. The 'outcome' element is the final component of the proposed concept, which pools all aspects concerning results of the crowdsourcing process (Pedersen et al. 2013, 582 ff.; Zuchowski et al. 2016, 168 f.).

Knop et al. (2017) take on the elements described above and order them under the theoretical lens of socio-technical systems. This systematization approach follows a premise outlined by Baxter and Sommerville (2011) whereupon the system to be described reflects a process that takes into account both social and technical factors that have an original influence on the functionality and use of IT-based systems. Beese et al. (2015) refer in this context to the enormous complexity of socio-technical systems, which depend on a multitude of often non-linear and dynamic mechanisms relating to both social and technical subsystems (Knop et al. 2017, 2 f.). Within this approach, IC is described as a socio-technical system that can be divided into the five components 'Actors', 'Task', 'Structure', 'Technology' and 'Environment' (Knop et al. 2017, p. 3).

While the elements 'Technology/IT', 'People/Actors' and 'Problem/Task' seem to be more or less congruent in all their proposed functional aspects (or such a congruence is, at least, assumed for now, see: Pedersen et al. 2013; Zuchowski et al. 2016), Knop et al. (2017) renounce the elements 'Outcome', 'Process' and 'Governance' in favour of the elements 'Environment' and 'Structure'. Knop et al. (2017, p. 3) defining the element 'Structure' as

> Systems of communication, systems of authority, and systems of workflow. It further includes both the normative dimension, that is, values, norms, and general role expectations, and the behavioural dimension, that is, the patterns of behaviour as actors communicate, exercise authority, or work within the internal crowd.

It should be argued at this point that the element 'structure', insofar as more far-reaching and differentiating descriptions of the categories presented here are missing, is a synthesis of considerations by Pedersen et al. (2013) and Zuchowski et al. (2016) in relation to 'process' and 'governance'. A statement or explicit reference to the latter in relation to the extension or modification of the selected categories by Knop et al. (2017) could not be found.

Despite all the differences, the approaches outlined above towards describing an IC System clearly demonstrate an attempt to come up with a first functional differentiation. Furthermore, in the selected description categories, a functional alignment with respect to the application of IC becomes apparent, revealing an application-oriented perspective. Problems, solutions, desired goals, tasks, results and evaluations, in order to include some of the applied descriptions, arise terminologically from an economic or practice-oriented design framework. The research work on external and internal crowdsourcing has in common that it pursues a strongly innovation-centred approach, which is accompanied by description categories that are characterized by economic and business management aspects (Ebner et al. 2009; Keinz 2015; Garcia Martinez 2017; Palin and Kaartemo 2016; Zhu et al. 2014, 2016; Zuchowski et al. 2016; Thuan 2019). This also results in the circumstance that many research projects in the context of (internal) crowdsourcing are 'applied science' projects which, as consortia, often focus primarily on economic perspectives (Blohm et al. 2018; Zhu et al. 2016; Thuan 2019). It is this aspect that explains the inherent logic of theoretical IC System descriptions within the empirical research, where research objectives are generally oriented towards understanding organizational practices, coordination mechanisms and organizational patterns, control and leadership mechanisms as well as management implications for innovation generation.

For Pedersen et al. (2013), Zogaj et al. (2014) and Zuchowski et al. (2016), it seems clear that this application-oriented, target-control aspect of crowdsourcing activities is suitable for describing one fundamental aspect of an IC System which should be labelled 'governance'. According to Pedersen et al. (2013, p. 582)

> Governance is the actions and policies employed to effectively manage the crowd and steer them toward the desired solution.

Based on this, Pedersen et al. (2013, p. 582) draft four governance challenges ('Effective task break-down mechanism', 'Effective task integration mechanisms', 'Effective incentive mechanism', 'Effective quality assurance system') and five governance mechanisms ('Right Incentive Mechanism', 'Managing Submissions', 'Loss of Control', 'Quality of the Ideas', 'Creating Trust'*)*. Why challenges are described as mechanisms, and mechanisms with, for example, 'loss of control' are summarized as challenges, seems to be due to an erroneous table heading, but ultimately cannot be understood. Apart from the quote above, Pedersen et al. (2013) offer no further matter suitable for an ongoing consolidation with respect to describable system fundamentals or distinctions with respect to the meaning of governance.

Zogaj and Bretschneider (2014) approach the governance problem by analysing the implementation of crowdsourcing on the basis of three practical examples in order to obtain information with regard to governance mechanisms in particular. Based on Dahlander et al. (2008, p. 118), governance mechanisms determine the nature and quality of participation in different 'online communities' to promote and generate innovation. In the context of citing Dahlander et al., Zogaj and Bretschneider (2014, p. 4) state, that

> [...] governance is carried out by means of different mechanisms, so-called governance mechanisms (Dahlander et al. 2008).

In order to describe governance itself, they essentially adopt a definition proposed by Markus (2007, p. 152) which seems to be based on a quotation by Lynn et al. (2001, p. 6). Zogaj and Bretschneider (2014, p. 4) define governance in crowdsourcing accordingly as a

> [...] means of achieving the direction, control and coordination of wholly or partially autonomous individuals on behalf of a crowdsourcing initiative to which they (jointly) contribute.

While Zogaj and Bretschneider base their definition on Markus, who adapts it for the context of Open Source Software (2007, p. 152), Markus for his part refers to Lynn et al, who explicitly refer to 'public-sector applications' for their definition framework (2001, p. 5). This provides a first indication of the origins of the scientific and theoretical reference framework in the application of the governance concept for crowdsourcing. Dealing with 'public-sector applications' describes a research focus originating in the political and administrative sciences.

Zuchowski et al. (2016, p. 171), who explicitly refer to the definition offered by Pedersen et al. (2013) and Zogaj and Bretschneider (2014), continue to stress the control and management-based understanding in their definition approach:

> We understand as 'governance' all actions and policies used to govern, manage, and steer the crowd and internal crowdsourcing.

In addition, they introduce the category 'crowdsourcing governance tasks'. Some of a total of six governance tasks are assumed to apply exclusively to internal crowdsourcing only. This is true for the first category '(a) management of corporate culture and change'. *The* other categories are titled '(b) incentive design; (c) task definition and decomposition; (d) quality assurance; (e) community management; and (f) management of regulations and legal implications' (Zuchowski et al. 2016, 171 f.). In summary Zuchowski et al. (2016, p. 172) conclude, that

> [. . .] the above discussion shows important differences between governance of internal crowdsourcing and external crowdsourcing and hierarchy-based work.

Notably, a functional differentiation of governance in crowdsourcing is made at this point, which is based on the scope of external in contrast to internal crowdsourcing. This need for differentiation based on structural differences between external and internal crowdsourcing is also supported by Knop et al. (2017, p. 2).

A final governance definition offered for IC is made by Blohm et al. (2018, p. 7) who, based on an analysis of governance mechanisms in 19 case studies, arrive at the following understanding:

> In crowdsourcing, governance involves structuring roles and responsibilities, formal and informal rules, standards and regulations, outcome control measures, communication processes, or matters of task allocation in order to achieve the crowdsourcer's goal.

On this basis, Blohm et al. (2018, 7 f.) define six classes—'Task Definition', 'Task Allocation', 'Quality Assurance', 'Incentives', 'Qualification' and 'Regulation' within which 21 governance mechanisms can be located and described. The authors' reference to previous studies (2018, p. 8), which have led to the *clear* identification of these 21 mechanisms, cannot be reproduced because:

> In order to ensure the possibility of a blind review, we do not cite these studies.

Based on the above, some subcategories and aspects for the description of a crowdsourcing system can be identified. (1) Crowdsourcing as a system or concept consists of framework conditions, elements or components (Pedersen et al. 2013; Zuchowski et al. 2016). These frameworks, elements and components, as Knop et al. (2017) propose, can be interpreted through the lens of socio-technical systems theory, which is a first reference to suitable theory frameworks. (2) All approaches are united in that they presuppose the attribution of a system-inherent manoeuvrability towards a 'desired solution' (Pedersen et al. 2013, p. 582) that implicitly defines the purpose of the system, namely, to achieve 'the crowdsourcer's goal' (Blohm et al. 2018, p. 7). (3) In order to achieve this, as described and sufficiently quoted above, governance is required. (4) Governance, in turn, can be subdivided into individual mechanisms (Zogaj et al. 2014; Blohm et al. 2018) or 'crowdsourcing governance tasks' (Zuchowski et al. 2016, p. 171). (5) A functional and structural distinction is made between external and internal crowdsourcing, including in the application of governance mechanisms (Zuchowski et al. 2016; Knop et al. 2017).

2.2 *In the Governance Trap?*

The identification of proposed description categories only reflects first premonitions of what it is that constitutes an IC System. If, however, the aim was to achieve definitional and conceptual clarity in order to come up with a meaningful and orderly overall set of aspects that constitute a dependable IC System as a cornerstone for a goal-oriented academic discourse, this clarity is still lacking.

For example, if Knop et al. (2017, p. 3) defined 'Structure' as communication systems, authority systems and workflow systems, which include both normative dimension (values, norms and general role expectations) and behavioural dimension (behaviour patterns, communication, authority), and the governance term according to Blohm et al. (2018, 7 f.) subsumes structuring roles and responsibilities, formal and informal rules, norms and regulations, measures to control outcomes, communication processes and matters of task allocations to achieve a crowdsourcer's goal, the question arises as to what is explicitly not included? The breadth of the proposed definitions makes it impossible to figure out what is actually meant and how one differs from the other.

Of course, the aim to initially propose definitions that are rather comprehensive and wide is understandable and inevitable when approaching a new phenomenon. It is, however, desirable to condense the initial uncertainty into clarity. As already mentioned in the introduction, it may be useful to choose interdisciplinary approaches in order to examine whether existing knowledge, for example, in the form of existing theoretical and terminological applications, is suitable for the present case. At this point, a discussion of the significance and scope of control categories in crowdsourcing appears to be urgently required. Since a lot of the introduced aspects of IC—frameworks, mechanisms, elements and components—seem to circle around the idea of steering or managing a crowdsourcing process as an action which is described by the term governance, understanding the latter must be the focus.

Of interest are the relationships between control subject and control object, as they are reflected in the governance definitions of crowdsourcing presented above. It is important, however, to first define the meaning and scope of the term governance itself. Since the only substantial reference to governance, namely, the reference to Lynn et al. (2001), points in the direction of political science, the following section will examine the range of definitions within this discipline and examine their transferability.

2.3 Governance in Political Science

According to Peters (2010, p. 2) the concept of governance can be considered as the most fashionable term—perhaps even a 'fetish'—in political science in recent years. The ambiguity of the concept is the reason for its success, because (Peters 2010, ibid.):

> [. . .] it can be shaped to conform to the intellectual preferences of the individual author and therefore to some extent obfuscates meaning at the same time that it perhaps enhances understanding.

The scope of the governance concept can be extended almost arbitrarily by additional attributes (Offe 2009, p. 557). One can find texts about '*sectoral governance*', 'good governance', 'corporate governance', 'public governance', '*multi-level governance*', '*sustainable governance*', 'global governance', '*environmental governance*', '*cultural governance*', 'earth system governance' or 'polycentric governance in telecoupled resource systems' to name but a few (Biermann et al. 2019; Newig et al. 2019; Brunnengräber et al. 2004; Grande 2012). Is governance therefore the all-purpose weapon for every kind of (social) regulatory problem as Grande (2012, p. 566) suspects? In fact, although it is a concept that is acknowledged as being unclear, fundamental common features in the characteristics of governance applications can be identified (von Blumenthal 2005; Lembcke et al. 2016).

It is clear that even if 'control' and 'governance' are used interchangeably at times, such an equivalent would imply that *governing* and *governance* are the same (Mayntz 2004). However, in contrast to their historical application, *governance* and *governing* cannot be applied synonymously in the sense of a hierarchy-bound control ideal, because, as will be shown, governance means control as cooperation and coordination (Mayntz 2008, 45). Thus governance concepts in political science are more than just 'empty signifiers' (Offe 2009). Following Grande (2012, 566 f.) there is a conceptual core that can be described as the common denominator of the various approaches, which can be summarized on the basis of five characteristics:

> The first and most important feature is the emphasis on non-hierarchical forms of production of public goods.
>
> Second, this is associated with a critique of the state as the exclusive producer of public goods. What is characteristic of governance concepts [...] is that non-state actors and organizations [...] are gaining in importance.
>
> This critique of hierarchies as a control principle and the inclusion of private actors in the production of public goods is interpreted as a necessary consequence of interdependence, which would be the third common feature.
>
> Fourth, because of this increasing interdependence, but also because of the loss of significance of territorial and functional boundaries for action, the complexity of political action has increased considerably.
>
> [...] All of this has resulted in a considerable increase in the necessity and importance of cooperation and coordination between a wide range of actors.

The empirical origin of governance concepts lies, inter alia, in the observation of increasing interdependencies between social subsystems and territorial levels of action (Grande 2012, ibid.). In the second half of the last century, the understanding of a traditional conceptualization of the public sector, according to which the state as the most important actor influences the economy and society, came under pressure. Part of the burden on national governments has resulted in the increased importance of international policy spheres and a diminished ability of national governments to protect their economies and societies from global pressures or to tackle global challenges alone (Peters and Pierre 1998, p. 223). In addition, the arenas and structures of negotiation processes within national arenas are subject to increasing demands for dialogue and participation between state and society, state and the economy, state and non-governmental organizations and national and supranational or international institutions. The European Union, while questioning the classical unity of law and politics in the nation state and leading to a multi-level system with a wide variety of constellations of actors and institutional architectures, is repeatedly cited as an example for this (Mayntz 2008; Brunnengräber et al. 2004; Grimm 2001; Peters and Pierre 1998).

An essential contribution to governance research is the argument that the development towards governance is a three-step process from 'planning' to 'control' to 'governance' (Schuppert 2016; Mayntz 2008; Grande 2012). While at first planning was at the centre of a state that actively controlled all social processes, planning semantics were soon replaced by control semantics and transformed into a control theory (Steuerungstheorie) (Schuppert 2016, p. 151). In control theory, the concept of hierarchical control is the fundament of the analytical framework. (Mayntz 2008, 43):

> This concept allowed a clear distinction to be made between control subject and control object; control objects are social subsystems or groups whose behaviour is to be steered in a certain direction.

If the central assumption of control theory is therefore the existence of a control subject, it is important to realize that governance is understood as something fundamentally different. In governance regimes, so Grande (2012, p. 581),

> [...] there is no actor any more who could function as an autonomous controlling instance of the overall process—neither real nor imaginary. [...] But if such a steering body no longer exists, then it no longer makes sense to speak of steering—and in cases where such a steering body still exists, governance should not be spoken of.

Even a nonhierarchical relationship between state and society is understood as 'control' *in the* sense of control theory (Grande 2012, p. 584). The intentional control desire by a control subject remains essential. Even though governance can be defined as 'the intentional regulation of social issues' (Mayntz 2008, 55), it remains open how 'in complex, dynamic governance structures one can sensibly speak of control intentions' (Grande 2012, p. 581).

2.4 Interim Conclusion

If the understanding of governance presented here in the context of political science is transferred to the de facto application within the crowdsourcing literature, some problems arise. In fact, as described before, the steering intention is an essential feature not only of the crowdsourcing process itself, but—more importantly—of the descriptive intention for which the word governance is used. As already stated, all descriptive approaches to crowdsourcing have in common that they assume a claim to control that is bound by the goal of achieving a 'desired solution' (Pedersen et al. 2013, p. 582) that is 'the crowdsourcer's goal' (Blohm et al. 2018, p. 7). Functionally, participants in crowdsourcing can always be divided into two roles: the 'crowdsourcer' and the 'crowdsourcee'. The 'crowdsourcer' is a client who is looking for a solution to a given problem; the *crowdsourcees* are members of the crowd who are supposed to work out a solution (Leimeister et al. 2015). This applies to both external and internal crowdsourcing, both of which must be regarded as a closed system in this context. Thus, they fit ideally into the understanding of control subject ('crowdsourcer') and control object ('crowdsourcee'), as a group whose behaviour is to be steered in a certain direction), as assumed in control theory. This understanding is clearly reflected in the following governance definition for crowdsourcing (Pedersen et al. 2013, p. 582):

> Governance is the actions and policies employed to effectively manage the crowd and steer them toward the desired solution.

Clearly governance for the description of crowdsourcing systems here actually means control. However, in the sense of a political science application, this terminology cannot be meaningfully transferred because, despite the diversity of governance applications, governance explicitly means something other than linear, hierarchical control relations (see above).

Since it has been established that the research on external and internal crowdsourcing pursues a strongly innovation-centred approach, which points to a predominant examination by economic and business management scientific disciplines, it shall be investigated at this point whether interdisciplinary governance research in economics offers further definitions that can support the current understanding of the application of governance for crowdsourcing.

2.5 Governance in the Economy

Two general governance concepts in economics are briefly outlined below. On the one hand, the concept of 'corporate governance' and on the other hand, theoretical approaches to 'economic governance'. While debates in the context of individual companies are outlined within the first, the second aims at macroeconomic understandings (Brunnengräber et al. 2004, p. 22). For Lindberg et al. (1991, 5 f.),

'Economic governance' can be described as a phenomenon at the meso-level, i.e. in industrial sectors. Governance there can be seen as

> [...] a matrix of interdependent social exchange relationships, or transactions, that must occur among organizations, either individually or collectively, in order for them to develop, produce, and market goods and services. Thus, governance is an extremely complex phenomenon.

Like within the political science approach, the aspect of interdependence is also brought to the fore here (Brunnengräber et al. 2004, p. 24). The difference is that the objective is not to regulate social issues in a way that is in the public interest but rather to develop, produce and market goods and services (Lindberg et al. 1991, p. 6; Mayntz 2008, 45 f.).

Under 'corporate governance', various framework legislations and reporting obligations are subsumed as a legal and factual regulatory framework. The approach is also concerned with the question of—responsible, sustainable, long-term value creation-oriented—corporate management and control (World Bank 1996, XIV; Brunnengräber et al. 2004, p. 7). Following Bainbridge (2002, p. 15), all *corporate governance* concepts have one thing in common:

> They strive to answer two basic sets of questions: (1) As to the means of corporate governance, who decides? In other words, when push comes to shove, who ultimately is in control? (2) As to the ends of corporate governance, whose interests prevail? When the ultimate decisionmaker is presented with a zero-sum game, in which it must prefer the interests of one constituency class over those of all others, which constituency wins?

At its core, therefore, *corporate governance is* also concerned with the problems of control intentions and hierarchies in a multi-level system. This is particularly evident in the case of stock corporations, shareholder claims and multinational companies with many regulatory and territorial levels of action. Even though the corporate constitution of companies is more reminiscent of the unity of law and politics in the sovereignty of the nation state in the late nineteenth and early twentieth centuries, it is also true for companies that the arenas and structures of negotiation processes are subject to major changes. Finally, the term 'corporate governance' does not refer to the internal order, i.e. the corporate constitution, but addresses problems within the framework of the integration of the company into its environment (Werder 2018).

In summary, it can be stated that—even though governance research is much less pronounced in economics *and* heterogeneous conceptual approaches can be observed for both disciplines—the traditional division of disciplines into political and economic subsystems is blurred in governance research (Brunnengräber et al. 2004, p. 24):

> The market, state and society are increasingly being placed in relation to one another by referring to the interdependencies and complex interdependencies between the social spheres. The various levels and systems of action (multi-level governance) are important in both political and economic concepts. The consideration of many actors and forms of interaction is addressed in the same way as the problem constellations, which are increasingly differentiating globally.

2.6 Lessons from Governance Research

For the discussion at hand, neither economic nor political science definitions for governance support the proposed use of the term governance for the description of control activities in crowdsourcing systems. More so, analysing the governance discourse in those disciplines opens a new perspective which renders it necessary to save the term in its political and economic meaning for a later use in the description of crowdsourcing.

If governance concepts, as models of new cooperative network management, *are* expressions of 'long-term structural changes in the modes of production of collective goods in modern contemporary societies' (Grande 2012, p. 585; Mayntz 2008, 46), then it makes sense to take a closer look at crowdsourcing itself as an expression of this structural change. Crowdsourcing then becomes an indicator of a systemic transformation through digitization, in which internal crowdsourcing possibly describes changes in the internal organization and external crowdsourcing possibly describes the relocation of work from the classical company organization. If such a transformation process—which cannot (yet) be observed—leads to a situation in which the roles 'crowdsourcer' and 'crowdsourcee' can no longer be assigned to a subject and object relation in a control-theoretical sense, i.e. if crowdsourcing creates 'relatively autonomous, functional subsystems' (Mayntz 2008, 48), then it is not only sensible but necessary to introduce the governance concept in the sense of crowd governance for steering purposes in multi-level crowdsourcing systems.

A similar approach is introduced by Fenwick et al. (2018, p. 9), albeit from a legal, market regulatory perspective, that propose to further the approach of *corporate governance* towards a *platform governance*:

> Given the proliferation of platforms, we seem to be living through a shift from a world of firms to a new world of platforms. In the same way that the 'firm' came to replace 'contracts' for many business activities in the context of the industrial revolution, 'platforms' are now replacing 'oldworld firms' in the context of the digital transformation.

In order to meet the resulting challenges for the economy, Fenwick and Vermeulen (2019, p. 2) deem it necessary to develop modern guidelines and regulations in the sense of '*corporate governance*' as a 'platform governance'.

With regard to the influence of crowdsourcing on the future constitution of companies (and its effect on hierarchy-dependent steering aspirations), some considerations have also been made by Schröter (see chapter 'Good Practice at GASAG-Group: Recommendations for the Application of Internal Crowdsourcing from a Business Perspective'):

> As virtual transaction spaces and platforms that were previously standalone grow together over time, new potentials of crowdsourcing unfold as part of modern crowdworking. Thinking and working in an order-related manner as well as a move away from focussing on purely vertical towards mainly horizontal value-creation chains in future, together with models of partially autonomous and agile working, will lead to a dominant culture of crowdsourcing applications. The boundaries between internal and external crowdsourcing are becoming blurred and both dynamics will merge with one another. Due to the

progressive removal of boundaries in company operations, the division between internal and external utilizations will slowly fade.

In order to be able to depict and describe such potential future phenomena in crowdsourcing system theory, the term governance, as it has been coined by political science during the last 50 years, may be appropriate and should consequently be reserved (Fig. 1).

2.7 Crowdsourcing Management

There is a clear recommendation that the term 'governance', as used in the definitions of crowdsourcing by Pedersen et al. (2013), Zogaj et al. (2014), Zuchowski et al. (2016) and Blohm et al. (2018), should be replaced by the word 'management'.

This applies consequently to the conceptions presented by Pedersen et al. (2013) and Zuchowski et al. (2016) with respect to model elements or components, here to the description of 'governance mechanisms' (Pedersen et al. 2013; Blohm et al. 2018) or 'crowdsourcing governance tasks' (Zuchowski et al. 2016).

It should be noted that it is not a question of replacing one term 'only' because another is more appropriate. Much more importantly, it is assumed that the future description of a crowdsourcing systems requires the description of a crowdsourcing governance and resulting governance mechanisms in the sense of an understanding shaped and presented by political and economic science. The term should in any case not be introduced to describe control principles and mechanisms, which of necessity would lead to misunderstandings, especially in interdisciplinary approaches (which constitute the norm for scientific approaches to crowdsourcing).

With regard to the question of how and whether already described subcategories and aspects of an IC System can be meaningfully described and placed in an orderly overall relationship, it is now advised to go back to the proposed description categories of an IC System for which management is anticipated. Earlier some subcategories and aspects for the description of a crowdsourcing system had been identified. (1) Crowdsourcing as a system or concept consists of framework conditions, elements or components (Pedersen et al. 2013; Zuchowski et al. 2016). These frameworks, elements and components, as proposed by Knop et al. (2017), can be interpreted through the lens of socio-technical systems theory, which is a first reference to suitable theory frameworks. (2) All approaches are united in that they presuppose a system inherent manoeuvrability towards a 'desired solution' (Pedersen et al. 2013, p. 582) that implicitly defines the purpose of the system, namely, to achieve 'the crowdsourcer's goal' (Blohm et al. 2018, p. 7). (New 3) In order to achieve this, as should be stated from now on, management is required. (New 4) Management, in turn, should be subdivided into individual mechanisms—based on suggestions by Zogaj et al. (2014) and Blohm et al. (2018)—or crowdsourcing management tasks, based on suggested crowdsourcing governance tasks by Zuchowski (2016). (New 5) A functional and structural distinction is made

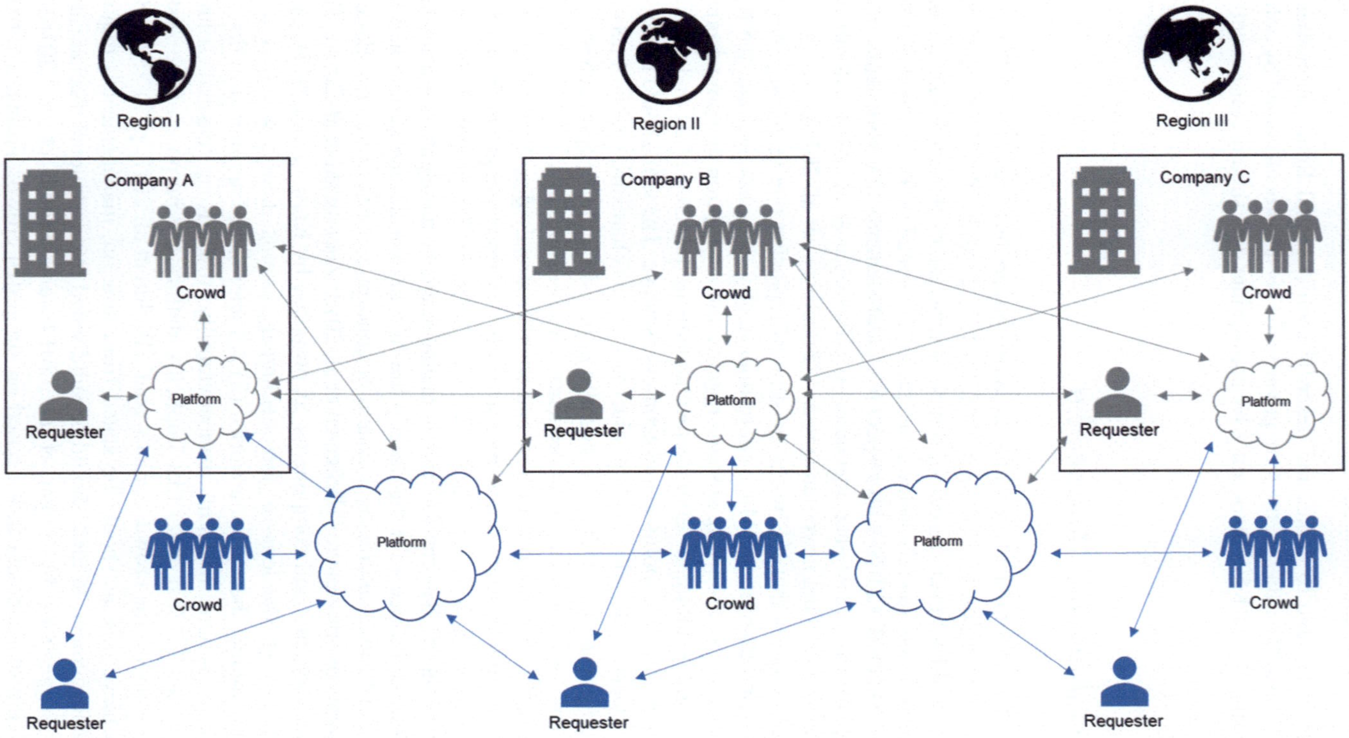

Fig. 1 Example of multi-level crowdsourcing system with a need for crowd governance

between external and internal application and implementation of crowdsourcing management (Zuchowski et al. 2016; Knop et al. 2017).

To start with the derivation of constitutive factors for an IC System, a closer look will now be taken at the meaning of the supposed framework conditions, elements, components and theory frameworks suggested above.

2.8 Crowdsourcing Theory Frameworks

Starting with suitable framework ascriptions to internal crowdsourcing, two kinds of frameworks have been mentioned so far: theory frameworks and systemic framework conditions.

With respect to theory frameworks, their scope and application are uncontroversial. As compiled by Wedel (2016, 13 f.), the following are summarized: for Ostrom (2007, p. 25) frameworks provide a metatheoretical language that can be used to compare theories. While frameworks bound inquiry and focus attention on critical features of the social physical landscape by specifying classes of variables and their interrelations, they cannot in and of themselves provide explanations and predictions (Schlager 2007, p. 293). It is theories that 'place values on some of the variables identified as important in a framework, and make predictions about likely outcomes' (Schlager 2007, p. 296). Theories are compatible with different frameworks (Ostrom 2007, p. 26). As identified by Moravcsik and Schimmelfennig (2009, p. 68), sometimes a minimum of three theories, organized in a multistage model, are required to avoid monocausal interrelations. Indeed this can be favourable to allow for counterfactual reasoning and avoid serious analytical fallacies (Ladrech 2010, pp. 40–41).

With respect to the subject matter of internal crowdsourcing, a couple of theories and respective schools of thought can be identified that provide a metatheoretical language and focus attention on IC. For the sake of this article, it is rather obvious that aspects of political science theory (here e.g. and in particular control/hierarchy theory and governance theories with respect to variables in light of multi-level, international, supra- and international system descriptions) should to be incorporated into a crowdsourcing theory framework. As mentioned earlier, Knop et al. (2017) and Knop and Blohm (2018) suggest incorporating sociotechnical systems theory (STS) into an overall framework, because researchers in the past analysed phenomena that are similar to internal crowdsourcing—where complex interactions between humans, technology and environments were observed—through the lens of STS. Here the metatheoretical language informs the concept of socio-technical components as applied within crowdsourcing (Knop et al. 2017, pp. 2–3). Based on Reichwald et al. (1998), it is Simmert et al. (2020) who suggest that the effect of internal crowdsourcing be analyzed in terms of key performance indicators by way of an extended economic efficiency analysis taking into account qualitative benefits (time, quality, flexibility, human situation) in addition to various cost aspects.

While the identification of all distant theory remarks ever applied in the context of internal crowdsourcing research is beyond the scope of this article and would be a questionable exercise in terms of its informative value, some conclusions can be drawn at this stage, nonetheless. While Simmert et al. (2020) approach the subject matter through an information systems lens, with STS theory Knop et al. (2017) chose the lens of organizational sociology, while the bulk of authors analysed by Pohlisch (see chapter 'An Introduction to Internal Crowdsourcing') chose an economic, innovation-centred lens. The authors of this article are certainly shaped by a social sciences approach (political science and sociology). If future researchers would acknowledge this interdisciplinary, multistage framework for the analysis of internal crowdsourcing, drawing on economics, social science and computer science approaches, thereby allowing for counterfactual reasoning while avoiding serious analytical fallacies, it could lead to concise, helpful and robust research results. This is only true, however, if such an interdisciplinary theory framework is based on and united by binding, consensus-based applications of system categories and descriptions. To arrive at such a consensus, it certainly helps to understand by what theory frameworks the metatheoretical language is informed. It is then necessary to agree which terminologies (including their theory inherent and discipline dependent understanding) are accepted and applied for the description of IC Systems.

2.9 IC Framework Conditions

In order to finally approach a system description for IC, it is important to understand where the system begins and where it ends, which aspects lie outside the system and which components are part of the system.

When Pedersen et al. (2013) suggest a first conceptual model they identified the elements 'problem', 'people', 'governance', '*process*', 'technology' and 'outcome' as relevant categories. Zuchowski et al. (2016, 168 f.) refer to these elements and conceptual model as a 'general crowdsourcing framework' and adopt it as a 'conceptual framework for internal crowdsourcing' consisting of various components (*problems component, governance component, people component, IT component, process component* and *outcome component)* (Zuchowski et al. 2016, ibid.). Following this understanding, the framework seems to represent the system itself. Figures in respective research present the categories and elements as part of a closed system (Pedersen et al. 2013, p. 3; Zuchowski et al. 2016, p. 170).

This understanding seems to originate from computer science where, based on Johnson and Foote (1988), the design of a program is described in terms of program components, based on a collection of abstract classes and an object-oriented abstract design, which is also called framework. A framework is therefore an abstract design for a particular kind of application. For Dietzsch (2002, p. 77) frameworks are then abstract architectures, i.e. reference architectures for families of application systems.

While there is generally no reason to oppose incorporating this computer scientific understanding into an IC theory framework, and therefore regard a possible IC System as an IC Framework, two problems arise. First, the proposed components *problem* (input) and *outcome* are of a processual rather than architectural nature and should not be regarded as an inherent aspect of either a framework or a system, but, quite literally, as input and output of it. Secondly, an IC System itself has framework conditions which indeed influence the system but are not part of the system itself. This ultimately would add a framework to the framework, which could lead to terminological confusion.

As internal crowdsourcing takes place within a company (see chapter 'An Introduction to Internal Crowdsourcing' and 'Managing the Crowd—A Literature Review of Empirical Studies on Internal Crowdsourcing'), we identify and suggest three framework conditions with relevance to an IC System: external framework conditions, internal framework conditions and IC strategy framework conditions, with the latter two being part of an overall intracompany-specific environment.

External framework conditions subsume all external socio-economic aspects that shape a company's environment. Those are market, politics, law and regulations as well as society. We proceed from the assumption that it makes a difference to the particular IC System design whether internal crowdsourcing is applied in a market environment shaped by, e.g. grid-bound commodities (such as energy or railway markets), knowledge economies or various other products or service industries. Accordingly, different markets are subject to different degrees of political scrutiny and market regulation. The military industrial complex, the health sector or educational sector, to name but a few, are characterized by quite different requirements (e.g. national interest, protectionism, public welfare) and respective public and general interests. Practically this might favour or restrict, e.g. certain aspects of information and exchange flows within the crowd or between crowdsourcer and crowdsource which, in turn, will affect the IC System. To our knowledge, none of the proposed IC concepts or frameworks address these external extra-company framework conditions explicitly.

When Knop et al. (2017, p. 3) introduce the *environment* component they refer to those conditions that describe 'to what extent the internal crowdsourcing takes place in a certain organizational setting' which, according to our understanding, would be internal framework conditions. These conditions are shaped by respective business models, organizational structures, applied processes, given infrastructures (including in particular IT) and corporate culture (see also Astor et al. 2016; Kaiser et al. 2012; Hochfeld et al. 2014). Again, we assume that aspects such as, inter alia, company size (multinationals, SMEs, start ups, etc.), business layouts (shareholder driven, family business, social business, non-profit, etc.), application environments (high-tech, R&D driven, not R&D driven), culture (high performance, conformist, traditional, change oriented, etc.) and leadership style (authoritarian leadership, cooperative leadership, participatory leadership, delegating leadership, etc.) influence aspects of a particular IC System design.

Finally, against the backdrop of external and internal framework conditions, it is the strategy framework that most decisively influences the application design of an IC System. Here objectives of and strategies for IC are defined. As an important finding from previous research (Ulbrich and Wedel 2019), the identified and considered target dimensions of IC applications shape its design. Dimensions such as employee participation, employee qualification or product, process and service innovation might lead to different processes (e.g. with respect to task typologies) and activities (assigned tasks and roles) within the IC System. This is equally important for potential works agreements for IC between trade unions and employers which in themselves define yet another framework for the application of IC within a company, such as has been the case within the ICU Research Project (Otte and Schröter 2019).

2.10 IC System

While framework conditions influence the application design of internal crowdsourcing, they do not alter nor change the fundamental logic of an IC System. We argue that each IC System consists of three components: process, activity and information technology.

We adopt the notion of an IC System as an STS system where all three components: process, activity and information technology are interdependent and where all components and interdependencies are distinct and describable.

Building on Pedersen et al. (2013) and Zuchowski et al. (2016), we would suggest that the process and technology components for an ideal typical IC System be adopted while neglecting the notion of a distinct problems, people, governance and outcome component. While, as stated above, problem and output are inputs and outputs to and of the system, governance could only exist as management and would be located in the intersection of the components activity and process, while people would be subsumed within the overall component activity (with respect to assigned tasks and roles).

With respect to Knop et al. (2017), we suggest that the STS approach and the technology component be adopted while neglecting the actors, task, structure and environment component. While the actors and task component can be subsumed within the activity component, structures and environments really refer to the internal framework conditions in the company with relevance for the IC System.

We argue that all component aspects described by Pedersen et al. (2013), Zuchowski et al. (2016) and Knop et al. (2017), which are neither part of the framework conditions (see above) nor input or output to and of the process flow, can be subsumed within these three overall components or located within the interplay of these three components. A detailed description of the component 'activity' and 'process' can be found in chapter 'Systematization Approach for the

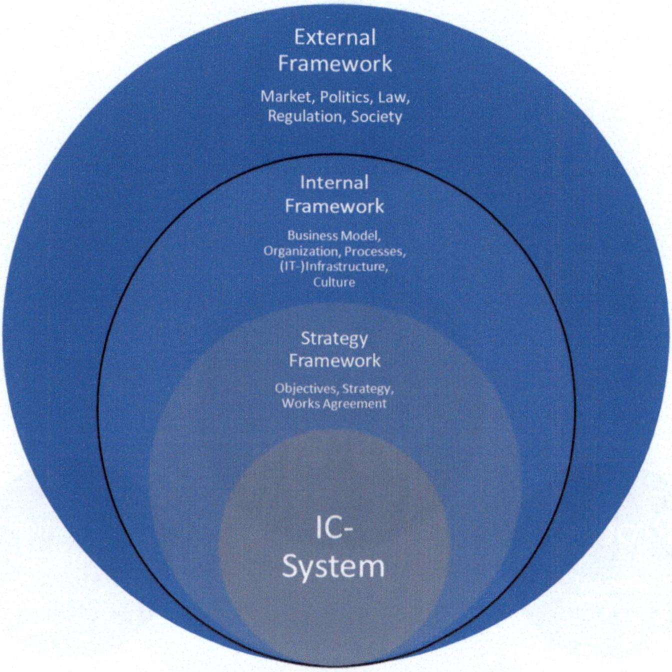

Fig. 2 Framework conditions for internal crowdsourcing

Development and Description of an Internal Crowdsourcing System' (Fig. 2). Further aspects with respect to IT implications and generic or specific crowd technology architectures for internal crowdsourcing can be found in chapter 'Design of a Process and Role Model for Internal Crowdsourcing' (Fig. 3).

Finally, we suggest that this three-component logic constitutes a simple yet solid basic IC System which can serve as a fundament for the description of theoretical IC principles. It is this three-component principle that is reflected in the IC definition by Zuchowski et al. (2016), whereas IC is an 'IT-enabled group activity based on an open call for participation in an enterprise'. Accordingly, we would argue the three components reflect this definition in so far as IC is in principle an IT-enabled activity based on a process.

Whether the interplay of the components, e.g. with respect to activity and process, is defined by five management challenges and mechanisms (Pedersen et al. 2013), six crowdsourcing management tasks (Zuchowski et al. 2016) or 21 management mechanisms (Blohm et al. 2018) are beyond the scope of this article and up for future discussion. It is, however, now of consequence for the suggested principle three-component layout of a basic IC System.

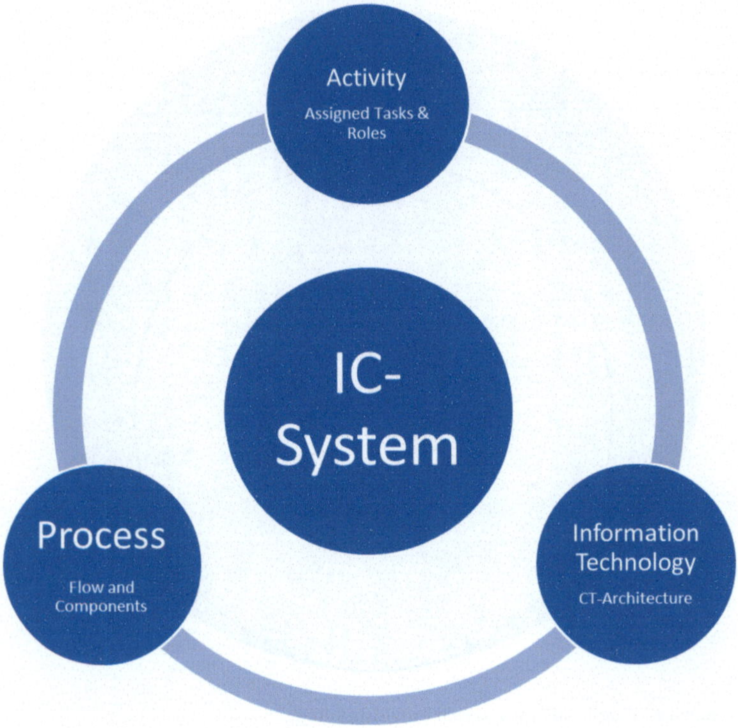

Fig. 3 Basic IC system (three components)

3 Conclusion and Suggestions

Considering the overall objective to systematize approaches towards developing a crowdsourcing system with binding system descriptions, the following is suggested in light of the deductions presented above:

1. Current IC theory frameworks are informed by an interdisciplinary, multistage analysis framework drawing on theories and leading to a meta-theoretical language informed by economics, social science and computer science approaches.
2. Each IC System consists of three components: process, activity and information technology. All additional aspects referred to as components in the IC literature that are neither part of the framework conditions nor input or output to and of the process flow can be subsumed within these three overall components or located within the interplay of these three components.
3. Every IC System is exposed to framework conditions: external, internal and strategy framework conditions, with the latter two describing overall intracompany framework conditions. While framework conditions influence the application design of internal crowdsourcing, they do not alter or change the fundamental logic of an IC System.

4. IC is characterized by the logic of a system-inherent manoeuvrability towards a desired solution which is clearly attributed to a directional relationship (crowdsourcer → crowdsourcee) and shaped by management processes.
5. There is a functional and structural difference between internal and external applications of crowdsourcing and crowdsourcing management.
6. Neither internal nor external crowdsourcing applications can be described through a governance perspective.
7. Potential future multi-level crowdsourcing systems, within which directional dependencies (crowdsourcer → crowdsourcee) can no longer be clearly attributed, ought to be comprehended through a governance perspective.

The guiding questions have been: (How) Can the already described subcategories and aspects of an IC System be meaningfully described and placed in an orderly overall relationship? What needs to be added to the existing system descriptions, if at all?

As summarized above, we propose the terminologies 'IC Theory Framework', 'IC Framework Conditions' (external, internal and strategic) and 'IC System' (with the components process, activity and information technology) as a first approach to binding system descriptions. With respect to existing research we consider the actual IC System—that is sometimes referred to as a framework, which we do not recommend for concern it might cause confusion—to be rather simple and concise, consisting 'only' of three components (see above). We attribute many aspects elsewhere labelled as framework or system components to the framework conditions (as explained above) because, while these referred to circumstances are influencing the application design of IC, they do not constitute the system itself. We finally highly recommend that future crowdsourcing researchers adopt the terminological distinction and respective application between crowdsourcing governance and management in the future discourse.

This first approach towards the development of a crowdsourcing system with binding system descriptions can only be considered an initial contribution towards a needed theory-bound discussion with respect to the phenomenon of crowdsourcing.

References

Astor M, Rammer C, Klaus C, Klose G (2016) Innovativer Mittelstand 2025—Herausforderungen, Trends und Handlungsempfehlungen für Wirtschaft und Politik: Studie im Auftrag des Bundesministeriums für Wirtschaft und Energie. https://www.bmwi.de/Redaktion/DE/Publikationen/Studien/studie-endbericht-innovativer-mittelstand-2025.html. Accessed 3 Feb 2020

Bainbridge SM (2002) Director primacy: the means and ends of corporate governance. SSRN Electron J. https://doi.org/10.2139/ssrn.300860

Baxter G, Sommerville I (2011) Socio-technical systems: from design methods to systems engineering. Interact Comput 23(1):4–17. https://doi.org/10.1016/j.intcom.2010.07.003

Beese J, Kazem H, Aier S (2015) On the conceptualization of information systems as socio-technical phenomena in simulation-based research. https://pdfs.semanticscholar.org/63ed/4e594c732636f2b52327efee89fd288b557e.pdf
Biermann F, Betsill MM, Burch S, Dryzek J, Gordon C, Gupta A, Gupta J, Inoue C, Kalfagianni A, Kanie N, Olsson L, Persson Å, Schroeder H, Scobie M (2019) The Earth System Governance Project as a network organization: a critical assessment after ten years. Curr Opin Environ Sustain 39:17–23. https://doi.org/10.1016/j.cosust.2019.04.004
Blohm I, Zogaj S, Bretschneider U, Leimeister JM (2018) How to manage crowdsourcing platforms effectively? Calif Manag Rev 60(2):122–149. https://doi.org/10.1177/0008125617738255
Brunnengräber A, Dietz K, Hirschl B, Walk H (2004) Interdisziplinarität in der Governance-Forschung. https://www.ioew.de/publikation/interdisziplinaritaet_in_der_governance_forschung/
Dahlander L, Frederiksen L, Rullani F (2008) Online communities and open innovation. Ind Innovat 15(2):115–123. https://doi.org/10.1080/13662710801970076
Dietzsch A (2002) Frameworks. In: Dietzsch A (ed) Systematische Wiederverwendung in der Software-Entwicklung. Deutscher Universitätsverlag, Wiesbaden, pp 77–89
Ebner W, Leimeister JM, Krcmar H (2009) Community engineering for innovations: the ideas competition as a method to nurture a virtual community for innovations. R&D Manage 39 (4):342–356. https://doi.org/10.1111/j.1467-9310.2009.00564.x
Fenwick M, Vermeulen EPM (2019) A sustainable platform economy & the future of corporate governance. SSRN Electron J. https://doi.org/10.2139/ssrn.3331508
Fenwick M, McCahery JA, Vermeulen EPM (2018) The end of 'corporate' governance: Hello 'platform' governance. SSRN Electron J. https://doi.org/10.2139/ssrn.3232663
Garcia Martinez M (2017) Inspiring crowdsourcing communities to create novel solutions: competition design and the mediating role of trust. Technol Forecast Soc Change 117:296–304. https://doi.org/10.1016/j.techfore.2016.11.015
Grande E (2012) Governance-Forschung in der Governance-Falle?—Eine kritische Bestandsaufnahme. Politische Vierteljahresschrift 53(4):565–592. https://doi.org/10.5771/0032-3470-2012-4-565
Grimm D (2001) Die Verfassung und die Politik: Einsprüche in Störfällen. Beck, München
Hochfeld K, Kaiser S, Schraudner M (eds) (2014) Unternehmenskulturen verändern—Vielfalt erreichen. Fraunhofer, Stuttgart
Johnson R, Foote B (1988) Designing reusable classes. J Object Orient Program 1(2):22–35
Kaiser S, Hochfeld K, Gertje E, Schraudner M (2012) Unternehmenskulturen verändern—Karrierebrüche vermeiden. Fraunhofer, Stuttgart
Keinz P (2015) Auf den Schultern von ... Vielen! Crowdsourcing als neue Methode in der Neuproduktentwicklung. Schmalenbachs Zeitschrift für betriebswirtschaftliche Forschung 67 (1):35–69. https://doi.org/10.1007/BF03372915
Knop N, Durward D, Blohm I (2017) How to design an internal crowdsourcing system. https://www.alexandria.unisg.ch/252020/1/JML_672.pdf
Ladrech R (2010) Europeanization and national politics. Palgrave Macmillan, Basingstoke, Hampshire
Leimeister JM, Zogaj S, Durward D (2015) New forms of employment and IT—crowdsourcing. In: Conference of the regulating for decent work network.
Lembcke OW, Ritzi C, Schaal GS (eds) (2016) Zeitgenössische Demokratietheorie. Springer Fachmedien Wiesbaden, Wiesbaden
Lindberg LN, Campbell JL, Hollingsworth JR (1991) Economic governance and the analysis of structural change in the American economy. In: Campbell JL, Hollingsworth JR, Lindberg LN (eds) Governance of the American economy. Cambridge University Press, Cambridge, pp 3–34
Lynn LE, Heinrich CJ, Hill CJ (2001) Improving governance: a new logic for empirical research. Georgetown University Press, Washington, DC
Markus ML (2007) The governance of free/open source software projects: monolithic, multidimensional, or configurational? J Manag Govern 11(2):151–163. https://doi.org/10.1007/s10997-007-9021-x

Mayntz R (2004) Governance Theory als fortentwickelte Steuerungstheorie? Max-Planck-Institut für Gesellschaftsforschung, Köln. http://hdl.handle.net/10419/44296

Mayntz R (2008) Von der Steuerungstheorie zu Global Governance. In: Schuppert GF, Zürn M (eds) Governance in einer sich wandelnden Welt. VS Verlag für Sozialwissenschaften, Wiesbaden, pp 43–60

Moravcsik A, Schimmelfennig F (2009) Liberal Intergovernmentalism. In: Wiener A, Diez T (eds) European integration theory. Oxford University Press, Oxford

Newig J, Lenschow A, Challies E, Cotta B, Schilling-Vacaflor A (2019) What is governance in global telecoupling? Ecol Soc 24(3). https://doi.org/10.5751/ES-11178-240326

Offe C (2009) Governance: an 'empty signifier'? Constellations 16(4):550–562. https://doi.org/10.1111/j.1467-8675.2009.00570.x

Ostrom E (2007) Institutional rational choice: an assessment of the institutional analysis and development framework. In: Sabatier PA (ed) Theories of the policy process, 2nd edn. Westview, Boulder, CO, pp 21–64

Otte A, Schröter W (2019) Lebende Konzernbetriebsvereinbarung als soziale Innovation: Internes Crowdsourcing in der GASAG-Gruppe. Bedeutung - Bewertung - Wortlaut. In: Schröter W (ed) Der mitbestimmte Algorithmus: Impulse zur Demokratisierung der Arbeitswelt 4.0. Talheimer, Mössingen-Talheim, pp 185–212

Palin K, Kaartemo V (2016) Employee motivation to participate in workplace innovation via in-house crowdsourcing. Eur J Workplace Innovat 2(2):19–40

Pedersen J, Kocsis D, Tripathi A, Tarrell A, Weerakoon A, Tahmasbi N, Xiong J, Deng W, Oh O, de Vreede G-J (2013) Conceptual foundations of crowdsourcing: a review of IS research. In: 2013 46th Hawaii international conference on system sciences (HICSS), Wailea, HI, USA, 07.01.2013–10.01.2013. IEEE, pp 579–588. https://doi.org/10.1109/HICSS.2013.143

Peters G (2010) Governance as political theory. http://regulation.huji.ac.il/papers/jp22.pdf

Peters BG, Pierre J (1998) Governance without government? Rethinking public administration. J Public Admin Res Theor 8(2):223–243. https://doi.org/10.1093/oxfordjournals.jpart.a024379

Reichwald R, Engelberger H, Moeslein K (1998) Telekooperation im Innovationstest—Strategieorientierte Evaluation von Pilotprojekten. Wirtschaftsinformatik 40(3):214–222

Sabatier PA (ed) (2007) Theories of the policy process, 2nd edn. Westview, Boulder, CO

Schlager E (1995) Policy making and collective action: defining coalitions within the advocacy coalition framework. Policy Sci 28(3):243–270. https://doi.org/10.1007/BF01000289

Schlager E (2007) A comparison of frameworks, theories, and models of policy processes. In Sabatier PA (ed) Theories of the policy process, 2nd edn. Westview, Boulder, CO, pp 293–319

Schuppert GF (2016) Governance in der Demokratietheorie. In: Lembcke OW, Ritzi C, Schaal GS (eds) Zeitgenössische Demokratietheorie. Springer, Wiesbaden

Simmert B, Eilers K, Peters C, Leimeister M (2020) Interne Crowd Work als Baustein einer Empowerment-orientierten Arbeitsorganisation. In Daum M, Wedel M, Zinke-Wehlmann C, Ulbrich H (eds) Gestaltung vernetzt-flexibler Arbeit. Beiträge aus Theorie und Praxis für die digitale Arbeitswelt. Springer, Berlin

Thuan NH (2019) Business process crowdsourcing: concept, ontology and decision support. Springer, Cham

Ulbrich H, Wedel M (2019) Development of employee-friendly internal crowdsourcing is more than innovation management: first findings from the ICU application. https://www.researchgate.net/publication/333396719. Accessed 1 Oct 2019

von Blumenthal J (2005) Governance—eine kritische Zwischenbilanz. Zeitschrift für Politikwissenschaft 15(4):1149–1180

Wedel M (2016) The European integration of RES-E promotion: the case of Germany and Poland. Springer Fachmedien Wiesbaden, Wiesbaden

Werder A v (2018) Corporate governance: definition. https://wirtschaftslexikon.gabler.de/definition/corporate-governance-28617/version-367554. Accessed 19 Sept 2019

World Bank (1996) Governance: the World Bank's experience, 2nd edn. World Bank, Washington, DC

Zhu H, Djurjagina K, Leker J (2014) Innovative behaviour types and their influence on individual crowdsourcing performances. Int J Innovat Manag 18(06):1–18. https://doi.org/10.1142/S1363919614400155
Zhu H, Sick N, Leker J (2016) How to use crowdsourcing for innovation?: A comparative case study of internal and external idea sourcing in the chemical industry. In: Kocaoglu DF (ed) Technology management for social innovation: PICMET'16 : Portland international conference on management of engineering and technology: proceedings. IEEE, Piscataway, NJ
Zogaj S, Bretschneider U (2014) Analyzing governance mechanisms for crowdsourcing information systems: a multiple case analysis. In: Avital M, Leimeister JM, Schultze U (eds) ECIS 2014 proceedings: 22th European conference on information systems, Tel Aviv, Israel, 9–11 June 2014. AIS Electronic Library
Zogaj S, Bretschneider U, Leimeister JM (2014) Managing crowdsourced software testing: a case study based insight on the challenges of a crowdsourcing intermediary. J Bus Econ 84 (3):375–405. https://doi.org/10.1007/s11573-014-0721-9
Zuchowski O, Posegga O, Schlagwein D, Fischbach K (2016) Internal crowdsourcing: conceptual framework, structured review, and research agenda. J Inform Technol 31(2):166–184. https://doi.org/10.1057/jit.2016.14

Dr. Marco Wedel is a Political Scientist (Dipl.rer.pol., Dr. phil.) and Senior Researcher at the Department of Vocational Education, Technology and Participation at the Technical University of Berlin. In addition to study visits to Boston, Constance and Berlin, he has worked in the Energy Sector (BASF) and in Science Management (Falling Walls Foundation), among other things. His current research activities focus on the topics future of work, entrepreneurship, digitalization and media competence. His long-term research focuses on European integration, democratic competence and sustainable development. Marco Wedel is co-editor of the science journal 'Innovation—The European Journal of Social Science Research'.

Hannah Ulbrich holds a Degree in Sociology (Dipl. Soz.—Bielefeld/Berlin) and is a Senior Researcher at the Department of Vocational Education, Technology and Participation at the Technical University of Berlin. There, she is the project leader of the BMBF- and ESF-funded research project 'ICU—Internal Crowdsourcing in Companies'. In addition to her work as a project manager, she is a scholarship holder of the Berlin Professional School of Economics and Law where she is currently completing a part-time MBA programme. Her research focus is on entrepreneurship and innovation, new work and agility and digital transformation and leadership.

Design of a Process and Role Model for Internal Crowdsourcing

Hannah Ulbrich and Marco Wedel

Abstract The successful implementation of internal crowdsourcing (IC) in a company requires a precise description and definition of the personnel responsibilities for the various process levels and process components within each process phase of IC. As part of the research project 'ICU—Internal Crowdsourcing in Companies', we have developed a new role model for internal crowdsourcing based on a practical application of IC in the company GASAG AG, an energy provider located in Berlin, Germany. The aim of this article is to present the main features of this role model (Some aspects of this article will also be published in German. Please be referred to Daum, M., Wedel, M., Zinke-Wehlmann, C., Ulbrich, H. (ed.) (2020): Gestaltung vernetzt-flexibler Arbeit. Beiträge aus Theorie und Praxis für die digitale Arbeitswelt. Berlin: Springer Vieweg). It is based on the roles of the agile model of Scrum, because partial aspects of the internal crowdsourcing process and certain process steering tasks have similarities with the procedure and task descriptions of Scrum. Scrum, as a mature and practice-proven set of rules with role descriptions, rules, events and artefacts, provides helpful implications for the design of an internal crowdsourcing role model as we will prove in further detail.

Keywords Internal crowdsourcing · Corporate crowdsourcing · Management · ICU system · IC process phases · IC process components · IC campaign · ICU role model · Scrum role model

1 Introduction

As a direct consequence of the technological developments of the last 10 years, internal crowdsourcing (IC) represents a new, digital form of internal knowledge networking and cross-functional collaboration. IC means that employees of a

H. Ulbrich (✉) · M. Wedel
Institute for Vocational Education and Work Studies, Technische Universität Berlin, Berlin, Germany
e-mail: hannah.ulbrich@tu-berlin.de; marco.wedel@tu-berlin.de

H. Ulbrich et al. (eds.), *Internal Crowdsourcing in Companies*, Contributions to Management Science, https://doi.org/10.1007/978-3-030-52881-2_5

company (the crowd) generate ideas and solutions that contribute to the improvement of existing products, processes and services or their new developments (innovations) in exchange via a digital platform. This makes IC both a tool for innovation management and employee participation and at the same time an implementation method.

In various forms and with different designations, the digitally mediated process has meanwhile established itself in numerous companies in Germany (Pohlisch 2019). Regardless of the form in which internal crowdsourcing is used in a company, the role model is essential for the practical implementation in all cases. Together with the IC Process and the technical solution, the so-called Crowd Technology Architecture (CTA), it forms the ICU System (see Wedel and Ulbrich, chapter 'Managing the Crowd: A Literature Review of Empirical Studies on Internal Crowdsourcing' in this book). It describes the division of responsibilities for the different process levels and process components of the individual process phases, as well as the associated steering tasks. The role model also specifies what support from other areas of the company is required for successful execution. As part of the research project 'ICU—Internal Crowdsourcing in Companies', such a role model has been realized on the basis of a prototypical application of IC.

The aim of ICU is to develop a cross-industry reference model for Good Practice in internal crowdsourcing with a focus on employee-friendly design of the application. The so-called ICU Model consists of a process strategy addressing the dimensions of innovation management, employee participation as well as employee qualification and an ICU Platform. In their role of industry partner in the ICU Project, the GASAG AG, an energy service provider based in Berlin, Germany, applied that model in its own company. The model development took place in stages: first a basic model was realized and tested as a pilot (first iteration); then the optimized model was revised by GASAG AG and further developed into a Good Practice example (second iteration). The Good Practice Model was then transformed into a cross-industry reference model of IC.

In this article, we will present the main features of the role model that have emerged from the research project. We deliberately based the design of the ICU Role Model on Scrum's role concepts, because in the light of the ICU pilot phase, we came to a fundamental realization. Partial aspects of the IC Process as well as necessary activities of process control and the principles inscribed in it show parallels to the procedure, principles and the task descriptions of the agile method Scrum. Therefore, Scrum had an exemplary character for us in developing a functional and differentiated ICU Role Model. In order to better understand the presentation of our ICU Role Model, first we will examine the IC Process with regard to its characteristics and then highlight the existing similarities between IC and Scrum. On this basis, we will then derive and describe in detail the ICU Role Model in discussion with the Scrum role approach.

2 Process Design of Internal Crowdsourcing in ICU

Scrum, especially used for agile software development, has never been considered from a process perspective because its developers Ken Schwaber and Jeff Sutherland described it as a method or better as:

> A framework within which people can tackle complex adaptive tasks consisting of Scrum Teams and their associated roles [Scrum Master, Product Owner, Development Team], Events [Sprint Planning, Daily Scrum, Sprint Review, Sprint Retrospective], Artifacts [Product Backlog] and Rules [Principles, Values]. The rules [...] define relationships and interactions between roles, events and artifacts. (Schwaber and Sutherland 2017)

However, the aforementioned elements of the framework structure the working activities in a certain way and thus, despite the freedom of design of the individual elements in terms of content, provide a predefined workflow. Using the definition of Petersen et al., which describes a process as a series of activities carried out by all participants to achieve a particular result or solve a particular problem (Pedersen et al. 2013, p. 581), it is safe to say that Scrum can be classified as a process.

In contrast, internal crowdsourcing as a technology-based procedure model is referred to either as a method, process or tool, depending on which aspect is put in the foreground. This is due to the different components that make up an ICU System. As explained by Wedel and Ulbrich earlier in this book, there are a number of possibilities for systematizing IC, whereby the postulated concepts, the selection of components and their relationship to one another vary. Our understanding of an ICU System in this article comprises only the three components of 'activity' (method), 'process' (process) and 'information technology' (tool).

In order to be able to explain the deliberately created similarities between IC and Scrum roles, the 'naturally' existing similarities between the IC and Scrum processes must be identified first. We will demonstrate this by describing the IC Process developed in ICU, i.e. describing the process phases, process components and process levels, and relating them to the corresponding process elements and the role descriptions of Scrum. Building on this, we describe the ICU Role Model at the end.

2.1 *Main Phases and Components of an IC Process*

There is a wealth of contributions in research dealing with the description of crowdsourcing processes. Thuan et al. divide these process descriptions, which are primarily aimed at external crowdsourcing, into two categories: studies with analytical approaches of high granularity and studies with analytical approaches of low granularity (Thuan et al. 2017, pp. 4; Thuan 2019, pp. 27).

Those in the high granularity group focus on conceptualization and strive to design the crowdsourcing process as a whole, also to recognize events at the macro level and to bring them into a temporal sequence (establishment of process models and framework conditions). According to Thuan et al., this group includes the works of Brabham (2008), Leimeister et al. (2009), Geiger et al. (2011), Zogaj et al. (2014) and Zogaj et al. (2015). In contrast, the research activities with low granularity are concerned only with partial aspects of the process. They highlight specific components with a focus on the associated workflows at the micro level (definition of tasks and procedures), such as studies on mechanisms of selecting and matching the appropriate target group with the right task like the work of Erickson et al. (2012), Geiger and Schader (2014) and Cullina et al. (2016) or studies on motivation and incentive systems like the work of Andrae (2012), Zhao and Zhu (2014), Machine and Ophoff (2014), Spindeldreher and Schlagwein (2016) and Feng et al. (2018).

Against this background, only the high granularity perspective is relevant for the following description of the IC Process with its process phases and process components, which we have developed in the ICU Project. Since for internal crowdsourcing the number of process-oriented investigations is manageable, we will build on fundamental features of existing process models for crowdsourcing in general (for an in-depth literature overview). In particular, we will use the phased model of Gassmann et al. (2013a, 2017) and supplement the missing steps and linkages. Zuchowski et al. have made a proposal specifically for structuring IC (Zuchowski et al. 2016, p. 169), but it does not close the gaps that we have identified in ICU with regard to the IC Process. Therefore, Zuchowski et al. will not be considered in the further explanations.

Gassman et al. (2013b, 2017, pp. 29) divide the process flow of a crowdsourcing project into five phases, starting with:

1. **Preparation**: The starting point is that a company has a problem that it wants to solve for itself. The first step is therefore to become clear about the desired result, i.e. what should be achieved and in what way should it be delivered in the end [process component: *target definition*][1]. It is also important to clarify who the adequate target group for the task to be worked on is, which platform is suitable and whether it is worthwhile in perspective to build up an own community [process component: *community management*]. After weighing up these aspects, the basic decision for or against a crowdsourcing project is made.
2. **Initiation**: Next, the task is published to the crowd on the platform of choice and the idea generation starts. This is preceded by the appropriate preparation of the tasks [process component: *task design*] and by determining the remuneration [process component: *motivation mechanisms/incentive systems]*.
3. **Implementation**: The crowdsourcing project is underway, and the first ideas are beginning to develop. These must be communicated to the relevant people in the company, and any resistance that may arise must be addressed and resolved [process component: *process monitoring*]. The activities of the crowd must also be managed to steer the dynamics in the desired direction.

[1]The terms in the square brackets are component names borrowed from the ICU Model and inserted by the authors.

4. **Evaluation**: Once the crowdsourcing activities on the platform have been completed, the solutions submitted will be evaluated. At this point it must be clear who is responsible for the evaluation and which criteria are to be applied.
5. **Utilization**: The final step is to compile the results, so they can be used further or developed and integrated into ongoing business processes [process component: *decision*]. Idea contributors should be informed about how their ideas will be used further. Sharing this information as an act of transparency contributes to building and maintaining the community [process component: crowd/*community management*].

As the previous explanations make clear, a process phase is the sum of its individual components, because it is impossible to describe individual process phases without simultaneously describing their process components. As a matter of fact, we define process components as events that occur within a process phase.

In the phased model of Gassmann et al., components were not explicitly pointed out as such. However, highlighting and naming the process components is important in order to be able to better distribute the responsibilities to the roles later on. If you do not have these clearly in mind, the role descriptions will get lost in the maze of individual workflows. Workflows are the action-oriented design of the process components and referred to in ICU as steering tasks. They belong to the 'activities' element of an ICU System (see chapter 'Managing the Crowd: A Literature Review of Empirical Studies on Internal Crowdsourcing'). Steering tasks can vary from company to company, but also over time within a company, as they have to be continuously adapted to the respective framework conditions in place. Process components, on the other hand, are constant in time and for all application contexts.

2.2 ICU Phases and Components

In principle, we were able to build the prototypical ICU Model roughly on the process flow of Gassmann et al. presented above. However, for the special form of internal crowdsourcing, we had to supplement and differentiate the process phases and components as well as rearrange the chronological order.

Our understanding of internal crowdsourcing in the ICU Project is not only about the one-sided mobilization of employees' knowledge and experience to solve a company's problems. It is also about striving for internal cooperation and employee participation. That is why the IC Process does not begin with a given problem per se, but rather with a proposal for an existing or prospective issue. With that in mind, the ICU Process is structured as follows:

1. **Impetus**: Employees from all areas of the company as well as executives, management and employee representatives are entitled to name topics. They submit potential topics either digitally via the ICU Platform or by email or face to face to the responsible department in the company, the so-called crowd team [process component: *topic proposal*].

   The responsible people in the crowd team, the Campaign Owner and the Crowd Master, filter the incoming proposals according to their relevance for the company. The relevance results from the target goals for internal crowdsourcing set by the management board [process component: *probing*].

   Then there is a discussion within the crowd team about which department might be interested in one of the topics. The Crowd Master reaches out to the head/key player of the potential department and makes agreements regarding the subject matter and the Content Ownership [process component: *exploratory talks*]. If an employee approaches the crowd team directly on behalf of a business unit, the steps of a probing and exploratory talks can be omitted.
2. **Decision (No/Go)**: The decision to pursue a topic and to set up a crowdsourcing project, in ICU and hereinafter referred to as a campaign, depends on two conditions: firstly, whether there is a need in one of the company divisions for the results that will be developed on the topic and, secondly, whether a division will take over Content Ownership for it [process component: *content ownership*]. If no one in the company takes Content Ownership, the campaign cannot be embedded in ongoing activities in a useful way. Nor could the principle of process transparency be guaranteed.

   Process transparency means that the participating employees can clearly understand at any given point in the process, what interest the company/department has in the topic, what are the objectives of the specific campaign and how the efforts of the crowd, i.e. the results, are being utilized.
3. **Conceptualization**: Once the decision to start a campaign has been made, the campaign team must develop a campaign concept. In doing so, the team must take various aspects into account. In order to productively exploit the potential of the crowd, the Campaign Owner must prepare the topics in a structured and targeted manner, so that the crowd can handle it in a meaningful way and produce usable results.

   First of all, it is therefore necessary to clarify what the aim of the campaign should be. This goes hand in hand with the definition of the expected results to be presented at the end. The Content Owner, together with the Campaign Owner, has to consider in which form the retrieved knowledge should be available at the end of the campaign, for example, as a prototype, a concept draft or a forecast [process component: *target definition*]. Directly related to this is the definition of the criteria according to which the delivered results are selected [process component: s*election of criteria*]. This also includes considerations of how the selected results can then be integrated into the Content Owner's work activities. This depends, of course, on the complexity of the campaign's objective. In most of the cases, it will be a list of ideas of how to tie in acquired knowledge. The concrete use can only be determined based on the results obtained further on [process component: intention of utilization].

Furthermore, it must be decided how employees are to be motivated to participate and what incentives are appropriate. According to Palin and Kaartemo (2016, p. 27), there are five factors that influence the extrinsic and intrinsic motivation of employees: (1) well-being in the work environment, (2) incentive system, (3) feedback from superiors and time windows for task dedication, (4) user experience and functionalities of the technology and (5) marketing and communication regarding the process and the platform (goal of site/results of site) (Palin and Kaartemo 2016). In the ICU Project, we were also able to identify these factors through employee surveys and participatory workshops. In our experience, the biggest influencing factor was 'marketing and communication'. Specifically, process transparency, which enables a comprehensive understanding of the activities on the platform, was of particular importance.

In conclusion, internal crowdsourcing does not necessarily require extrinsic incentives for employees to participate. Intrinsic motivation is far more important and can be stimulated through open communication and process transparency. Against this background, the process component 'incentive system' is closely linked to the process component 'crowd/community management' [process component: motivation mechanisms/incentive system].

The preceding process components provide the prerequisites for developing the task design. The task design is composed of different aspects. These include the description of the task in which the overriding interest is made clear, the goal definition, result definition, possible incentives, selection criteria, possible exploitation of results and the time schedule. It also includes the selection of task types.

A basic typology of tasks has been introduced by Pohlisch earlier in this book (see chapter 'Introduction to "Internal Crowdsourcing: Theoretical Foundations and Practical Applications"'). In the ICU Project, we have applied a total of five different types of tasks. These correspond largely to the basic types mentioned by Pohlisch, but we have also integrated other types that we also find frequently in the research literature (Chiu et al. 2014; Leimeister and Zogaj 2013; Zogaj et al. 2015; Brabham 2008; Jaafar and Dahanayake 2015):

- **Crowdstorming**—The crowd is called upon to point out facets of content in the set topic and to identify opportunities and challenges. The objective of the call is to explore the issue at hand.
- **Crowdvoting**—The crowd is called on to give ratings, votes, opinions or recommendations concerning set topics. The objective of the call is to gather estimations and forecasts.
- **Crowdsolving**—The crowd is called upon to develop solutions to problems to benefit the company's existing services, products and processes. The objective of the call is to optimize the portfolio offer.
- **Crowdcreation**—The crowd is called on to create new ideas and concepts for products, services and processes. The objective of the call is to generate innovation.

- **Crowdtesting**—The crowd is used to test prototypes for services, products and processes with regard to usability and user experience. The objective of the call is to obtain constructive feedback and suggestions for improvement.

Depending on the overall objective of the campaign, task types can be selected as independently implemented measures, so-called standalones. But more often, the campaign team chooses a task combination according to the mix & match principle. This combination of different types of tasks enables a multistage, iterative development of results by continuously increasing the degree of complexity in the activity required of the crowd. The mix & match principle is depicted in Fig. 1 [process component: *task design*].

The success of a campaign depends on its visibility within the company. In order to draw attention to a campaign and encourage participation, it must be advertised internally using all available communication channels: digital, such as social media applications and the intranet, and analogue, such as events, posters and flyers. To achieve the greatest possible reach in the company, strategic planning is necessary. The campaign team must select appropriate communication measures and determine the launching order [process component: *marketing strategy*]. In addition to that, the team needs to coordinate the marketing activities with the sequence of the selected task types and the accompanying events, which are specified in the campaign schedule. The schedule also defines the start, end and duration of the individual phases of the campaign, for example, the duration for participation in a campaign, results evaluation and results publication. At the end of the conception phase, the technical implementation of the campaign concept is due [process component: *IT template*].

4. **Execution**: As a prequel to the campaign, marketing starts with a teaser announcing the topic and its background information. Subsequently, a call is issued. The call goes out to every employee in the company. The group of employees are the so-called crowd or the community. In ICU we make a distinction between these two terms. In our view the term community refers to the sum of all employees, while the term crowd addresses the specific part of the community that actively participates in an IC campaign. In other words, we understand the crowd to be the active subset of the community, whereas the community represents potential crowd participants not activated yet [process component: *crowd/community management*]. Once the campaign has started, the campaign team must coordinate the process activities [process component: *process coordination*].

   In addition, continuous process monitoring is required with regard to IT functionalities, progress and scheduling. The team must report continuously to the Content Owner, who can give feedback to steer the campaign in the right direction [process component: *process monitoring*].

   At the technical level, processes must be set up and configured to ensure that the campaign runs smoothly. These must be continuously monitored and

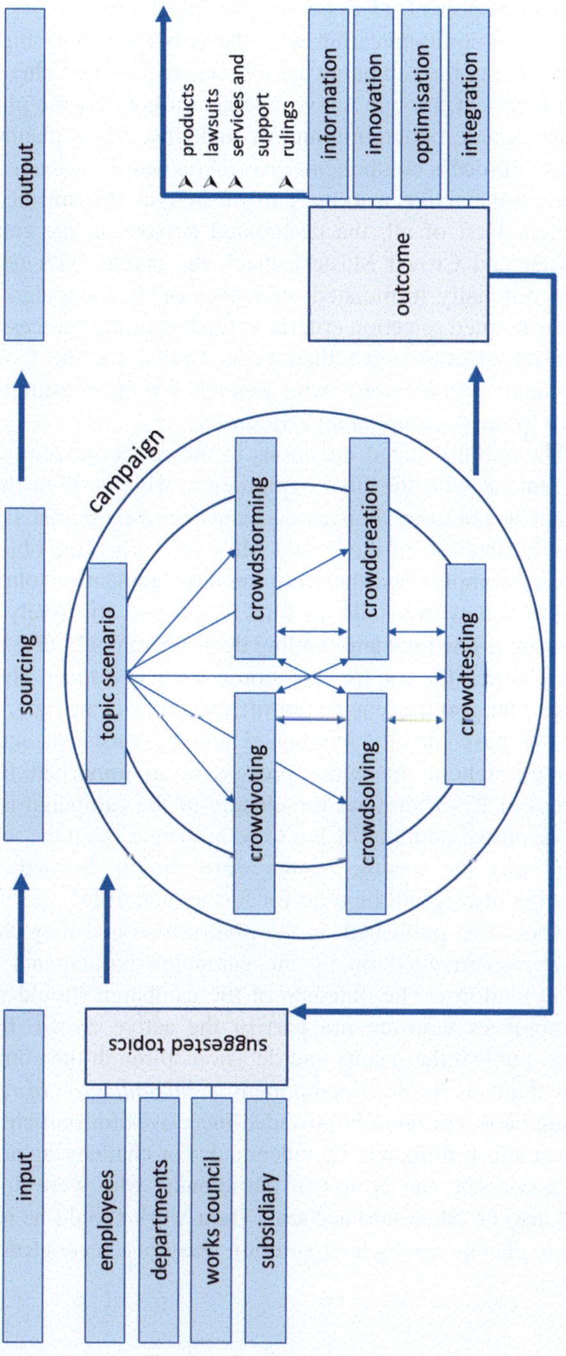

Fig. 1 Task design using the mix & match principle (own representation)

supported. In addition, the content, such as the definition of tasks, must be managed [process component: *IT & content management*].

Ongoing and open communication with the crowd has very high priority in this phase. At this point, the campaign team is seeking to strengthen and keep up the crowd's commitment through active interaction both on the platform in the manner of feedback and moderation and at analogue events planned for in the marketing strategy [process component: *crowd/community management*].

5. **Assessment:** When the active working part of the crowd is finished, the results must be evaluated. First of all, the designated persons in the campaign team (Campaign Owner and Crowd Master) check the results with regard to their relevance to the originally formulated objectives of the campaign. They do so on the basis of the defined selection criteria in the beginning [process component: *selection*]. This preselection must then be compiled for the Content Owner [process component: *preparation*], who evaluates it in consultation with his department team [process component: *evaluation*].
6. **Exploitation**: The initially stated intentions to utilize the outcomes of the campaign can be identical with the final exploitation. This is often the case when departments want to compare their assessments on a particular issue with the assessments and evaluations of the crowd. However, when the objectives of the campaign are more complex and therefore the development of solutions is more open, the question of how to handle the final results and effectively exploit them has to be raised again. The final and binding decision can only take place in view of the results available at the end [process component: *decision*]. The campaign's output, of course, can also become a spin-off for a new campaign.
7. **Feedback:** As we have already mentioned above, consistent and transparent communication throughout the entire process is an important factor for the long-term success of IC. Therefore, the closure of the campaign is an essential last step. First, the crowd/community has to be informed about the selected results and the reasons why the specific results were chosen. Second, it has to be announced how the results will be used for further activities.

   The results should be published on the platform so that they can be viewed and, if necessary, commented on by the campaign participants and all staff registered on the platform. The outcome of the campaign should also be made available to employees who are not part of the active crowd. It is therefore advisable to also publish the results and decisions through the company's other communication channels [process component: *communication of results*].

   If the campaign concept initially provided incentives for participation such as prize draws, these must ultimately be redeemed. For challenging activities, such as developing a concept, the efforts of participants who were not selected as winners should also be taken into account. Their work should be recognized by giving them an explanation why their solution was not selected [process component: *honouring*].

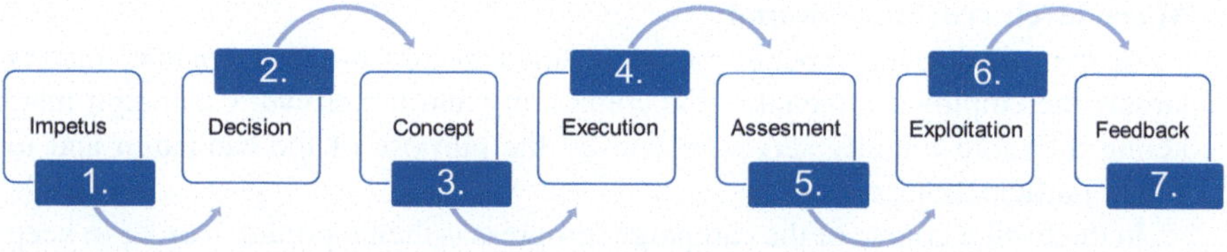

Fig. 2 Phases and process flow of the ICU model (own representation)

One observation we have made in the ICU Project is that the steering tasks within the individual process components take place in parallel or can be combined. However, the process components themselves remain the same (Fig. 2).

2.3 *ICU Process Levels*

It is clear from the above that the successful implementation of internal crowdsourcing requires a high level of communication and coordination. In the ICU Model, we have identified three different levels of process communication addressing different aspects and target groups:

- **Macro level: overall process**

  At the macro level, it is important to represent the idea and the spirit of internal crowdsourcing within the company and to show the value added by the process for current business activities (process marketing). Here, the focus is on looking at the overall process and ensuring that the defined framework conditions for IC in the company are in line with the progress of the process and that process integrity is guaranteed. The target group for process communication is senior management, the executive board and the works council.
- **Meso-level: campaign**

  The IC campaign represents the operational implementation of an IC topic and thus forms the core of the ICU Process. It consists of 'visible' process phases with communication activities running in the foreground (execution, final feedback) and 'non-visible' process phases with communication activities running in the background (conception, evaluation, exploitation).

  While the 'visible' phases take place at the micro level, the 'non-visible' process phases are located at the meso-level and are aimed at defining and coordinating the sense and purpose of the campaign in a selected circle. Here, process communication is aimed at the corporate divisions involved in the conception and implementation of the campaign.

- **Micro level: crowd/community**
  At the micro level, process communication in the so-called 'visible' phases targets the employees, meaning the community and the crowd. Campaign marketing therefore initially serves to convey the purpose of the campaign and to solicit participation.
  In the further course of the campaign, progress is then reported in order to keep the crowd activities going and to maintain the principle of transparency. There is also direct interaction within the campaign in the form of moderation on the platform or IT support.

The distinction made here between the process levels is helpful in order to be able to better differentiate the responsibilities of the roles and clearly assign control activities later on.

3 Parallels Between Internal Crowdsourcing and Scrum

In this section we first compare the components of the Scrum process relevant for the IC and then introduce the roles defined in Scrum. Based on this we present and explain the ICU Role Model. There are two main similarities that suggest a role distribution for the IC that is similar to Scrum.

3.1 Process Levels

A basic agreement between IC and Scrum exists in the different process levels on which process communication takes place. This fact is only indirectly expressed in Scrum literature (Goll and Hommel 2015; McKenna 2016; Schwaber and Sutherland 2017; Maximini 2018). This is because Scrum is seen as a set of rules and is not viewed from a process-oriented perspective. But, as already shown in the explanations on IC, Scrum also has a macro level, meso-level and micro level on which separate communication activities are carried out.

- **Macro level: overall process**
  As with IC, the macro level is also about representing Scrum with its principles, practices, rules and values in the company and making the added value of the process model comprehensible to everyone (process marketing). This level is also where the set of rules is located that determines the teamwork on the micro level.

- **Meso-level: product definition**
  The product is designed on the meso-level. Here a catalogue of requirements is created, the so-called product backlog. It defines which problem the product should solve for the customer, which properties it should have, how it should perform and what it should look like.
- **Micro level: product development**
  The requirements recorded in the product backlog are implemented on the micro level in an iterative procedure, the so-called sprint[2]. Here it must be decided which requirements from the product backlog are to be realized in a sprint (creating a sprint backlog) and how the work on the upcoming tasks is to be organized.

3.2 *The Principle of Transparency*

The Scrum framework not only includes guidelines such as practices and rules but also specifies values and principles for the teamwork. One of the three principles is transparency. Ken Schwaber and Jeff Sutherland define transparency in 'The Scrum Guide' (2017) as follows:

> The essential aspects of the process must be visible to those responsible for the outcome. Transparency requires that these aspects be defined according to a common standard, so that viewers share a common understanding of what they see. (Schwaber and Sutherland 2017, p. 7)

Transparency therefore means that everyone involved knows at all times in the work process what the current development status is. They know which features and problems are being worked on specifically, who is carrying out which activities and how the individual components contribute to the final product. Transparency is created by events such as the Daily Scrum, in which the team members (process participants at the micro level) discuss the status of their work on a daily basis and compare it with the set sprint goals (Schwaber and Sutherland 2017, p. 12). The fact that everyone has an overview of the work process and the progress made creates trust in the teamwork and the process, which motivates the team members (McKenna 2016).

In the ICU Project, we also conducted employee surveys and workshops on this issue. These revealed that process transparency is the key component in building a stable internal crowdsourcing process, ensuring that employees (crowd/community) have trust and confidence in the process and are highly motivated. Transparency also has a great influence on the perception of the employees' personal engagement as useful, because they can comprehend what happens with their effort and feel

[2]Sprints are work cycles in which selected items from the product backlog are processed within a defined timeframe. The outcome as a sprint is a 'potentially deliverable product increment' (sprint goal). By rule of thumb, a sprint lasts 2 weeks, but it can be individually adapted depending on the industry and work context (Schwaber and Sutherland 2017, p. 9).

appreciated. These findings are in line with the knowledge provided in the recent research literature as well (Garcia Martinez 2017, p. 298; Bañón-Gomis et al. 2015, p. 114; Schön et al. 2011, pp. 12; Abdul-Rahman and Hailes 2000, pp. 2; Ebner et al. 2009, p. 347). This leads us to conclude that the transparency of the process is achieved firstly through the open exchange of campaign objectives and background information with employees; secondly, by making it clear how the results and the individual steps within the campaign are used, so that employees can understand; and lastly by showing that the process serves a useful purpose in the company.

3.3 Scrum Role Model

The process levels just described refer to specific areas of responsibility that need to be managed or steered. In Scrum there are three roles that perform the following tasks:

3.3.1 Scrum Master (Macro Level)

The Scrum Master (SM) is responsible for representing the basic idea as well as the practices, rules and values of Scrum in the company (function: ambassador). The SM has to implement them and make them align with existing company values and structures (function: business developer). As coach and servant leader, the SM helps employees at different levels to understand and apply the agile framework. For example, the SM supports the Scrum Team in its work to always adhere to the agile principles and, if necessary, refers to the correct implementation of the rules. The SM assists the Product Owner with the setup and management of the product backlog and the communication with the Scrum Team. Furthermore, the SM teaches employees and managers outside the Scrum Team how they can interact with them in a way that is meaningful to them and increases the productivity of the Scrum Team (Schwaber and Sutherland 2017, pp. 7).

3.3.2 Product Owner (Meso-level)

The Product Owner (PO) is the communicative interface between the Scrum Team, the customers and the rest of the company (function: stakeholder manager). The core task of the PO is to exchange information with the customers about the desired product and to create a catalogue of requirements for product development, the so-called product backlog. The requirements are presented in the form of user stories, which the PO has to develop and present to the Scrum Team. As a representative of the customer's perspective, the PO is solely responsible for the product backlog and decides whether to accept or drop further requirements from outside. Also, the PO holds the position that can influence the course of action during the sprint. Starting from the product backlog, the PO is the one that checks the potentially deliverable product increments for compliance and then accepts or rejects them. In addition, the PO must also manage the financial aspects and keep an eye on key performance indicators (KPIs) such as ROI (return on investment) (McKenna 2016, p. 39; Schwaber and Sutherland 2017, p. 6).

3.3.3 Scrum Team (Micro Level)

The Scrum Team is a cross-functional development team that is self-organized in its work. The team members usually do not have defined roles. The idea behind it is that everybody should be able to do everything in a sprint meaning writing, testing, documenting and delivering software. Together the team decides which items from the product backlog are the most relevant at the moment and are to be implemented in the upcoming sprint transferring them to the sprint backlog (steps: sprint planning and sprint goal). During the sprint, the team works self-sufficiently. The SM and optionally also the PO only check in with the team during the Daily Scrum, which is used to jointly check and ensure the development progress. At the end of the sprint, the team members present their potentially deliverable product increment (step: sprint review) to the PO and all the stakeholders, who give feedback. Afterwards, the team has a sprint retrospective with the SM present. This serves the purpose of analysing the completed sprint (steps: lessons learned and how to improve), so that the team can improve their next sprint process (McKenna 2016, p. 42; Schwaber and Sutherland 2017, p. 7).

The principle of transparency in Scrum can be understood as a cross-cutting task for which all roles bear equal responsibility. However, the implementation of transparency looks different on every process level and results in different requirements for the individual roles:

> All of the team's success and failure is out in the open for all to see. The team is operating in a transparent manner and sharing information; the Product Owner is also being transparent and sharing. The Scrum Master posts all relevant team information on information radiators so that stakeholders can easily find out how the Sprint is progressing. [. . .] Instead of hiding information, a Scrum Team broadcasts everything about what they are up to. (McKenna 2016, p. 36)

3.4 Design of the ICU Role Model

The role model that we have developed in the ICU Project is essentially based on the division and design of roles described in Scrum but also has other actors. It describes the division of responsibilities for the different process levels as well as process sections and the associated steering tasks. In addition, it indicates the relations to other company divisions, which are needed as support for a successful execution of

IC. With reference to Porter's process model (Porter 1985), they are referred to here as 'primary' and 'secondary' units.

3.4.1 Primary Roles

We have identified three main roles that are essential for the successful implementation of IC: (1) Crowd Master, (2) Campaign Owner and (3) Crowd Technology Manager[3]. Together they form the so-called crowd team. It is the department of contact for the topic in the company and is responsible for the entire process. In concrete terms, the three roles perform the following tasks:

Crowd Master (Macro Level/Meso-level)

The Crowd Master (CM) is responsible for the general direction and the implementation of IC in the company. To this end he consults with the Board of Directors, senior management and the workers' representatives [process component: *marketing strategy*]. The CM ensures that the established framework conditions are adhered to and that the integrity and quality of the process are guaranteed [process component: *process monitoring*].

The idea of IC is promoted by the CM in the company in order to create an awareness of the possible use cases, the structure and process of internal crowdsourcing campaigns as well as to establish them as everyday working routines (ambassador function). The CM does this through direct discussions and organizing workshops or information events [process component: *marketing strategy*]. As an advocate for IC, the CM proactively networks within the company and establishes rapport with the people in the so-called specialist departments. Thus, the CM forms alliances with important key players and creates potential commitment with regard to Content Ownership [process component: *exploratory talks*].

The CM is a supportive sparring partner to the Campaign Owner during the development and implementation of campaigns as well as during the preselection of campaign results. In this context the question of employee motivation is of great importance. The CM summarizes the incentive mechanisms common in the company in a kind of catalogue and makes further adjustments to the incentive system [process component: *incentive system/employee motivation*].

In order to ensure support within the company, especially from the board of directors and senior management, the CM must create regular reports and document success using significant KPIs, for example, number of registered employees,

[3]In Fig. 3, the dotted green lines indicate that, depending on the resources available in the company, the Crowd Master and the Campaign Owner or the Crowd Technology Manager and the IT counterpart can form a personal union.

number of active campaign participants, satisfaction of Content Owners and so forth [process component: *process monitoring*].

Campaign Owner (Meso-level/Micro Level)

The Campaign Owner (CO) is the linchpin at the operational level and is responsible for the development and implementation of internal crowdsourcing campaigns. The CO works together with the Content Owner to define the goals, intention of utilization and content design of the campaign [process component: *target definition; intention of utilization*]. Based on their exchange, the CO drafts the task design for the specific campaign, selecting task types and formulating task descriptions [process component: task design; selection criteria], and chooses the appropriate incentives from the incentive catalogue created by CM best to motivate participation [process component: *incentive system/employee motivation*].

When planning the single steps of the campaign communication, the CO coordinates with the secondary units and integrates all activities into a higher-level campaign plan. The CO shares the campaign plan with the entire team, so that the process is transparent for everyone involved [process component: *marketing strategy; process coordination*]. The Crowd Technology Manager (CTM) is informed of the task design by CO so that they can set up the campaign technically, and they receive the task description to enter into the IT template [process component: *IT template*] (Fig. 3).

During thc implementation phase, the CO coordinates all activities, carries out campaign monitoring and is in touch with the crowd, for example, moderating on the

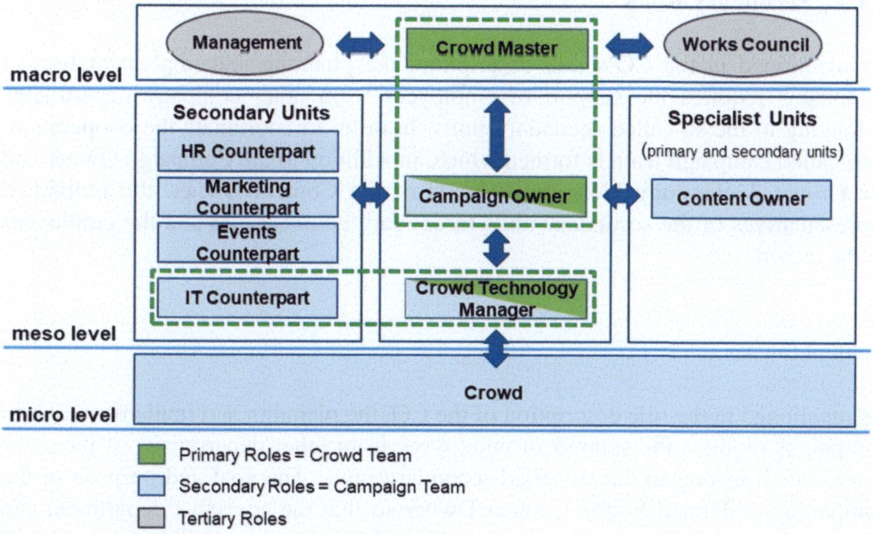

Fig. 3 ICU role model (own representation)

platform or answering questions [process component: *crowd/community management*].

After the active work phase for the crowd has been completed, the CO, in tandem with the CM, preselects the results with the established selection criteria in mind. The CO processes the results, so that Content Owner and a selected committee can evaluate them. Once the decision has been made, the CO acknowledges the campaign participants for their efforts (feedback, award ceremony, etc.) and prepares the information for the final feedback [process component: *selection; preparation; evaluation; decision; communication of results; honouring*].

Crowd Technology Manager (Meso-level/Micro Level)

The Crowd Technology Manager (CTM) configures the IT process of the campaign and is responsible for the technical implementation of the campaign guided by the Campaign Owner. Based on the given task design, the CTM builds an IT template and manages the content provided by the CO (uploads, changes) [process component: *IT template*]. The CTM is also in charge of the communication activities on the platform, initiating the go-live of campaigns, announcing the different work phases (first crowdvoting, then crowdstorming, etc.) and publishing information regarding the campaigns [process component: *IT & content management*].

The CTM ensures a flawless run of the platform and a smooth user experience (continuous bug fixing) providing user support in case of technical problems with the platform or campaigns.

3.4.2 Secondary Roles

As mentioned in the CO's role description, the planning and implementation of campaigns requires the support of employees from other company departments belonging to the so-called secondary units. In order to coordinate the cooperation, a so-called campaign team is formed which, in addition to the Campaign Owner and the Crowd Technology Manager, consists of the Content Owner, the individual representatives of the secondary units (secondary counterparts) and the employees in the crowd.

Content Owner

As mentioned in the role description of the CO, the planning and implementation of campaigns requires the support of employees from other departments of the company, which belong to the so-called secondary units. The goal and purpose of the campaign are defined by the Content Owner so that the specialist department can then continue working with the results achieved [process component: *target definition; selection criteria; task design*].

The Content Owner may or may not be the same person who submitted the topic to the crowd team. In principle, all employees can suggest topics for which they can take responsibility/ownership but are not obliged to do so. If there is no ownership, the CM and the CO must ask a suitable specialist unit in the company to take over the ownership and provide a Content Owner. When evaluating the results, the Content Owner is part of the selection committee [process component: *evaluation; decision*].

Secondary Counterparts

The CO seeks support for the planning and implementation of campaigns from the relevant experts in the company. When developing a suitable communication strategy for a campaign, for example, the CO contacts the internal marketing or employee communication department with a draft so that they can work together on the details (marketing counterpart). For the implementation of offline community events to accompany the digital internal crowdsourcing campaigns, the CO seeks the support of the department that conducts internal events and participative formats (events counterpart). For further training formats or qualifying initiatives in connection with campaigns, the CO works together with the HR department (HR counterpart). The Crowd Technology Manager works actively with the IT department to adapt the platform to the guidelines of the company's IT architecture (IT counterpart).

The areas of the company where the necessary internal contacts are located depend on the structure of the company.

Crowd

Although the crowd in the ICU Role Model is assigned to the campaign team, it is not a conventional team member like the others shown above. The crowd is the general condition to execute campaigns. It is the role that accomplishes the tasks set in the campaign and produces results. Since the crowd is just active during the campaign and a mutual exchange with the conventional team members can only take place within this situation, it is rather a component in the campaign team than a team member.

3.4.3 Tertiary Roles

The success of IC essentially depends on the commitment of the (7) Board of Directors or senior management and the support of the (8) employee representatives or works council. Together with the CM, these two stakeholders must negotiate and define the framework conditions for IC in the company and clearly demonstrate that they believe in the process and its benefits.

4 Conclusion

In this article we have presented a new process and role model for the application of internal crowdsourcing in companies, which we have derived from the practical implementation in the ICU Research Project. Based on Gassmann et al. (2013a, 2017), we developed differentiated process phases and components (ICU Process) and combined them with a process management approach described as the ICU Role Model. Due to the demonstrated similarities with Scrum, we were able to identify and formulate roles for internal crowdsourcing with specific task descriptions in relation to the developed ICU Process. The role distribution is ideal-typical and can be scaled according to the circumstances and the availability of resources in the company. This means that some of the roles can be performed by one person, depending on the workload. This is true for the roles of the Crowd Master and Campaign Owner, or the Crowd Technology Manager and IT Counterpart, especially in the initial phase of applying internal crowdsourcing.

The ICU Process and role model are intended to assist companies interested in applying internal crowdsourcing and therefore indicate how to plan if internal crowdsourcing is to be implemented successfully. As part of the IC System, introduced in chapter 'Managing the Crowd: A Literature Review of Empirical Studies on Internal Crowdsourcing' of this book, it is primarily aimed at companies that need a stronger orientation in their individual transformation journey and want to use digital processes to mobilize internal knowledge and competencies to connect and process them faster, so they can be useful for ongoing business processes.

References

Abdul-Rahman A, Hailes S (2000) Supporting trust in virtual communities. In Sprague RH (ed) System sciences 2000. Proceedings of the 33rd annual Hawaii international conference, Maui. HICSS33: Hawaii international conference on system sciences, Maui, HI, USA, 4–7 Jan 2000. IEEE Computer Society Press, Los Alamitos, CA, p 9

Andrae M (2012) Einsatz von Gamification zur Motivation in Crowdsourcing-Projekten

Bañón-Gomis AJ, Martínez-Cañas R, Ruiz-Palomino P (2015) Humanizing internal crowdsourcing best practices. In: Garrigos-Simon FJ, Gil-Pechuán I, Estelles-Miguel S (eds) Advances in crowdsourcing. Springer, Cham, pp 105–117

Brabham DC (2008) Crowdsourcing as a model for problem solving: an introduction and cases. Convergence 14(1):75–90. https://doi.org/10.1177/1354856507084420

Chiu C-M, Liang T-P, Turban E (2014) What can crowdsourcing do for decision support? Decis Support Syst 65:40–49. https://doi.org/10.1016/j.dss.2014.05.010

Cullina E, Conboy K, Morgan L (2016) Choosing the right crowd: an iterative process for crowd specification in crowdsourcing initiatives. In: 2016 49th Hawaii international conference on system sciences (HICSS), Koloa, HI, USA, 05.01.2016–08.01.2016. IEEE, pp 4355–4364

Ebner W, Leimeister JM, Krcmar H (2009) Community engineering for innovations: the ideas competition as a method to nurture a virtual community for innovations. R&D Manag 39 (4):342–356. https://doi.org/10.1111/j.1467-9310.2009.00564.x

Erickson LB, Petrick I, Trauth EM (2012) Hanging with the right crowd: matching crowdsourcing need to crowd characteristics. In: Proceedings of the eighteenth Americas conference on information systems

Feng Y, Ye J, Hua, Yu Y, Yang C, Cui T (2018) Gamification artifacts and crowdsourcing participation: examining the mediating role of intrinsic motivations. Comput Hum Behav 81:124–136. https://doi.org/10.1016/j.chb.2017.12.018

Garcia Martinez M (2017) Inspiring crowdsourcing communities to create novel solutions: Competition design and the mediating role of trust. Technol Forecast Soc Change 117:296–304. https://doi.org/10.1016/j.techfore.2016.11.015

Gassmann O, Friesike S, Häuselmann C (2013a) Crowdsourcing: Eine kurze Einführung. In: Gassmann O (ed) Crowdsourcing. Innovationsmanagement mit Schwarmintelligenz; Interaktiv Ideen finde; Kollektives Wissen effektiv nutzen ; mit Fallbeispielen und Checklisten, 2nd edn [elektronische Ressource]. Hanser, München, pp 1–21

Gassmann O, Winterhalter S, Wecht CH (2013b) Praktische Durchführung: Hürden und Tipps. In: Gassmann O (ed) Crowdsourcing. Innovationsmanagement mit Schwarmintelligenz; Interaktiv Ideen finden; Kollektives Wissen effektiv nutzen ; mit Fallbeispielen und Checklisten. 2nd edn [electronic resource]. Hanser, München, pp 176–194

Gassmann O, Friesike S, Daiber M (2017) Crowdsourcing Methode und Prozess. In: Pechlaner H, Poppe X-I (eds) Crowd entrepreneurship. Springer, Wiesbaden, pp 23–39

Geiger D, Schader M (2014) Personalized task recommendation in crowdsourcing information systems—current state of the art. Decis Support Syst 65:3–16. https://doi.org/10.1016/j.dss.2014.05.007

Geiger D, Seedorf S, Schulze T, Nickerson RC, Schader M (2011) Managing the crowd: towards a taxonomy of crowdsourcing processes. In: Seventeenth Americas conference on information systems, Detroit, MI, 4th–7th Aug 2011. http://aisel.aisnet.org/amcis2011_submissions/430

Goll J, Hommel D (2015) Mit Scrum zum gewünschten System. Springer, Wiesbaden. http://www.springer.com/

Jaafar N, Dahanayake A (2015) Software architecture for collaborative crowd-storming applications. In Morzy T, Valduriez P, Bellatreche L (eds) New trends in databases and information systems. 19th East-European conference on advances in databases and information systems]; ADBIS 2015 short papers and workshops BigDap, DCSA, GID, MEBIS, OAIS, SW4CH, WISARD, Poitiers, France, 8 11 Sept 2015; proceedings, Communications in computer and information science, vol 539. Springer, Cham, pp 268–278

Leimeister JM, Zogaj S (2013) Neue Arbeitsorganisation durch Crowdsourcing. Eine Literaturstudie. Hans-Böckler-Stiftung (Arbeitspapier Nr. 287)

Leimeister JM, Huber M, Bretschneider U, Krcmar H (2009) Leveraging crowdsourcing. Activation-supporting components for IT-based ideas competition. J Manag Inform Syst 26 (1):197–224. https://doi.org/10.2753/MIS0742-1222260108

Machine D, Ophoff J (2014) Understanding what motivates participation on crowdsourcing platforms. In: Proceedings of the e-skills for knowledge production and innovation conference 2014, Cape Town, South Africa. http://proceedings.e-skillsconference.org/2014/e-skills191-200Machine820.pdf

Maximini D (2018) The scrum culture. Introducing agile methods in organizations, 2nd edn. Springer (Management for Professionals), Cham. https://doi.org/10.1007/978-3-319-73842-0

McKenna D (2016) The art of scrum. Apress, Berkeley, CA

Palin K, Kaartemo V (2016) Employee motivation to participate in workplace innovation via in-house crowdsourcing. Eur J Workplace Innovat 2(2):19–40

Pedersen J, Kocsis D, Tripathi A, Tarrell A, Weerakoon A, Tahmasbi N, et al (2013) Conceptual foundations of crowdsourcing: A review of IS research. In: 2013 46th Hawaii international conference on system sciences (HICSS), Wailea, HI, USA, 07.01.2013–10.01.2013. IEEE, pp 579–588

Pohlisch J (2019) Bericht—Innovationsaktivitäten Deutscher Unternehmen. Technische Universität Berlin, Fachgebiet Innovation Economics, Berlin. https://tubcloud.tu-berlin.de/s/2m2BzwNyR3T9s8a#pdfviewer

Porter ME (1985) Competitive advantage. Creating and sustaining superior performance. Free Press, New York

Schön S, Güntner G, Markus M (2011) Online-Gemeinschaften und Crowds in Unternehmen. HMD 48(4):6–15. https://doi.org/10.1007/BF03340601
Schwaber K, Sutherland J (2017) The scrum guide. https://www.Scrumguides.org/docs/Scrumguide/v2017/2017-Scrum-Guide-German.pdf
Spindeldreher K, Schlagwein D (2016) What drives the crowd? A meta-analysis of the motivation of participants in crowdsourcing. In: PACIS 2016
Thuan NH (2019) Business process crowdsourcing. Concept, ontology and decision support. Cham: Springer International Publishing (Progress in IS)
Thuan NH, Antunes P, Johnstone D (2017) A process model for establishing business process crowdsourcing. Australasian Journal of Information Systems, 21, Zugegriffen am 10.10.2019 https://journal.acs.org.au/index.php/ajis/article/view/1392/782.
Zhao YC, Zhu Q (2014) Effects of extrinsic and intrinsic motivation on participation in crowdsourcing contest. Online Inf Rev 38(7):896–917. https://doi.org/10.1108/OIR-08-2014-0188
Zogaj S, Bretschneider U, Leimeister JM (2014) Managing crowdsourced software testing: a case study based insight on the challenges of a crowdsourcing intermediary. J Bus Econ 84 (3):375–405. https://doi.org/10.1007/s11573-014-0721-9
Zogaj S, Leicht N, Blohm I, Bretschneider U, Leimeister JM (2015) Towards successful crowdsourcing projects: evaluating the implementation of governance mechanisms. In: Thirty sixth international conference on information systems, Fort Worth
Zuchowski O, Posegga O, Schlagwein D, Fischbach K (2016) Internal crowdsourcing. Conceptual framework, structured review, and research agenda. In J Inf Technol 31(2):166–184. https://doi.org/10.1057/jit.2016.14

Hannah Ulbrich holds a Degree in Sociology (Dipl. Soz. – Bielefeld/Berlin) and is a Senior Researcher at the Department of Vocational Education/Technology and Participation at the Technical University of Berlin. There, she is the Project Leader of the BMBF- and ESF-funded research project 'ICU—Internal Crowdsourcing in Companies'. In addition to her work as a project manager, she is a Scholarship Holder of the Berlin Professional School of Economics and Law where she is currently completing a part-time MBA programme. Her research focus is on entrepreneurship and innovation, and agility and digital transformation and leadership.

Dr. Marco Wedel is a Political Scientist (Dipl.rer.pol., Dr. phil.) and Senior Researcher at the Department of Vocational Education/Technology and Participation at the Technical University of Berlin. In addition to study visits in Boston, Constance and Berlin, he has worked in the Energy Sector (BASF) and in Science Management (Falling Walls Foundation), among others. His current research activities focus on the topics 'future of work', entrepreneurship, digitalization and media competence. His long-term research focuses on European integration, democratic competence and sustainable development. Marco Wedel is coeditor of the science journal *Innovation: The European Journal of Social Science Research*.

An Empirical Analysis of an Internal Crowdsourcing Platform: IT Implications for Improving Employee Participation

Neslihan Iskender and Tim Polzehl

Abstract Crowdsourcing has become one of the main resources for working on so-called microtasks that require human intelligence to solve tasks that computers cannot yet solve and to connect to external knowledge and expertise. Instead of using external crowds, several organizations have increasingly been using their employees as a crowd, with the aim of exploiting employee's potentials, mobilizing unused technical and personal experience and including personal skills for innovation or product enhancement. However, understanding the dynamics of this new way of digital co-working from the technical point of view plays a vital role in the success of internal crowdsourcing, and, to our knowledge, no study has yet empirically investigated the relationship between the technical features and participation in internal crowdsourcing. Therefore, this chapter aims to provide a guideline for organizations and employers from the perspective of the technical design of internal crowdsourcing, specifically regarding issues of data protection privacy and security concerns as well as task type, design, duration and participation time based on the empirical findings of an internal crowdsourcing platform.

Keywords Internal crowdsourcing · Enterprise crowdsourcing · Technology implications · Employee participation

1 Introduction

Thanks to the widespread use of the Internet, a fast and relatively inexpensive resource, so-called microtask crowdsourcing, has emerged, meaning that the cost and time barriers of qualitative and quantitative laboratory studies, controlled experiments, challenges in innovation and product enhancement can be easier overcome (Kittur et al. 2011; Gadiraju 2018). Microtask crowdsourcing has been primarily

N. Iskender (✉) · T. Polzehl
Quality and Usability Lab, TU Berlin, Berlin, Germany
e-mail: neslihan.iskender@tu-berlin.de; tim.polzehl@qu.tu-berlin.de

H. Ulbrich et al. (eds.), *Internal Crowdsourcing in Companies*, Contributions to Management Science, https://doi.org/10.1007/978-3-030-52881-2_6

used for simple, independent tasks such as image labelling or digitizing print documents (Kittur et al. 2011). One of the well-known examples of crowdsourcing is Wikipedia, where crowdsourcing is used to gather knowledge from people from all over the world. They bring together a collection of images, links and topics, tag the content, sort it into categories and link and recommend content to each other. Inspired by the results of microtask crowdsourcing, some researchers have begun to investigate crowdsourcing for complex and expert tasks such as writing, translating, product design or product innovation (Kittur et al. 2013; Valentine et al. 2017; Zuchowski et al. 2016). Progressive digitization and the global networking associated with it are also leading to a change in the professional world, meaning that the use of crowdsourcing in enterprises has increased substantially as a direct result of widespread use of Internet applications and digitalization.

This new form of digital agile work, both in terms of collaboration and the knowledge transfer processes, has aroused the interest of many enterprises where the same pattern of online working is used internally. In that way, crowdsourcing has evolved and created a new form which is referred to as 'internal crowdsourcing'. It involves outsourcing certain work steps and tasks from the daily tasks, production or innovation processes or any kind of topic that might be interesting for employees, via company-owned online platforms or intermediaries to a predefined group of company employees (Zuchowski et al. 2016; Erickson et al. 2012; Vel et al. 2018). In this case, value-added activities are not outsourced to an indefinite mass of people, the so-called external crowd, but to a closed group of people such as employees or other stakeholders (Leimeister et al. 2015).

This also has far-reaching consequences for companies and the way they use the Internet for their diverse work processes. This new way of digitalization and work organization is increasingly becoming an alternative to the traditional way of working in organizations, especially in the innovation and participation domain (Benbya and Leidner 2016; Benbya and Leidner 2018; Malhotra et al. 2017). Apart from collecting information on any topic, organizations can apply internal crowdsourcing for complex tasks such as idea creation, product evaluation or innovation generation, which are mostly quite complex and require special knowledge and skills. This new concept is implemented in practice at numerous large companies. For example, the American consumer goods producer Procter & Gamble, the pharmaceutical company Bayer HealthCare and the toy manufacturer LEGO use the crowdsourcing strategy to achieve higher-quality, cheaper and faster innovation processes (Zuchowski et al. 2016).

The idea that the innovation or idea creation processes are opened to all the employees (not just the employees of strategy or innovation department) is interesting for many companies because this type of crowdsourcing uses the principle of the 'wisdom of the crowd'. This is the phenomena whereby a heterogeneous group of individually decisive people can produce qualitatively better solutions than certain experts under certain conditions (Lüttgens et al. 2014). In that way, organizations can benefit from the internal knowledge and personal experience of all employees and involve them in the innovation process without any additional costs. For example, Dieter Zetsche—the Chairman of the Board of Management of Daimler

AG—recently announced that 20% of the employees will be transformed into an internal crowd to operationalize a series of innovation tasks (Daimler 2017). However, designing and building such a large internal crowd involves a significant organizational transformation process that needs to be managed (Malhotra and Majchrzak 2014). Allianz UK has shown how tedious this change can be when they launched an internal crowdsourcing platform for innovation development (Benbya and Leidner 2016; Benbya and Leidner 2018). More than 8 years have passed from commissioning to the efficient use of the platform.

Since internal crowdsourcing is not yet a standardized procedure, the internal crowdsourcing task design, the foundation of the employee's motivation to participate, the measures of quality and success for internal crowdsourcing as well as ground rules for protecting employee rights and privacy should be established for an ethical and successful operationalization of internal crowdsourcing (Zuchowski et al. 2016). Chapters 'Introduction to "Internal Crowdsourcing: Theoretical Foundations and Practical Applications"' and 'Systematization Approach for the Development and Description of an Internal Crowdsourcing System' provide the theoretical background for internal crowdsourcing; however, to our knowledge, no study has yet empirically investigated the effects of crowdsourcing campaign topics, the estimated timeframes involved, the time and day for employee participation in the campaign or the question types to be used in the campaign concerning the participation of employees in the internal crowdsourcing. As such, the empirical results of internal crowdsourcing should be further investigated to find out what kind of relationship exists between the technical characteristics of an internal crowdsourcing platform and employee participation.

This chapter aims to provide some initial insights about how to shape and communicate the rules regarding data protection, privacy and security concerns of employees as well as the guidelines for technical implementation of such a platform and its daily operation. Its anticipated contribution towards the practical implementation is the establishment of ground rules for fair internal crowdsourcing to lower the barriers to employee participation. The following section of the chapter explains the review and synthesis of the external and internal crowdsourcing in the literature. The subsequent section then presents the basic function of an internal crowdsourcing platform based on an empirical example of it. The penultimate section highlights the research methods and internal crowdsourcing tasks that have been conducted using an internal crowdsourcing platform and provides an empirical analysis of these. In the last section, the discussion and conclusion of the empirical results are presented.

2 Theoretical Background

The term 'crowdsourcing' was first used by the American journalist Jeff Howe (2006) in an article entitled 'The Rise of Crowdsourcing', which was published in the technology magazine Wired (Howe 2006). It is a neologism from the words 'crowd' and 'outsourcing', and Howe describes it as follows:

> The technological advances in everything from product design software to digital video cameras are breaking down the cost barriers that once separated amateurs from professionals. Hobbyists, part-times, and dabblers suddenly have a market for their efforts, as smart companies in industries as disparate as pharmaceutical and television discover ways to tap the latent talent of the crowd. The labor isn't always free, but it costs a lot less than paying traditional employees. It's not outsourcing; it's Crowdsourcing. (Howe 2006)

So, crowdsourcing is a form of participatory online activity involving an individual, an institution, a charity or a company—an undefined group of individuals—through a flexible open call to perform a task voluntarily or in return for some monetary benefit (Geiger et al. 2012).

Brabham takes the results of Howe and focuses on the crowdsourcing from the company's perspective saying that:

> A company posts a problem online, a large number of individual solutions to the problem, the winning ideas are some form of a bounty, and the company mass products the idea for its own gain. (Brabahan 2008)

It becomes clear that Brabahan (2008) considers the crowdsourcing process particularly as a problem-solving method, thus emphasizing the crowd's swarm intelligence. However, the authors Lopez, Vukovic and Laredo limit the crowdsourcing principle only to the company's own perspective and see crowdsourcing as an Internet-based production model that enables distributed and Web-based human collaboration (Lopez et al. 2010).

Taking the above definitions into account, three main components of crowdsourcing can be identified: (1) requester or initiator (crowdsourcer), (2) crowd or Internet users (crowdworker) and (3) Internet-based crowdsourcing platform. This is distinguished from outsourcing in that it has a mediator (Internet-based crowdsourcing platform) which enables the communication between an unknown group of people, crowdworkers and the requester (Leimeister et al. 2015). In the case of outsourcing, the requester knows exactly who the task executer is and instructs him/her by giving a certain task in return for monetary payment. In contrast to outsourcing, in external crowdsourcing, the crowdsourcers outsource certain tasks to an Internet-based platform for processing. The undefined mass of people or the so-called crowdworkers take over the processing of outsourced tasks voluntarily or in return for a monetary benefit (Leimeister and Zogaj 2013; Hirth et al. 2012). The entire process, as well as the interaction between crowdsourcers and crowdworkers, takes place on Internet-based crowdsourcing platforms (Blohm et al. 2014; Hoßfeld et al. 2012). It follows that if the crowdworkers are a defined group of people such as employees, stakeholders or members of an organization, then we talk about 'internal crowdsourcing' (Leimeister and Zogaj 2013).

In the light of the above definitions, crowdsourcing is defined as a mechanism of task sharing, especially the outsourcing of tasks or orders by crowdsourcers to a wide crowd (crowdworkers) via an open call to solve a particular problem as quickly and effectively as possible. Following that, we separate crowdsourcing based on the crowdworkers into two categories: external and internal crowdsourcing. External crowdsourcing, as explained in chapter 'Introduction to "Internal Crowdsourcing:

Theoretical Foundations and Practical Applications"', deals with an undefined open, heterogonous and usually unskilled crowd. However, the crowd in internal crowdsourcing describes a closed group of people with certain skills, usually the employees of the company, defined by the requester (Benbya and Leidner 2018).

2.1 Internal Crowdsourcing

In recent years, the still relatively new strategy of *crowdsourcing* has become increasingly interesting for companies in various industries as a way to redesign and speed up innovation processes and to benefit from the unused internal knowledge of the employee in an organization (Howe 2006, 2009; Hammon and Hippner 2012; Blohm et al. 2014; Simula and Ahola 2014). This type of crowdsourcing is referred to as 'internal crowdsourcing' (IC), which is defined according to Zuchowski et al. (2016) as follows:

> Internal crowdsourcing is (a) IT-enabled (b) group activity based on (c) open call for participation (d) in an enterprise.

By definition, certain work steps and tasks of a production or innovation process are outsourced using internal crowdsourcing via company-owned online platforms or intermediaries to a predefined group of employees who participate voluntarily in the completion of these crowd tasks online (Leimeister and Zogaj 2013). These are then used to produce innovative, marketable products and services, thus contributing towards increasing the company's efficiency and profit.

Internal crowdsourcing is still a poorly researched practical phenomenon. Although corporate crowdsourcing is a lucrative process from a corporate perspective, there is an imbalance between the burden and the benefits of crowd activity from the employee's point of view. For this reason, an incentive system should be developed so that employees can motivate themselves or see benefits in the process as a whole. To ensure that crowdsourcing for employees does not lead to an extra workload, the labour law framework for internal crowdsourcing should also be defined. Also, there are no standards or standardized procedures for task design, task decomposition, task typology, technical requirements for an internal crowdsourcing platform and measurement of the quality of results in internal crowdsourcing. For this purpose, methods that can be used to measure the quality of a creative process are also to be explored. Finally, an ideal process flow (workflow) is needed, which takes into account all aspects of internal crowdsourcing and in an optimal order with associated roles and resources.

2.2 Employee Motivation

In the case of internal crowdsourcing, the incentive system is more diversified, as employees are generally financially secure due to their employment in the company. Fundamentally, there are intrinsic and extrinsic motivations to contribute to the crowdsourcing task from the employee perspective. Intrinsic motivations are when carrying out an action is rewarding for the employee himself, for example, because it brings satisfaction, while extrinsic motivation comes from the expectation of a reward from the outside world as a consequence of an action (Meffert et al. 2018).

One of the intrinsic motivations for employees is their enjoyment of the activity, for example, having fun while testing an internal software, contributing to the ideation of a new product or being intrigued by the competitive nature of crowdsourcing projects (Leimeister and Zogaj 2013). The prospect of helping to shape products in line with their own wishes and ideas and to influence their development can also be crucial from the employee's perspective (Sixt 2014). This motivation is particularly evident in crowdsolving and crowdcreation, where the motivation here is not in the material reward but in the positive feeling that arises from being involved in the task. Another intrinsic motivation is social exchange within the crowd where the desire to exchange and interact with like-minded people serves as an incentive (Leimeister and Zogaj 2013). Brabham (2013) also mentions the following as essential motivations for participating in crowdsourcing initiatives: 'to network with other creative professionals' and 'to socialize and make friends'. Another intrinsic motivation for participating in internal crowdsourcing is the opportunity to learn within the crowdsourcing engagement and thus enhance personal skills, competencies and experiences through the exercise of relevant tasks so that creative skills can be improved by tackling complex tasks and gaining experience.

Extrinsic motivation comes from the outer world, and the desire for appreciation by other people can also serve as an essential extrinsic motivation in internal crowdsourcing (Leimeister and Zogaj 2013). To feel appreciated by the outside world, e.g. managers and colleagues, crowdsourcing contributions should be visible to other participants, like in competitions where the winner is chosen by the community itself. Participants hoping for recognition from the crowd (their colleges) and company (their employers) are usually motivated to generate high-quality contributions to gain prestige in the company (Franke and Klausberger 2010). Another extrinsic motive is the desire for self-expression or self-marketing. In addition to showing their own contributions to other members of the crowd, self-marketing through crowdsourcing may also improve an employee's own career opportunities by opening up the possibility that the employer becomes aware of an employee's high-quality contributions (Leimeister and Zogaj 2013). Monetary rewards can be mentioned as a last extrinsic motive. These can be in the form of monetary compensation, benefits in kind, discounts or certain premiums (Franke and Klausberger 2010).

2.3 Labour Law Framework

As this new way of working sets in motion a fundamental shift in work organization and in the division of labour, minimum standards for fair work in the crowd and fair digital work environment should be defined. To avoid additional workload, the crowd concepts should be designed in a way that takes into account labour policy /legal requirements such as works constitution law, occupational health and safety, trade association regulations, collective bargaining agreements and data protection regulations. Therefore, it is recommended that an official company agreement that regulates all these aspects be drawn up. One of the latest group-wide company agreements for internal crowdsourcing in Germany, 'Lebende Konzernbetriebsvereinbarung als soziale Innovation' (the living group works council agreement as social innovation), establishes the rules for a fair crowdsourcing environment for employees (Otte and Schröter 2018). According to Otte and Schröter (2018), the following rules can be applied to any internal crowdsourcing environment:

- The participation of employees in the internal crowdsourcing is voluntary, and employees are not affected by participation or non-participation.
- The participation of employees in the internal crowdsourcing takes place during working hours. The time working on the platform is working time.
- Accessibility to internal crowdsourcing is provided at work via mobile phones or laptops and guaranteed by the company in employees' home offices as well. There will be no additional IT accesses or IT jobs provided. Employees without IT access can place IC initiatives directly through the crowd manager.
- The participation of employees in group-public or employer-public points or ranking systems is always voluntarily. Participants have the right to use their real name or a pseudonym.
- The company is committed to handling data security and data protection in a highly sensitive manner that goes beyond the regulations of the national data protection law. Any and all platform data will be made available for use only in an aggregated and anonymized form to the corporate bodies as well as department heads and supervisors and, upon request, to the research community. A person-related breakdown of data does not take place. The aim is to strengthen employees' right to determine themselves what happens to their information and to reinforce their confidence in the company and its careful corporate culture.
- In order to protect employees' privacy, there will be no online tracking or controlling of employee performance or behaviour.
- Innovation ideas by employees that are brought into an internal crowdsourcing platform are legally transferred to the company. The idea providers are entitled to appropriate remuneration.

2.4 Tasks in Internal Crowdsourcing

Tasks in internal crowdsourcing are usually like crowdsolving and crowdcreation as described in chapter 'Systematization Approach for the Development and Description of an Internal Crowdsourcing System'. In larger and more segmented enterprises, it is difficult to match people to the right problem. However, with the help of internal crowdsourcing, the unutilized or unnoticed knowledge of employees can be used by the company internally to generate faster innovation processes, improve existing products or solve current problems in the organization (Lopez et al. 2010; Benbya and Van Alstyne 2010; Gaspoz 2011). In this way, a social innovation community can be built, and the quality of social capital in an enterprise can be improved with the help of internal crowdsourcing (Bharati et al. 2015).

The content of the internal crowdsourcing tasks is determined by the needs of the company and is therefore highly varied. For example, IBM established a platform called 'InnovationJam' to drive innovation and collaboration by providing a platform to discuss innovative ideas (Bjelland and Wood 2008). In the InnovationJam platform, the idea creators must first consider concrete aspects such as costs, quality and deadlines, simulate planned projects and then reach the declared goal. After that, every employee gets a virtual wallet and uses their budget to invest in their colleagues' ideas and vote for them. If the virtual test run is successful, the company decides to follow through with a real implementation.

Similarly, Allianz UK uses an internal crowdsourcing platform to generate as many different ideas as possible while also encouraging the submission of 'smaller' ideas, as these are more common in the financial services sector (Benbya and Leidner 2016). Idea generation takes the form of idea campaigns, and the idea campaigns are geared to the needs of the respective area to increase employee participation. Qualitative feedback mechanisms, in particular, ensure that the ideas submitted are treated with respect and provide for a close exchange between the employees who are involved in the process and those responsible for the process of developing the ideas.

Telekom AG has been conducting so-called forecast markets for product innovation since 2012 (Zuchowski et al. 2016). Their platform is accessible to all employees, and, instead of an employee, a department places various topics and problems in the platform. Usually, tasks that are placed in Telekom's platform, such as sales channels, target groups, benefits analysis, product design or market potential, would be outsourced to external market research agencies. However, due to the short trading time of the questions that have been asked, that is, within 5 working days, results from the forecast markets are available faster and generally exceed the quality of conventional market analyses. The individual contributions by the employees are aggregated into an overall contribution whereby the calculation basis for the forecast is formed from the median of all individual forecasts.

SAP uses internal crowdsourcing to make a social impact and aims to use the ideas of SAP employees to improve the lives of one billion people on the planet by 2020 (Durward et al. 2019). In doing so, SAP technologies should be used to promote sustainable ideas of social significance that are economically feasible at the same time. For this purpose, SAP APJ invests 1 million € annually to finance social start-ups within SAP. The orientation of the foundations focuses mainly on the business areas of health and disaster management.

2.5 *Crowdsourcing Forms*

Depending on the task characteristics and skill demands, crowdsourcing can generally be divided into two categories: microtask and macrotask crowdsourcing.

Microtask Crowdsourcing In the case of microtask crowdsourcing, crowdworkers collectively work on a large number of tasks so that the traditional human resource requirements of requesters can be reduced. In doing so, the online crowdsourcing platform splits the big tasks of the requester into small subtasks, which are as small as possible so as to ensure quick and easy processing. This process is then referred to as 'microtasks' or 'micro-jobs' (Difallah et al. 2015). In the end, all subtasks are brought together again and sent back to the requester. Amazon Mechanical Turk is one of the best-known platforms for this type of activity.

This kind of crowd task is used by requesters to handle less complex, often repetitive, tasks such as image tagging and video tagging or the transcription, translation or digitation of documents that are easy for humans to process but cannot be processed easily by machines (Geiger et al. 2011). However, the task description should contain all the necessary information about the task execution because crowdworkers only see a small portion of a bigger task which they do not know about, and they usually do not have an opportunity to contact the requester for further information about the task (Deng et al. 2016; Felstiner 2011; Leimeister et al. 2016). Therefore, it is extremely important to formulate the task as concretely and specifically as possible to obtain high-quality solutions (Deng et al. 2016).

Macrotask Crowdsourcing In macrotask crowdsourcing, the task is divided into units that are quite large and therefore still relatively complex and require preprocessing. It is an interactive form of service delivery that is organized collaboratively or competitively and involves a large number of extrinsically or intrinsically motivated actors using modern ICT systems. Among other things, this variant of crowdsourcing uses the principle of the 'wisdom of crowds', which James Surowiecki described in his book in 2005 (Surowiecki 2005). It states that the solution achieved and the decision-making are often better when information is accumulated in a heterogeneous group of individuals than when it is given by a single expert. Macrotasks are difficult to take apart, and the solutions for macrotasks require a great deal of sharing of contextual information or dependencies on intermediary results. Therefore, creative tasks such as design contests or coding challenges are executed in the form of macrotasks (Niu et al. 2019).

In contrast to microtask crowdsourcing, macrotask crowdsourcing promotes collaborative working among crowdworkers because of its complex subtasks.

Different abilities and skills meet in the crowd and connect productively to one or more end solutions. In this way, both innovation ability, generation and preservation are promoted.

2.6 Process Management

Crowdsourcer Institutions, e.g. public authorities or universities, non-profit organizations or an individual may act as crowdsourcers (Leimeister and Zogaj 2013). Typically, an organization passes one task on to more than one external crowdworker and uses the results from their work to complete the crowdsourcing process. The 'crowdsourcer' (requester, client) usually designs the process by defining the task typology, the required crowdworker profile, the budget and time constraints and by executing the task decomposition. After the task is completed, the crowdsourcer analyses the results based on the predefined evaluation criteria (Difallah et al. 2015) (Fig. 1).

Crowdworker Generally, the crowdworkers consist of an undefined large group of people who have participated in the completion of a given task voluntarily or in return for monetary compensation (Difallah et al. 2015). The optimal number of crowdworkers depends on the type of crowdsourcing task, the task specifications and the information and skills needed to solve the problem (Leimeister and Zogaj 2013). The crowdworkers' expertise and abilities can determine the quality of the results; therefore the credentials and experience of crowdworkers might play an important role when the requester is selecting the right crowd (Allahbakhsh et al. 2013).

Platform Crowdsourcing platforms provide the medium of interaction and thus the (only) point of contact between the requesters and the crowdworkers. These platforms control all processes starting with the registration of a crowdworker on the platform, then continuing with the placing of the crowdsourcing task defined by the requester on the platform, assigning of the task to the given crowdworker profile, providing support with technical issues and collecting the answers from the crowdworkers (Difallah et al. 2015). The crowdsourcing platforms can be divided into the following types:

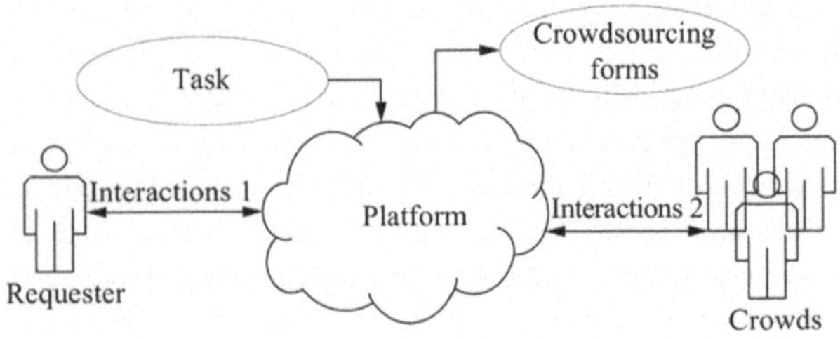

Fig. 1 A simple crowdsourcing process (Niu et al. 2019)

- *Microwork platforms:* These platforms are mostly designed for microtask crowdsourcing. These tasks are of low complexity and high granularity. The best-known platforms for microtasks today are Amazon Mechanical Turk, Clickworker and CrowdFlower.
- *Development, test and marketing platforms*: Tasks are (very) complex and have low granularity. The best-known platforms for this are rapidusertests and Testbirds.
- *Innovation platforms:* Tasks may have both low and high complexity. The best-known platform for this is InnoCentive.
- *Internal crowdsourcing platforms*: Tasks are business-driven and may have low or high complexity. There is no generally known platform for internal crowdsourcing; each company uses its own platform or one of the platforms of the external providers.

As explained in chapter 'Systematization Approach for the Development and Description of an Internal Crowdsourcing System', the *ICU Process and Role Model* describes the process of internal crowdsourcing, in particular the individual steps that are necessary to solve an explicit task. Exploiting the full potential of the employees, the following steps should be designed by the requester, usually a department in a company or an employee: (1) impetus; (2) decision; (3) conceptualization; (4) execution; (5) assessment; (6) exploitation and (7) feedback (see chapter 'Systematization Approach for the Development and Description of an Internal Crowdsourcing System').

Stage 3 in particular plays an important role in the success of internal crowdsourcing and should be defined before the task execution. The definition, decomposition, integration and allocation of tasks are crucial in this process because the task should be explained unambiguously, in a focused manner and precisely so that employees can understand it easily by reading it in an online environment and so that they can complete the task in a short timeframe (Bailey and Horvitz 2010). Additionally, the bigger picture that lies behind the task should be communicated beforehand so that the employees can understand the context better and feel appreciated by contributing to something bigger (Simula and Ahola 2014). After the task is completed, the results evaluation and the quality control can be performed either by employees in the form of a crowdrating or by the requester (the department or an individual employee) or by an expert in the given domain (Thuan et al. 2017). Another important aspect is that the final results and the next steps with the achieved results should be communicated clearly to the employees.

2.7 Role of IT in Internal Crowdsourcing

The internal crowdsourcing platforms can be divided into two categories: *generic social IT platforms* (i.e. multipurpose tools such as social networking sites or wikis) and *specific crowdsourcing IT platforms* (i.e. tools developed specifically for crowdsourcing, possibly even for a particular purpose in a particular enterprise) (Zuchowski et al. 2016).

Generic Social IT Platforms In the case of generic social IT platforms, the company uses an internal social platform such as wikis, intranet, yammer or slack as a tool for internal crowdsourcing (Stocker et al. 2012; Rohrbeck et al. 2015). These platforms are established not only for crowdsourcing; it is also easier to reach out to all of the employees in the company by integrating internal crowdsourcing into existing IT infrastructures. Since the employees are already using them and information about how to use the platform is already established, the entry barriers will be low.

However, it can also be challenging if specific IT features are needed to perform the internal crowdsourcing task. Specific IT requirements cannot be implemented in most cases, and the company needs to work with the given IT structure (Rohrbeck et al. 2015). Different user interfaces and new question and data entry types that are not offered by the generic platform cannot be implemented. Also, the other postings regarding the company may distract the attention of the employees, e.g. the most recent internal crowdsourcing task might be shown at the bottom of the webpage because of other postings which lead to lower participation and attention. Furthermore, it is harder to reach out to a specific group of employees if a generic social platform is used.

In addition, security guidelines and regulations (e.g. privacy, barrier-free access) might be a problem in most cases (Rohrbeck et al. 2015). Large companies especially have strict regulations regarding the security and use of companywide IT platforms that can be accessed by a large number of employees. The data shared on the platform might include sensitive data regarding both the company strategy as well as personal information of employees the sharing of which with third-party organizations is not permitted.

Specific Crowdsourcing IT Platforms Specific IT platforms enable repeatable and well-defined internal crowdsourcing processes that have the same characteristics (Geiger et al. 2011). These platforms can typically be adjusted to the enterprise's very particular needs, and new IT features can be developed specifically for the particular problem category crowdsourcing is addressing (intelligence, design, decision) (Zuchowski et al. 2016). Having an expert platform that is specifically designed for the company's own needs might enhance the motivation of employees to participate, since the user experience on such platforms is usually better than on generic social IT platforms for internal crowdsourcing. Moreover, the security and privacy issues can be addressed and designed in line with the company's requirements. However, maintaining such a platform, developing new features if needed and providing technical support 24/7 are very time-consuming and costly for an enterprise.

Additionally, the entrance barriers for employees are usually higher than a generic platform because of the aversion to 'yet another platform'. Creating another account and using another tool might be seen as a burden, especially in big corporate organizations, since the employees are already overloaded with the IT tools

(Rohrbeck et al. 2015). Another challenge that organizations might face is that the organization itself is constantly changing. Together with this change, the IT requirements for the internal crowdsourcing platform also change, while an IT tool cannot be developed as fast as the change requires. Therefore, a flexible and configurable IT implementation is an important aspect for specific crowdsourcing IT platforms.

For our study, we chose to implement a specific internal crowdsourcing platform because it enhances the effectiveness of internal crowdsourcing in avoiding security and privacy issues and offers the opportunity to adjust the platform to the specific needs of the application partner.

3 An Internal Crowdsourcing Platform: Idealab

Based on the findings in the literature explained earlier, a German energy company, the industry partner, established a specific internal crowdsourcing platform to support innovation activities, promote employee participation in the internal decision processes and identify the undiscovered competencies of its employees. The platform is a white-label version of an external crowdsourcing platform, specifically designed for this industry partner in that it has all the functionalities that an external crowdsourcing platform might have. Before the platform was developed, the strategy, incentive mechanisms and roles in the platform were carefully defined and discussed so that the IT requirements, the technical feasibility of these requirements and their prioritization could be planned and addressed precisely.

At first, the possibilities of IT integration into the industry partner's IT, the concrete requirements for data protection and intellectual property rights, terms of use, use of pseudonyms, feedback functions of the platform and registration process were discussed and established. The use of the platform is completely voluntarily, and the opportunity to stay anonymous is provided if desired. To protect the internal information in the company and block people who are not an employee of the industry partner, the employees were allowed to register on the platform using only their work email address. When registering, they were asked to fill out the fields for username (it could be their real name or pseudonym), email, password and checkbox asking if they were using their real name. In addition, there were optional fields for age group, gender, the position at the company and the occupation. To inform the employees about privacy and security regulations, the terms of use and unbundling regulations were presented during registration, and employees were asked to accept the conditions of use and unbundling regulations. They were not allowed to create an account without accepting these regulations and filling out the required fields (Fig. 2).

After confirming registration per email, the employees see a landing page where the active tasks (called campaigns) and the results of the past tasks are placed using card user interface design (see Fig. 2). In the first row of the landing page, the active campaigns are listed with a title, short description and remaining duration of the task. A preview of the next active campaigns can be also placed here to inform the

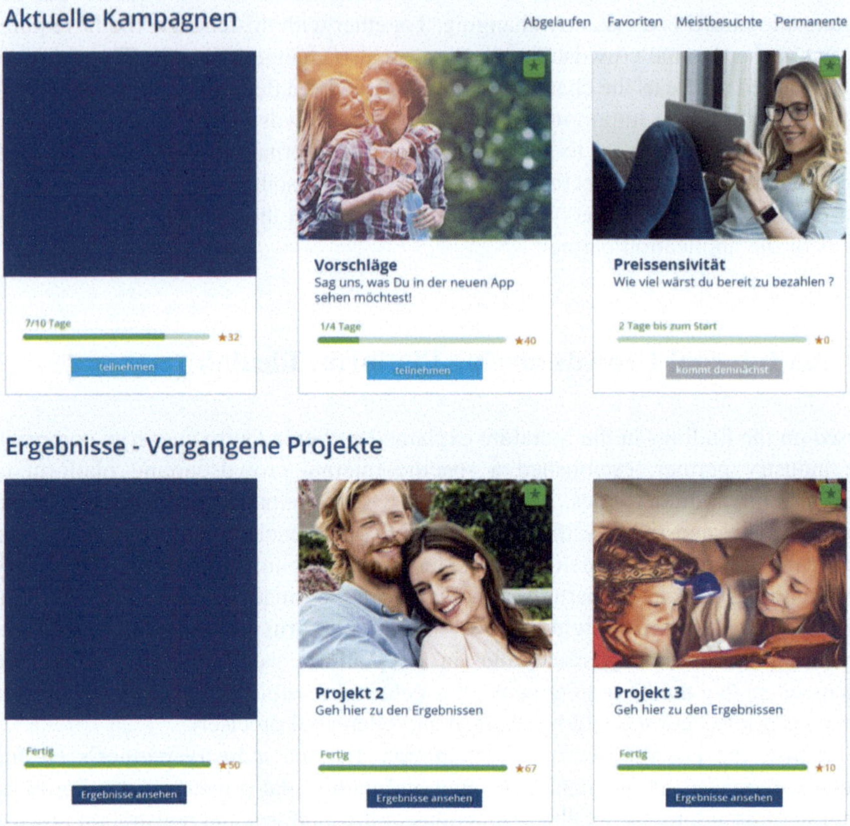

Fig. 2 The Idealab landing page

employees about the next topics. Following that, the results of past campaigns are displayed in the second row on the landing page (Fig. 3).

In the last row on the landing page, there is relevant information about the platform, rules about the platform use and the internal crowdsourcing activities of other enterprises along with two different kinds of feedback button (see Fig. 3). One of these feedback buttons was designed to collect technical feedback about the platform such as bug reporting, suggestions for new desired features and also general feedback about the campaigns that have been or are being executed on the platform. The other feedback button offers the opportunity to suggest new campaign ideas anonymously and to influence the use and topic direction of the platform together with the employees.

Fig. 3 Last row on the landing page

3.1 Data Protection: Privacy and Security

The privacy and security concerns of employees are one of the most important barriers to using the platform. For this reason, special regulations regarding these issues were established during the commissioning of the platform (Rohrbeck et al. 2015; Zuchowski et al. 2016). These regulations were communicated clearly to the employees to win their trust in the platform at every stage of platform use, starting with registration and continuing with active participation.

At first, internal crowdsourcing netiquette was shaped as a code of good behaviour on the platform. To ease online communication, it is suggested that people desist from using abbreviations and capital letters, that the correct sentence structure and spelling be followed, that quotation sources be named and that the already existing contributions be read before participation in order to avoid double contributions. Additionally, the employees were informed that inappropriate posts, e.g. if they deviate significantly from the netiquette or if they make factually untrue statements that could lead to confusion among the workforce, will be removed. Following that, a security and privacy policy was created in line with the European Union General Data Protection Regulation for 'natural persons'. This includes the following information: sources and data use on the platform, the legal base for the data processing, access to user data, data storage, privacy rights and also the use of cookies.

While using the platform, the IP address of the user, the date and time of the activity, the number of tabs clicked on in the platform and the name of the downloaded files as well as the scope of transmitted data are temporarily stored and used in a log data file. This data is stored for statistical purposes and also to prevent or detect unauthorized access to the platform components. After leaving the platform, this temporary data is deleted. There is no link between any other data from other sources and the personal data of employees. While actively using the platform, in particular, further personal data may be exchanged and stored if the employee uses the feedback buttons or contacts the requesters through other communication channels. However, this happens voluntarily and is based on employee initiative.

Nonetheless, if necessary, the processing of personal data might go beyond the scope that is described above. The reasons for this might be to review and optimize needs analysis procedures, to ensure the IT security and IT operation of the systems, to assert legal claims and provide defence in legal disputes, to prevent crime, to carry out business management measures and to further develop offers and services. As part of the system optimization, key figures about the platform use are recorded and analysed and might include such items as the number of registered users, participants per campaign, cancelled campaigns, help/feedback use and new campaigns. Fully automated decision-making according to data protection law GDPR (including fully automated profiling) is not used on the platform.

The personal data and the data pertaining to employee use of the platform are not disclosed to the industry partner, in order to ensure the full anonymity of employees, unless they want to provide this information. The platform use data and the platform activity data are only made available in an aggregated and anonymized way to the company committees as well as department heads and supervisors. Consequently, no tracking of personal information takes place, thus ensuring employees' rights of self-determination rights, reinforcing their confidence in the company and creating a trusted corporate culture.

However, the external platform provider has access to this personal data to provide IT support and maintenance, archiving, document processing, call centre services, compliance services, controlling, data destruction, customer management, media technology, website management and accounting services. This data storage is limited to 3 years due to legal limitations. To ensure a high level of usability on the platform, cookies are used for remembering settings between the various visits to the platform, preventing the username and password from having to be entered repeatedly and analysing the use of the platform for further improvements.

3.2 Technical Task Typology

The task typology in internal crowdsourcing differs from external crowdsourcing since the complexity, knowledge and skills of employees and the incentives for participation differ a great deal from those in external crowdsourcing. Moreover, observing the task typologies from the technical point of view leads to a modified version of the task typologies explained in chapter 'Systematization Approach for the Development and Description of an Internal Crowdsourcing System'. In Idealab, the following task typologies are implemented: info question, free text input, single choice, multiple choice, vote and comment.

In the info question, the task description, the expected input from employees, the campaign initiator, the time schedule and the next steps are explained clearly so that employees can understand the task completely and no direct input from the employees is expected. In the open-ended text question, the employees are asked to write directly their responses to the questions, and their answers are not shown to other employees participating in the campaign. This type of technical question might

Table 1 Technical task typologies

Task type	Feedback from crowd necessary?	Text input	Selection input	Publicity
Info	No	No	No	No
Free text	Yes	Yes	No	No
Single choice	Yes	No	Yes, limited to 1	No
Multiple choice	Yes	No	Yes, more than 1 possible	No
Vote	Yes	No	Yes, more than 1 possible	Yes
Comment	Yes	Yes	No	Yes

be used for crowdsolving or crowdcreation if the answers of the participants are to be in full disclosure and creative ideas are desired. In single-choice and multiple-choice questions, the employees answer the questions by choosing one possible offered (single choice) or more than one of the answers offered (multiple choice) from the given list. This kind of question might be used in crowdrating campaigns, where all of the answers are treated equally and combined. Again, the answers given by employees are not shown to the other participants in single-choice and multiple-choice questions.

On the contrary, in the last two question types 'vote' and 'comment', the participants can see the other answers. In the vote question, employees can vote for an option or options, and every participant sees the aggregated votes for each option while voting. In the comment question, the employees are asked to leave a comment or question describing their ideas in detail using free text input, but their answers are seen by the other employees immediately. This enables a discussion between the participants which might be very helpful in ideation and creation tasks. The differences between these technical task typologies are illustrated in Table 1.

During the design process for an internal crowdsourcing campaign, the requester can select the question types described above and use more than one question type in a single crowdsourcing campaign. In addition to task typologies, the platform has the technical features for limiting the number of participations for an individual employee (max. assignment function), determining the duration of the campaign, limiting the total number of participants and setting conditions using profile keys to address the targeted group of employees if necessary. All the question types can be styled using HTML, and multimedia such as video, picture or documents can be added to the question descriptions.

3.3 *Roles and Tools for Platform Management*

Along with the roles defined in chapter 'Systematization Approach for the Development and Description of an Internal Crowdsourcing System', an internal

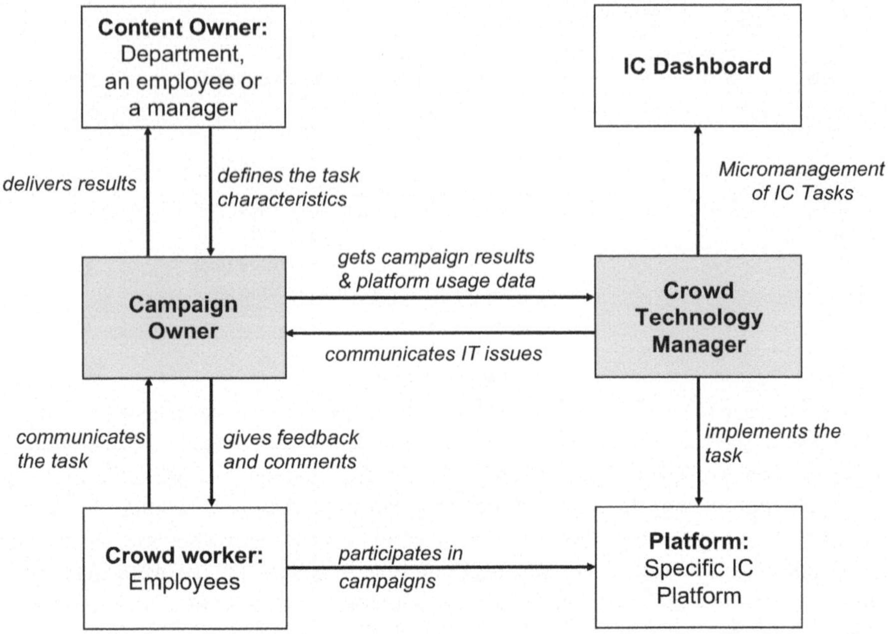

Fig. 4 Roles and tools for internal crowdsourcing

crowdsourcing platform needs additional roles such as crowd master, crowd technology manager and campaign master as well as a second technical platform, a dashboard, for the micromanagement of internal crowdsourcing tasks. Figure 4 shows the roles and their relationship to each other in an internal crowdsourcing environment.

The campaign owner might be an employee of the company who is assigned to manage the communication between the content owners, the crowd and the crowd technology manager. It is an objective position where the crowd master aims to create a free and fair internal crowdsourcing environment for employees and to provide solutions to the problems of campaign masters by designing an optimal internal crowdsourcing campaign. In addition to these, the campaign owner communicates all the technical problems regarding the platform and desired new features if necessary. During the course of platform management, we found out that a dashboard would be very beneficial to help the crowd technology manager micromanage the internal crowdsourcing tasks. These tasks might include creating new tasks, prolonging the duration of a task, making some text or style changes on active tasks, observing the answers and deleting the answers that violate the netiquette rules or other internal company regulations, activating or deactivating tasks or observing and reporting platform statistics.

4 Empirical Results: Case Studies

The platform was released in June 2018, and 11 different campaigns were realized between its release and October 2019. The communication of new campaigns, campaign results and news regarding the platform was carried out by the crowd master using the company's intranet, yammer and sending email newsletters to the registered user of the platform when there were new campaign releases, campaign results releases or news regarding the platform.

According to the latest figures provided by the industry partner, 1820 people are employed by the company. Out of 1820, 535 employees have registered on the platform with a registration ratio of 29.4%, which is quite high for a voluntary platform. After the release of each new campaign, an email newsletter and a post in internal communication channels were sent. In total, 11 different campaigns were released, and the number of participants on the platform has increased after each campaign release, as shown in Fig. 5. Additionally, out of a registered 535 users, 360 employees have voluntarily specified the information about their age group, gender, position and occupation at the company, and 50.8% of the employees have used their real names during the registration. This shows that the opportunity to use a pseudonym is an important feature from the employee's perspective. The campaign participants were mostly young employees working in governance or sales, with an almost equal number of males and females, as shown in Fig. 6. Surprisingly, employees over 40 years old were relatively active on the platform. However, employees with a management position were not as interested as employees without a management role.

Figure 7 shows the total work duration on the platform including all the answers completed for 11 campaigns. More than half of the contributions were done in under 160 s ~ 2.67 min, and the average work duration was 351 s ~ 5.85 min. Although the campaign complexity and durations vary a lot, this is not reflected in the average work duration because employees have chosen to participate mostly in short tasks and are not interested in long complex tasks.

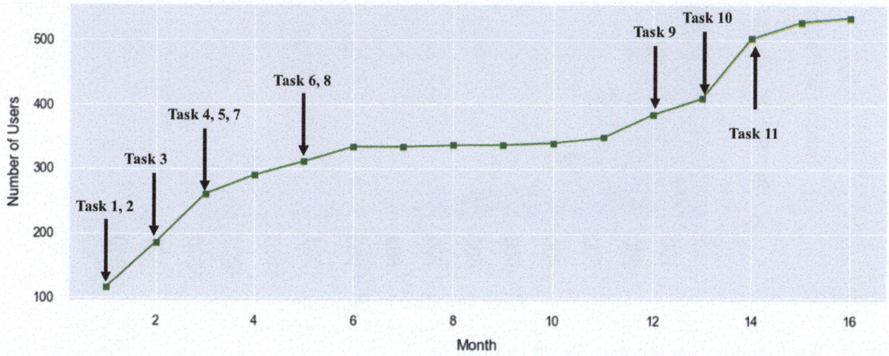

Fig. 5 Number of users over time

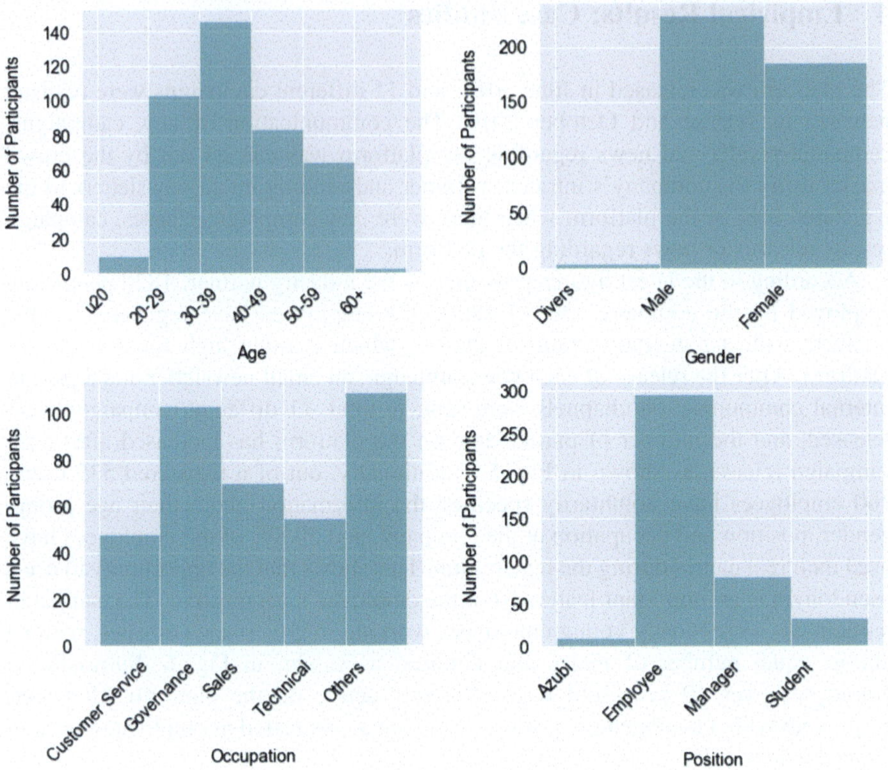

Fig. 6 Descriptive statistics about the campaign participants

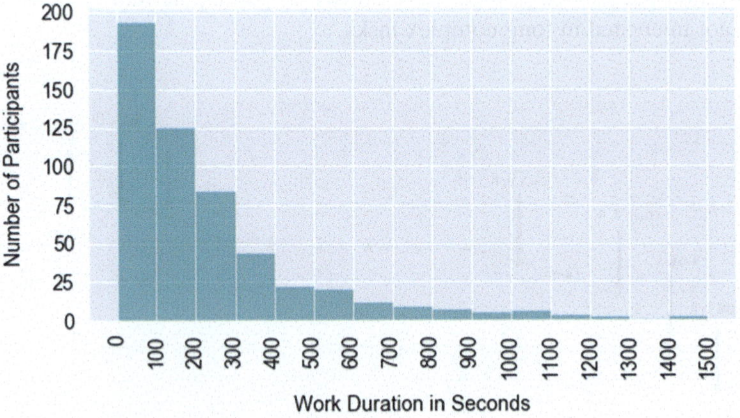

Fig. 7 Work duration in seconds for all campaigns

Table 2 displays the detailed participation statistics regarding 11 campaigns that were executed after the release of the platform. The campaigns are listed and numbered by release time, whereby they are categorized into four different topics: location, product, QA and survey. The technical task typologies used and the number of questions in each campaign are listed next to each other. The '*average work duration*' column shows the average completion time in seconds per campaign. Next to it, the '*started tasks*' column presents the number of task started without completing the task, meaning that employees did not proceed through to completion, although they clicked on the campaign and read the campaign description.

In some campaigns, employees were allowed to participate more than once, so the total number of submitted answers might be higher than the number of unique participants. To differentiate between these two figures, the '*completed tasks*' column presents the overall number of submitted answers without differentiating the uniqueness of the participants, and the '*unique users*' column shows the number of unique participants in campaigns. To measure the achievement of a campaign, we introduced the '*participation ratio*', which illustrates the task completion based on the number of registered users on the platform by the time of campaign release. Since the number of participants has increased over time, the absolute number of participants is not sufficient to describe the success of a campaign. The average participation ratio on the platform was 19.69%, with campaign number 5 having the highest participation ratio of 51.94%.

$$\text{Participation Ratio} = \text{Completed Tasks}/\text{Number of Registered Users}$$

Another ratio that we introduced is the '*task completion ratio*'. It helps to understand how many of the users continue and finish the campaign after starting it and how many read the campaign description. The 11 campaigns were started a total of 2,875 times but only completed 564 times, which results in an average task completion ratio of 19.62%, with campaign number 5 having the highest task completion ratio of 47.52%.

$$\text{Task Completion Ratio} = \text{Completed Tasks}/\text{Started Tasks}$$

Analysing the results by topics, the first topic contains all the campaigns related to the relocation of the industry partner employees to another building, called 'location'. In the context of the location topic, five different campaigns were released, and this topic was the most interesting in the platform with an average participation ratio of 27.25% and a task completion ratio of 26.86%. It was realized using only the comment and vote functions of the platform, meaning all the answers or rather results were directly shown to the participants. Additionally, the number of questions was one in four of the campaigns and four in one of the campaigns, leading to lower expected workload measured in time.

The second topic, called the 'product', contains all the campaigns related to the product, e.g. further development of an existing product, collecting new product ideas or collecting feedback about the existing product. In the context of the product,

Table 2 Overview of the participation numbers in internal crowdsourcing campaigns

Task ID	Topic	Task typology	# Questions	Average work duration	Started tasks	Completed tasks	Unique users	Participation ratio (%)	Task completion ratio (%)
1	Survey	Multiple choice	2	163	204	41	41	28.87	20.10
2	Location	Comment	1	159	349	61	27	45.86	17.48
3	Product	Single Choice, Multiple choice, Freetext	20	790	117	25	25	18.80	21.37
4	QA	Comment	1	264	221	14	7	6.36	6.33
5	Location	Vote	1	275	282	134	134	**51.94**	**47.52**
6	Product	Single Choice, Freetext	4	452	141	8	8	2.37	5.67
7	Product	Single Choice, Freetext	7	787	109	28	27	8.95	25.69
8	Location	Comment	4	1528	223	17	16	5.04	7.62
9	Location	Comment	1	207	195	51	30	13.18	26.15
10	Location	Vote	1	100	422	150	143	28.68	35.55
11	QA	Comment	1	1235	611	35	19	6.51	5.73

three campaigns were released and completed with an average participation ratio of 10.04% and an average task completion ratio of 17.58%, both lower than the ratios in the location topic. The campaigns contained multiple questions in the form of a single-choice, multiple-choice and open-ended questions. The reason for lower participation might be the higher expected workload because the average number of questions in campaigns was 10.3 and average work duration approx. 11 min, which are above the platform's overall average.

The third topic, called 'QA', is about campaigns that provide employees with the opportunity to ask questions or leave comments about the current issues in the company or to ask any question directly to the top management of the company. In the context of the QA topic, two different campaigns were released, and both campaigns contained one question in the comments. The average participation ratio was 6.43%, lower than the location topic, and the average task completion ratio was 6.03%. Although the expected workload measured in time was not so high, the participation ratio is quite a bit lower than the location topic. The low task completion ratio also shows that the number of started tasks was high, meaning that the employees were generally interested in this topic, but they did not want to participate although every contribution was stored anonymously. This shows the effect of the selected topic on participation and also shows that sensitive topics such as asking a question to the manager are quite interesting but perceived as being risky.

The last topic, called 'survey', contains one campaign which had two questions in multiple-choice format. The participation ratio was 28.87% and the task completion ratio 20.1%, similar to the location topic. This was the first campaign released on the platform, and the expected workload was low; therefore the participation ratio is quite high in comparison to the QA and product topics.

For further investigation, the campaigns are analysed based on two categories: topic and technical task typology. As shown in Table 2, the campaigns with task IDs 2, 5, 8, 9 and 10 belong to the topic location; with task IDs 3, 6 and 7 to the product topic; with task IDs 4 and 11 to the QA topic and with task ID 1 to the topic survey. For categorizing the technical task typologies, the campaigns with the technical task typologies single choice and multiple choice are considered as one category and called 'selection'. Campaigns with task IDs 1, 3, 6 and 7 belong to this category. The campaigns with task IDs 2, 4, 8, 9 and 11 belong to the technical task typology 'comment' and with task IDs 5 and 10 to 'vote'.

4.1 Work Duration and Participation

Figure 8 illustrates the boxplots of work duration categorized by topic (left) and technical task typology (right). Because of the non-normal distribution of the data, the Kruskal–Wallis test was conducted to find out differences between topics and task typologies in terms of working duration. There was a statistically significant difference (Chi-square = 85.511, $p = 0.000$, df = 3) among the four different categories of topics (location, product, QA, survey) regarding the work durations.

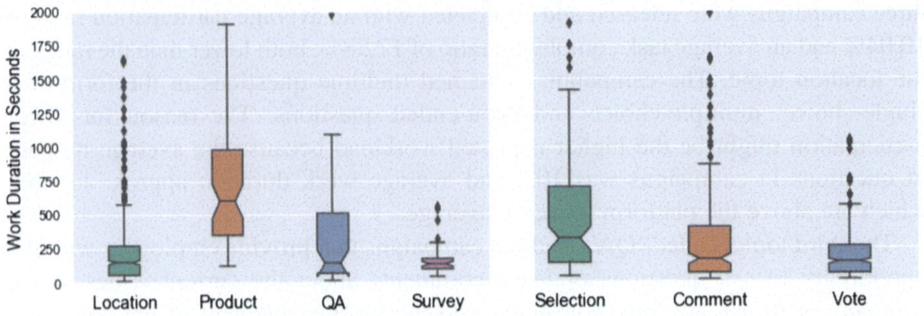

Fig. 8 Boxplots of work duration for categories topic (left) and technical task typology (right)

The post hoc test (Dunn criterion) revealed that the mean of product ($M = 745.12$) was significantly higher than the mean of survey ($M = 163.90$, $p < 0.05$) and higher than the mean of location ($M = 238.97$, $p < 0.01$). A second Kruskal–Wallis test showed that there were also significant differences (Chi-square = 49.095, $p = 0.000$, df = 2) among the categories of technical task typologies (selection, comment, vote). The post hoc test (Dunn criterion) revealed that the mean of vote ($M = 182.53$) was significantly lower than the mean of comment ($M = 529.91$, $p < 0.01$) and lower than the mean of selection ($M = 511.49$, $p < 0.05$).

Furthermore, the Spearman rank-order correlation coefficients are calculated to investigate the relationship between the average work duration in seconds and the participation ($N = 11$). There was a moderate negative significant correlation between the average work duration and completed tasks ($r_s = -0.618$, $p = 0.043$). This result confirms that the higher average work duration gets, the lower the number of completed tasks will be. The Spearman rank-order correlation coefficient between average work duration and the participation ratio shows a substantial trend towards significance with $p = 0.060$ and is negative with a moderate value of $r_s = -0.582$. Figure 9 illustrates this relationship in a regression plot.

4.2 Participation Day and Time

As shown in Fig. 10, the time of the day when participation takes place is mostly in the early mornings between 8 and 10 ($N_{8\text{–}10} = 197$), and the most popular day is in the middle of the week, Wednesday and Thursday ($N_{\text{Wednesday}} = 141$, $N_{\text{Thursday}} = 130$). This is a good indication of what time to publish an internal crowdsourcing campaign on the platform and when to announce it to the employees. Looking at the descriptive statistics, late Friday afternoons after 4 pm is not an optimal time to release a new crowdsourcing campaign on the platform.

To see if this pattern is applicable for all the categories of topic and technical task typology, Kruskal–Wallis tests were conducted. No significant differences were found between the four categories of topic (Chi-square = 5.025, $p = 0.170$,

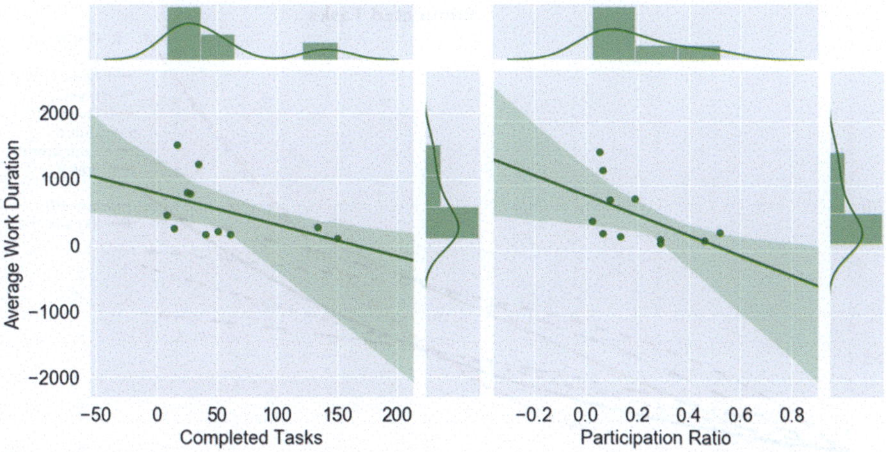

Fig. 9 Regression plot of average work duration and participation

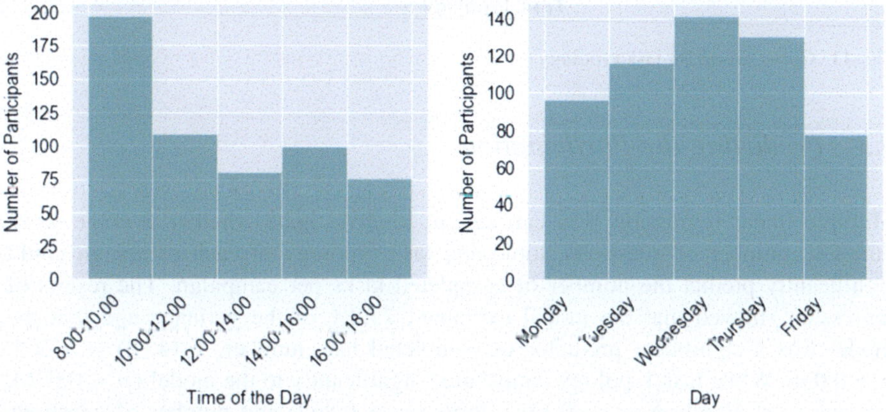

Fig. 10 Time of the day and the day of participation

df = 3) and between the three categories of technical task typology (Chi-square = 5.470, $p = 0.065$, df = 2) regarding the participation time of the day. Similarly, there was no significant difference between the four categories of topics (Chi-square = 0.901, $p = 0.825$, df = 3) and the three categories of technical task typology (Chi-square = 1.691, $p = 0.429$, df = 2) regarding the day of participation.

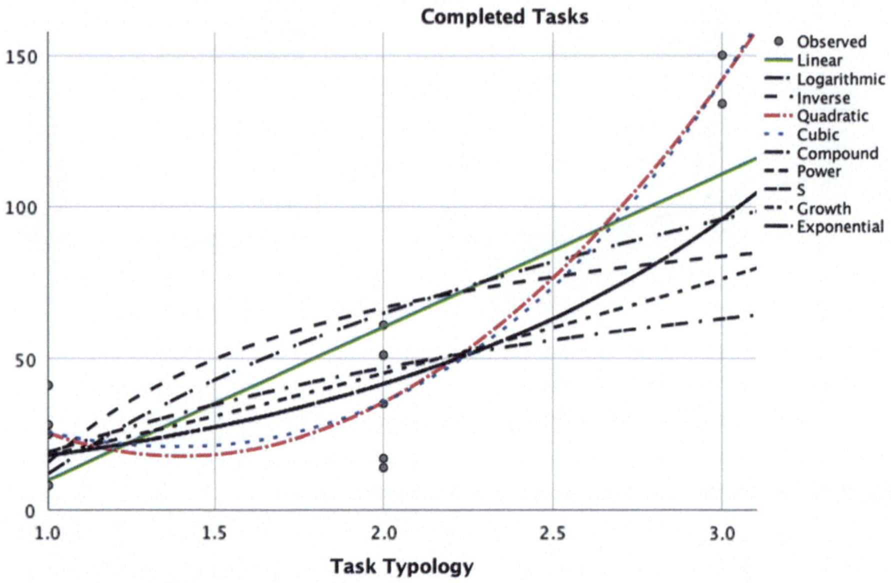

Fig. 11 Curve fitting for task typology

4.3 Predicting the Participation

Multiple linear regression was carried out to investigate whether average work duration, number of questions, topic and task typology of each campaign could significantly predict the number of completed tasks per campaign. The results of regression showed that the model explained 77.8% of the variance and that the model was a significant predictor of completed task number, $F\ (4, 6) = 5.265$, $p = 0.036$. While task typology contributed significantly to the model ($p = 0.036$), average work duration ($p = 0.112$), topic ($p = 0.862$) and number of questions ($p = 0.377$) did not. The final predictive model was:

$$\begin{aligned}\text{Completed Tasks} = {} & -33.037 - 0.037 \times \text{Average Work Duration} - 3.549 \\ & \times \text{Topic} + 57.359 \times \text{Task Typology} + 2.028 \\ & \times \text{Number of Questions}\end{aligned}$$

The task typology being the only significant predictor of the model was the strongest contributor to the model. Therefore, for further investigation of task typology, we carried out curve fitting and compared linear, logarithmic, inverse, quadratic, cubic, power, compound, S-curve, logistic, growth and exponential models based on their relative goodness of fit where the number of completed tasks is predicted by task typology. The results revealed that the quadratic and cubic models are the best fitting significant models with $R^2 = 0.895$ and $p = 0.000$ for both models. Figure 11 illustrates the different curve fittings for task typology.

Since a better portion of the variance in the number of completed tasks is explained by the quadratic model of task typology, quadratic regression was carried out to finalize the model coefficients. The results showed that the model explained 89.5% of the variance and that the model was a significant predictor of completed task number, $F\ (2,\ 8) = 34.253$, $p = 0.000$, and task typology also contributed significantly to the model ($p < 0.05$). The final predictive model was:

$$\text{Completed Tasks} = 111.7 - 134.35 \times \text{Task Typology} + 48.15 \times \text{Task Typology} \times \text{Task Typology}$$

5 Discussion

This chapter has analysed the use of internal crowdsourcing from the IT perspective based on the empirical results of the successful implementation of different kinds of internal crowdsourcing campaigns.

Our findings from the active use data of the internal crowdsourcing platform show that there is a general interest in using the platform proven by the relatively high registration ratio for a voluntary platform, although no specific incentive mechanisms or programmes were implemented. The only motivation to participate in the platform comes from enjoyment in the activity or the chance to shape products according to one's own wishes. This puts a specific emphasis on the topics to be selected for internal crowdsourcing campaigns on the platform. Therefore, the needs and wishes of the employees should be asked and considered while choosing and shaping crowdsourcing tasks. What is more, the number of registered users increased after the release of each campaign because of the active marketing of new campaigns via newsletters, intranet and yammer. This shows how important it is to communicate and actively promote the platform.

Looking at the profile of registered users, we observed that mostly young employees without a management role preferred to participate on the platform, which is a common pattern for new technologies introduced to companies, because technology affinity decreases with age. As a solution to this problem, onsite courses about how to use the platform could be given by the company. Following on from this, looking at the absolute number of started tasks and completed tasks in each campaign, we observed that the interest in starting a campaign was always high, while the task completion ratio was quite low in some cases. The reason for this might be the uninteresting topic, complex task design or employees being distracted by their daily tasks, which in most cases have higher priority.

In terms of participation ratio and task completion ratio, the most successful campaign was about voting on the name of the company's new building (ID 5). This is a perfect example of a successful task design and topic selection, because it was relevant for every employee in the company, easy to complete in under 3 min and the idea of naming the industry partner's new building motivated the employees intrinsically. As such, three important aspects of an internal crowdsourcing task—optimal duration, low complexity and interesting topic—were met in that way.

Furthermore, the findings about significant different average work durations between three technical task typologies could help by estimating the expected work duration and consequently optimizing the task design, as the average work duration negatively affects the number of completed answers. This shows that the employees of the industry partner are mostly interested in short tasks. If this is already known about employees, then complex tasks such as ideation, innovation or technical challenges might not be the right topic selections for this type of employee group, as these usually require longer timeframes to be completed.

Another important empirical finding was about the time and day of participation. The employees mostly preferred to participate in the middle of the week and early in the morning between 8 and 10, and they tended not to participate on Friday afternoons. There was also no difference in different kinds of topics or task typologies regarding the participation day and time. So, the optimal time for releasing all kinds of new campaigns would be Wednesdays in the early mornings, while Friday afternoons should be avoided.

Next, we tried to predict the number of participants based on the data that was available before releasing the campaign, e.g. work duration, topic, task typology and the number of questions. The most important factor is again task typology, explaining the variance in participation of up to 90% with a quadratic regression model. Apparently, task typology is the determining factor for the success of an internal crowdsourcing campaign and should be selected very carefully. Based on these findings, the crowd manager could estimate the expected number of completed tasks and accordingly predict the success of a crowdsourcing campaign in terms of participation.

6 Conclusion

In this chapter, we tried to find out empirically which kind of internal crowdsourcing task is desired by the employees. Although the scope of campaigns and variation of topics and typologies were limited, some preliminary results regarding the optimal work duration, ideal task typology and interesting topics could be found out.

The most important finding is that how interesting the internal crowdsourcing campaign is with respect to the intrinsic motivation of the employees determines the success of a campaign. Therefore, before introducing such a platform into a company, conducting surveys regarding the desired topics and motivating factors could help to select optimal topics. In addition to that, the task typology played an important role while predicting participant numbers, because indirectly the task typology determines the expected work duration. Therefore, the reasons for the desired low work duration should be investigated in detail. This might be due to the company culture: the company might not accept the time spent on internal crowdsourcing as working time, or other daily tasks might have a higher priority, or it might have to do with the general preference of employees. If the corporate culture limits the working duration, then special time slots for spending time on the platform could be defined.

Companies must understand how they can design and use an internal crowdsourcing system technically and from the employee's perspective (Fitzgerald and Stol 2015) so that the potential of internal crowdsourcing can be used effectively. To our knowledge, this study is the first to address this gap by summarizing and deriving requirements for the implementation of an internal crowdsourcing system comprehensively considering the privacy and security concerns of employees, company intern regulations regarding crowdwork and the technical aspects of an internal crowdsourcing task.

Concerning the limitations of the study, they are mainly due to the fact that the empirical investigation involved only 11 crowdsourcing campaigns with a narrow scope of topics and task typologies performed by a single company; thus, results are not generalizable, since corporate culture plays an important role in the preferences of employees regarding topics, task typologies and work duration. However, the aim of the study was not to provide a complete picture about the issue under analysis but to derive some preliminary insights that can provide some impulses to scholars and professionals and open the way to further research.

References

(2017) Daimler 2017: Daimler and the transformation of the automotive industry. 29 March. Accessed 18 Oct 2019. https://www.daimler.com/documents/investors/annual-meeting/daimler-ir-amspeechzetsche-2017.pdf

Allahbakhsh M, Benatallah B, Ignjatovic A, Motahari-Nezhad HR, Bertino E, Dustdar S (2013) Quality control in crowdsourcing systems: Issues and directions. IEEE Internet Comput 17 (2):76–81

Bailey BP, Horvitz E (2010) What's your idea?: a case study of a grassroots innovation pipeline within a large software company. In: Proceedings of the SIGCHI conference on human factors in computing systems

Benbya H, Leidner D (2016) Harnessing employee innovation in internal crowdsourcing platforms: Lessons from Allianz UK. In: Thirty seventh international conference on information systems. AIS, Dublin

Benbya H, Leidner D (2018) How Allianz UK used an idea management platform to harness employee innovation. MIS Q Exec 17(2):141–157

Benbya H, Van Alstyne MW (2010) How to find answers within your company. MIT Sloan Research Paper

Bharati P, Zhang W, Chaudhury A (2015) Better knowledge with social media? Exploring the roles of social capital and organizational knowledge management. J Knowl Manag 19(3):456–475

Bjelland OM, Wood RC (2008) An inside view of IBM's 'Innovation Jam'. MIT Sloan Manag Rev 50(1):32

Blohm I, Jan Marco L, Zogaj S (2014) Crowdsourcing and crowd work—Ein Zukunftsmodell der IT-gestützten Arbeitsorganisation? In: Wirtschaftsinformatik in Wissenschaft and Praxis. Springer, Heidelberg, pp 51–64

Brabahan D (2008) Crowdsourcing as a model for problem solving. Int J Res New Media Technol 14(1):75–90
Brabham DC (2013) Crowdsourcing. MIT Press, Cambridge, MA
Deng X, Joshi KD, Galliers RD (2016) The duality of empowerment and marginalization in microtask crowdsourcing: Giving voice to the less powerful through value sensitive design. MIS Q 40(2):279–302
Difallah DE, Catasta M, Demartini G, Ipeirotis PG, Cudré-Mauroux P (2015) The dynamics of micro-task crowdsourcing: The case of amazon mturk. In: Proceedings of the 24th international conference on world wide web
Durward D, Simmert B, Peters C, Blohm I, Leimeister JM (2019) How to empower the workforce-analyzing internal crowd work as a neo-socio-technical system. In: Proceedings of the 52nd Hawaii international conference on system sciences
Erickson LB, Trauth EM, Petrick I (2012) Getting inside your employees' heads: Navigating barriers to internal-crowdsourcing for product and service innovation. In: Thirty third international conference on information systems, Orlando
Felstiner A (2011) Working the crowd: employment and labor law in the crowdsourcing industry. Berk J Employ Labor Law 32:143
Fitzgerald B, Stol K-J (2015) The dos and dont's of crowdsourcing software development. In: International conference on current trends in theory and practice of informatics
Franke N, Klausberger K (2010) Die Architektur von Crowdsourcing: Wie begeistert man die Crowd. Crowdsourcing: Innovations management mit Schwarmintelligenz 1:58–71
Gadiraju U (2018) Its getting crowded! Improving the effectiveness of microtask crowdsourcing. Gesellschaft für Informatik eV.
Gaspoz C (2011) Prediction markets as web 2.0 tools for enterprise 2.0. In: AMCIS 2011
Geiger D, Seedorf S, Schulze T, Nickerson RC, Schader M (2011) Managing the crowd: towards a taxonomy of crowdsourcing processes. In: Proceedings of the seventeenth Americas conference on information systems, Detroit
Geiger D, Rosemann M, Fielt E, Schader M (2012) Crowdsourcing information systems-definition typology, and design. In: Thirty third international conference on information systems, Orlando
Hammon L, Hippner H (2012) Crowdsourcing. Bus Inform Syst Eng 4(3):163–166
Hirth M, Hoßfeld T, Tran-Gia P (2012) Analyzing a commercial microtask crowdsourcing platform from the involved actors' viewpoints. EuroNF Summer School, Würzburg
Hoßfeld T, Hirth M, Tran-Gia P (2012) Aktuelles Schlagwort: Crowdsourcing. Informatik Spektrum 35(3):204–208
Howe J (2006) The rise of crowdsourcing. Wired Mag 14(6):1–4
Howe J (2009) Crowdsourcing: Why the power of the crowd is driving the future of business (unedited ed). Crown Business
Kittur A, Smus B, Khamkar S, Kraut RE (2011) Crowdforge: Crowdsourcing complex work. In: Proceedings of the 24th annual ACM symposium on user interface software and technology. ACM. pp 43–52
Kittur A, Nickerson JV, Bernstein M, Gerber E, Shaw A, Zimmerman J, Lease M, Horton J (2013) The future of crowd work. In: Proceedings of the 2013 conference on computer supported cooperative work. ACM, pp 1301–1318
Leimeister JM, Zogaj S (2013) Neue Arbeitsorganisation durch Crowdsourcing: Eine Literaturstudie. Arbeitspapier, Arbeit and Soziales
Leimeister JM, Zogaj S, Durward D (2015) New forms of employment and IT crowdsourcing. In: 4th conference of the regulating for decent work network
Leimeister JM, Durward D, Zogaj S (2016) Crowd Worker in Deutschland: Eine empirische Studie zum Arbeitsumfeld auf externen Crowdsourcing-Plattformen. Study der Hans Böckler-Stiftung
Lopez M, Vukovic M, Laredo J (2010) Peoplecloud service for enterprise crowdsourcing. In: 2010 IEEE international conference on services computing
Lüttgens D, Pollok P, Antons D, Piller F (2014) Wisdom of the crowd and capabilities of a few: internal success factors of crowdsourcing for innovation. J Bus Econ 84(3):339–374

Malhotra A, Majchrzak A (2014) Managing crowds in innovation challenges. Calif Manag Rev 56 (4):103–123

Malhotra A, Majchrzak A, Kesebi L, Looram S (2017) Developing innovative solutions through internal crowdsourcing. MIT Sloan Manag Rev 58(4):73

Meffert H, Burmann C, Kirchgeorg M, Eisenbeiß M (2018) Marketing: Grandlagen marktorientierter Unternehmensführung Konzepte—Instrumente—Praxisbeispiele. Springer

Niu X-J, Qin S-F, Vines J, Wong R, Hui L (2019) Key crowdsourcing technologies for product design and development. Int J Autom Comput 16(1):1–15

Otte A, Schröter W (2018) Lebende Konzernbetriebsvereinbarung als soziale Innovation. 30 July. Accessed 20 Oct 2019. http://www.blog-zukunft-der-arbeit.de/wpcontent/uploads/2018/07/Lebende_KBV_Otte_Schroeter.pdf

Rohrbeck R, Thom N, Arnold H (2015) IT tools for foresight: The integrated insight and response system of Deutsche Telekom Innovation Laboratories. Technol Forecast Soc Change 97:115–126

Simula H, Ahola T (2014) A network perspective on idea and innovation crowdsourcing in industrial firms. Ind Market Manag 43(3):400–408

Sixt E (2014) Schwarmökonomie and Crowdfanding: Webbasierte Finanzierungssysteme im Rahmen realwirtschaftlicher Bedingungen. Springer

Stocker A, Richter A, Hoefler P, Tochtermann K (2012) Exploring appropriation of enterprise wikis. Comput Support Cooper Work (CSCW) 21(2-3):317–356

Surowiecki J (2005) The wisdom of crowds. Anchor

Thuan NH, Antunes P, Johnstone D (2017) A process model for establishing business process crowdsourcing. Australas J Inform Syst 21

Valentine MA, Retelny D, To A, Rahmati N, Doshi T, Bernstein MS (2017). Flash organizations: crowdsourcing complex work by structuring crowds as organizations. In: Proceedings of the 2017 CHI conference on human factors in computing systems. ACM, pp 3523–3537

Vel V, Park I, Liu J (2018) The effect of enterprise crowdsourcing systems on employees' innovative behavior and job performance. In: Proceedings of the 51st Hawaii international conference on system sciences, Hawaii

Zuchowski O, Posegga O, Schlagwein D, Fischbach K (2016) Internal crowdsourcing: conceptual framework, structured review, and research agenda. J Inform Technol 166–184

Neslihan Iskender received her Bachelor and Master of Science degree in Industrial Engineering and Management at KIT. Since May 2017, she has been employed as a research assistant at the Quality and Usability Lab of TU Berlin where she is working towards her PhD in the field of crowdsourcing. Currently, Neslihan is an awardee of a BMBF-funded Education programme for future IT and development leadership (Software Campus) involving partners such as MediaMarkt Saturn, Merck, Zeiss, Huawei, Holtzbrinck.

Dr.-Ing. Tim Polzehl studied Science of Communication at Berlin's Technical University and joined the Quality and Usability Lab as a researcher in 2008. He has worked in both industrial and academic projects with a focus on speech technology, machine-learning crowdsourcing solutions. In 2014, Tim was awarded a PhD for his work on the automatic prediction of personality attributes from speech and since 2014, he has been working as a Postdoc at QUL. At the same time, he is driving the start-up activity (Crowdee) and working on the development of crowdsourcing solutions.

Proposals for the Future of Internal Crowdsourcing: A Trade Union-Based Approach

Welf Schröter

Abstract The "FST" personnel network "Forum Soziale Technikgestaltung" (Forum for Social Forms of Technology) from the German Trade Union Confederation (DGB) of Baden-Württemberg has been examining the subjects informatization of work and digitization since 1991. More than 4600 women and men from works councils and staff councils, union representative bodies and the workforce, large companies, small- and medium-sized enterprises, the manual trades, as well as self-employed people have been involved in an exchange about their experiences in production and services and in administrations. Against this background, and drawing on the accumulated knowledge gained from experience, the following proposals for the future of internal crowdsourcing have been derived. The proposals represent a trade union-based approach.

Keywords Order-related innovation · External crowdsourcing · Open external crowdsourcing · Platform-related crowdwork

1 Proposals for the Future of Internal Crowdsourcing

1.1 Proposal 1

Platform-based crowdsourcing has seen continued pluralization and increased differentiation. Thanks to the new process flows emerging from the digital transformation, we will see crowdsourcing merge increasingly with crowdworking. This means that a specific crowdsourcing that is methodologically conceived in the narrower sense will become the exception in the everyday working scenario.

W. Schröter (✉)
Forum Soziale Technikgestaltung beim DGB, Baden-Württemberg, Mössingen, Germany
e-mail: schroeter@talheimer.de

H. Ulbrich et al. (eds.), *Internal Crowdsourcing in Companies*, Contributions to Management Science, https://doi.org/10.1007/978-3-030-52881-2_7

1.2 Proposal 2

Platform-based crowdworking is establishing itself increasingly in the area of industrial production, industry-related services, the private services sector, the civil service, the manual trades, and the financial sector.

1.3 Proposal 3

As virtual transaction spaces and platforms that were previously stand-alone grow together over time, new potentials of crowdsourcing unfold as part of modern crowdworking. Thinking and working in an order-related manner as well as a move away from focusing on purely vertical toward mainly horizontal value-creation chains in future, together with models of partially autonomous and agile working, will lead to a dominant culture of crowdsourcing applications. The boundaries between internal and external crowdsourcing are becoming blurred, and both dynamics are merging with one another. Due to the progressive removal of boundaries in company operations, the division between internal and external utilizations will slowly fade.

1.4 Proposal 4

The pluralization of user cultures is bringing forth different variants and models:

1. Internal crowdsourcing as voluntary internal innovation management
2. Internal crowdsourcing as order-related innovation
3. Internal, order-related crowdsourcing linked to selective external crowdsourcing
4. Internal crowdsourcing with permanently open external crowdsourcing
5. Flexible agile models of order-related crowdsourcing
6. Differing platform-related crowdwork

Evidence shows that the variants mentioned in nos. 2–6 will ultimately cover around two-thirds to three-quarters of the coming platform-based working environments.

1.5 Proposal 5

Among the big challenges facing us in the near future is the question of whether and how well the transitions between the variants named in nos. 1–6 will succeed from the point of view of the workforce. The interfaces between the variants present greater challenges than the inherent implementation within them. Working people will be forced to constantly change back and forth between these models. If the organizational models are not intelligent enough, not flexible enough, and not compatible, the result will be obstacles, time delays, errors, and failures. What is needed is an intelligent, inclusive self-management to handle these changes.

1.6 Proposal 6

Following on from Proposal 5, the question arises as to whether qualification strategies should concentrate more on the interfaces and on being able to manage these or more on the inherent processes within the respective variants.

1.7 Proposal 7

From current experiences with "self-learning" software applications and with "autonomous software systems," it can be concluded that the variants named in Proposal 4 (nos. 2–6) will be augmented and partly controlled by "self-learning" and "autonomous" systems (software) in the near future (Schröter 2019). This would underscore the relevance of order-related processes for value creation.

Reference

Schröter W (2019) Der mitbestimmte Algorithmus. Arbeitsweltliche Kriterien zur sozialen Gestaltung von Algorithmen und algorithmischen Entscheidungssystemen. In: Schröter W (ed) Der mitbestimmte Algorithmus. Gestaltungskompetenz für den Wandel der Arbeit. Talheimer Sammlung kritisches Wissen, vol 85. Talheimer, Mössingen, pp 101–150

Welf Schröter is the head of the personnel network "Forum Soziale Technikgestaltung" (in German "FST") at DGB Baden-Württemberg and acts as a partner in the Federal Ministry of Education and Research project "Internes Crowdsourcing in Unternehmen: Arbeitnehmergerechte Prozessinnovationen durch digitale Beteiligung von Mitarbeiter/innen" (Internal Crowdsourcing in Companies: Employee-Friendly Process Innovations Through the Digital Participation of Employees; in German "ICU").

Good Practice at GASAG Group: Recommendations for the Application of Internal Crowdsourcing from a Business Perspective

Florian Porth

Abstract Developing innovative and marketable products and services and maintaining innovation capacity are basic prerequisites for a company's economic success and present implicit challenges in the adaptation to twenty-first-century needs. These success factors are put at risk by silo mentalities and by insufficiently pronounced cross-departmental knowledge transfers. The GASAG Group as a typical organizational layout of medium-sized enterprises in Germany has been and still is confronted with these challenges as well. In order to face them, the GASAG Group decided to work on company culture as well as to develop an open and innovative mindset, prompting it to join the ICU (ICU stands for 'Internal Crowdsourcing in Enterprises' and is a joint project funded by the Federal Ministry of Research and Education (BMBF) and the European Social Fund (ESF) for a period of 3 years, from June 2017 to May 2020, under the funding measure 'Work in the Digitalised World' and supervised by the project management organization Karlsruhe. The project goal was the development of an employee-friendly cross-industry reference model for Internal Crowdsourcing.). Research Project in 2017. The aim of this chapter is to describe the ICU approach from the practical, company perspective of the GASAG Group and to map out identified success factors as well as provide general recommendations for the implementation of Internal Crowdsourcing in a business environment.

Keywords Good Practice · Platform development · Crowdsourcing campaigns · Success factors

---

F. Porth (✉)
GASAG AG, Berlin, Germany
e-mail: fporth@gasag.de

H. Ulbrich et al. (eds.), *Internal Crowdsourcing in Companies*, Contributions to Management Science, https://doi.org/10.1007/978-3-030-52881-2_8

1 Introduction

The GASAG Group is a leading energy service provider in the Berlin-Brandenburg metropolitan region with a tradition spanning 170 years. The group consists of 19 subsidiaries with 1600 employees. Their core business is the transportation, distribution and sale of energy and heat and, to an increasing extent, the provision of energy services and the generation of renewable energies. The GASAG Group's business activities involve the transportation, storage, distribution and sale of natural gas, heat, electricity and water, the production of biogas and electricity from renewable sources, the operation of facilities for distributed energy supply and the provision of energy services. The customer base includes private households, trade and industry, companies in the housing sector, hospitals and municipal entities, redistributors and users of gas transport services.

Despite being a successful company for more than 170 years, the GASAG Group faces the challenges presented by the typical organizational layout of small- and medium-sized enterprises in Germany as well as the challenges implicit in adapting to twenty-first-century needs (Pohlisch 2019),[1] especially when it comes to silo mentalities, and insufficiently pronounced cross-departmental knowledge transfers.

The feeling of affiliation among the employees of the GASAG Group was experienced as being stronger towards their own division or employer company, than to the corporate group as a whole. Therefore, the employee's knowledge and expertise, often spread beyond their usual ranges of duty, has often been skimmed within employees' own departments or divisions. There has been little use to date of the potentials offered by a cross-company knowledge transfer within the GASAG Group. Solutions to problems are generally generated within single departments or divisions. In short, the wisdom of the crowd hasn't been utilized to its full value, and the result has been that there is room for improvement in shortening processing periods, in increasing flexibility and agility and in promoting a bottom-up innovation culture.

As a reaction to these circumstances, the management board decided to take action to increase company activities offering employee participation, especially in the fields of idea generation, innovation and process improvement. Innovative ideas were to be discussed within a broader group of people beyond the boundaries of divisions and individual enterprises. Fast and agile collaboration methods were to be tested and encouraged, the goal being that these measures also improve cross-departmental communications and implementation speed and strengthen the corporate group identity.

At that time, the Technical University of Berlin introduced the ICU Research Project funded by the Ministry of Education and Research and the European Social Fund to the GASAG Group and proposed a scientific partnership to develop—

---

[1]Pohlisch, Jakob (2019). Bericht—Innovationsaktivitäten Deutscher Unternehmen. Technische Universität Berlin, Fachgebiet Innovation Economics. Berlin. Available online at https://tubcloud.tu-berlin.de/s/2m2BzwNyR3T9s8a#pdfviewer

together with the project consortium—a process as well as a digital and groupwide platform for Internal Crowdsourcing. The project consortium, the implementation partners and the extended project network aimed to design a cross-sector reference model for Internal Crowdsourcing.

Both, the Technical University of Berlin's research objectives and the GASAG Group's strategic corporate goals, had strong overlaps and the potential to support each other. For that reason, both institutions as well as other cooperation partners agreed to join the ICU Project.

2 Solution Approach: GASAG Good-Practice Model

The GASAG Group's specific objective within the research project was to put the theoretical model for Internal Crowdsourcing into practice and adapt, test and develop it in order to create a Good-Practice model for companies in the service sector. In addition, labour law and operational procedural standards were to be developed. All inner-company interest groups were involved in the project, from the workforce through the works council to corporate management.

The research layout, developed by the ICU Project's cooperation partners, concerning GASAG as the application and implementation case, can be sketched as follows: In the first step, an 8-month planning process was initiated. Several employee workshops and interviews were used to determine the platform's design and functionalities. Furthermore, in cooperation with the external project partners, strategies for the platform community management as well as incentive systems were developed, and a realization process for participation campaigns was designed.

This planning process was followed by another 8-month phase in order to test platform functionalities and participation campaign mechanisms within the corporate group. Within that phase, various data and statistics were gathered and analysed. The resulting, now more specific knowledge on participation rates as well as campaign and platform functionalities was used to review the initial strategies and plans regarding the digital platform.

The last phase carried out at the GASAG Group was the best-practice phase, where all lessons learned in the pilot phase were used to optimize platform functionalities and realization processes for participation campaigns.

2.1 Platform Development

To make sure the majority of the GASAG Group's employees have easy and fast access to the Internal Crowdsourcing approach at different locations, the approach is conducted on a technical Internet platform developed by the project partner Crowdee GmbH. To make sure the platform design and functionalities and Internal Crowdsourcing workflows fit the needs of the GASAG Group's employees, several workshops and focus interviews with employees and executives were held within the planning phase.

From an employee perspective, evaluating a submitted proposal required comprehensible, transparent decision criteria, as well as well-founded feedback concerning each rejected proposal, in order to express appreciation for the efforts made.

Furthermore, a high level of transparency regarding the benefits of everyone's own engagement was an important motivating factor. This meant that the effects of the ideas introduced had to be clearly documented on the platform and made public in order to stimulate the intrinsic motivation for further participations.

Each employee was also to decide individually whether their ideas were to be submitted anonymously or using their name, in order to prevent proposals from being evaluated based on their authorship and to give employees additional support in the event of conflicts with higher hierarchical levels. On the other hand, anonymous submissions might also encourage reluctant employees to participate and avoid discrimination.

Additionally, the employees questioned warned us not to overestimate the IT affinity of many colleagues.

Based on the insights gathered, a design concept and a content concept were developed as well as a requirements specification document for the technical developer.

The platform was intended to be as intuitive as possible with a self-explanatory menu structure and fewer submenus. Besides the menu areas for crowdsourcing campaigns and results, the content concept also contained additional information and details about the advantages of Internal Crowdsourcing as a collaboration method as well as practical examples from other companies already using Internal Crowdsourcing successfully. There is also a 'how-to' area that, among other things, includes the GASAG Group's internal works agreement on Internal Crowdsourcing. All three were intended to lend the by then quite unknown working method more credence and acceptance among the staff.

One lesson learned from the platform development is that it is necessary to fully integrate the technical platform in the company's IT infrastructure, meaning to have a single-sign-on workflow for the platform users. In the case of the GASAG Group, the single-sign-on functionality wasn't part of the requirement specifications in the first place. As a result, employees were required to create an individual user account what led to dissatisfaction with the additional effort as well as fear among employees that their personal data would be used for non-business purposes by external companies.

2.2 *Campaign Phases and the Internal Crowdsourcing Workflow*

Before the first Internal Crowdsourcing campaigns were carried out, it was necessary to modulate an ideal-typical implementation process. The ICU phased model, developed by the Institute of Vocational Education and Work Studies of the Technical University of Berlin (IBBA), was used as a guideline for the practical application at GASAG AG ensuring that the required steps of an Internal Crowdsourcing process were executed. It proposed the following steps: (1) impetus, (2) decision, (3) conceptualization, (4) execution, (5) assessment, (6) exploitation and (7) feedback (see chapter "Systematization Approach for the Development and Description of an Internal Crowdsourcing System"). This theoretical process model was transferred and adapted to the specific situation and needs at the GASAG Group.

1. *Impetus:* Ideally, within this process step, possible campaign topics are submitted to the crowd team by employees or the management via the Internal Crowdsourcing platform. Nevertheless, to get the Internal Crowdsourcing going within the GASAG Group, it was necessary to actively search for appropriate campaign topics within the company. Several roadshow formats were held in order to introduce this new collaboration method to departments, employees and managers. These roadshows also offered the possibility of brainstorming possible campaign topics.
2. *Decision:* A crowdsourcing campaign needed to fit certain criteria in order to underline it's meaningfulness from the perspective of potential participants. These criteria were, among others, a clear and comprehensible utility for the campaign owner and a concrete concept for further utilization of the campaign results.
3. *Conceptualization*: The campaign design included determining the task design (crowdstorming, crowdvoting, crowdsolving, crowdcreation, crowdtesting), formulating detailed job descriptions, choosing specific target groups, formulating campaign goals and expectations, deciding how to utilize the anticipated results, choosing appropriate incentive schemes and creating a campaign schedule (go-live, duration, deadlines, events, etc.). It was also very important in this process phase to develop a communication strategy, including selecting internal communication channels (online vs. offline) and defining a detailed action plan for the community and crowd management.
4. *Execution*: In this phase, the campaign concept was put into practice and monitored over the entire time. For GASAG AG, a mix between offline (posters, flyers) and online communications measures (intranet, email-newsletter) has had the greatest impact in promoting Internal Crowdsourcing campaigns. Campaign periods of 3–4 weeks with weekly participation reminders sent via internal communication channels delivered the best participation results. Periods of less than 3 weeks might possibly reduce the chance for every willing employee to participate due to office absence or simply due to time constraints. Campaigns

longer than 4 weeks did not increase participation rates significantly. Instead, they only prolonged the campaign without any additional benefits and increased the waiting period for campaign results. Another important lesson learned was that the original campaign period planned sometimes had to be increased while a campaign was running, due to a lack of participation.

5. *Assessment*: After completing the execution phase, the results were compiled and delivered to the content owner, who had to decide how to use them effectively. In order to communicate the results as fast as possible to the crowd and the community, it is necessary to set a deadline for the content owner. Also, providing assistance to the content owner in interpreting the results was helpful.
6. *Exploitation*: In this process phase, the content owner announced to the crowd team how the results would be used. This step is very important because it gives meaning to the input of each participant. If the final communication lacks information about the further exploitation of the campaign results, the participants may feel that the time they have spent is not valued and has therefore been badly invested. This might lead to them not participating in future campaigns again.
7. *Feedback:* The final communication including campaign description, results and further utilization was then compiled by the campaign manager and sent to the owner for final approval. Afterwards, the results were published on the Internal Crowdsourcing platform and communicated via GASAG's internal communication channels.

One lesson learned from the practical execution of the Internal Crowdsourcing process is that not every steering task described in the ideal ICU phased model is necessary or realizable for every campaign. Sometimes certain steps are set by default or cannot be executed due to internal limitations, for example, choice of internal communication channels and creation of a campaign schedule. Sometimes certain tasks are consolidated or have to be carried out in a different chronological order. Nevertheless, the process components as such remain the same, and the existence of a detailed theoretical process flow is still very helpful as a checklist.

2.3 Selection of Internal Crowdsourcing Campaigns

The implementation of Internal Crowdsourcing in the GASAG Group had three main objectives: (1) to increase activities that offered employee participation, (2) to support the innovation management and (3) to support employees in developing their skills. The campaign topics were specifically chosen in order to support these objectives.

Ten Internal Crowdsourcing campaigns were implemented as part of the project. Five of those campaigns can be associated with the task type 'crowdstorming'. One campaign can be seen as 'crowdvoting'. Three campaigns contained both crowdstorming and crowdvoting elements. One campaign was an example of 'crowdcreation'. The number of participants ranged from 8 to 147, while the number of registered users on the platform increased to 535 (about 30% of the workforce). The platform monitoring has shown that the majority of the registered employees monitor the Internal Crowdsourcing activities passively, while only a small number actively participate. Campaigns that targeted cultural aspects in the broadest sense and campaigns where employees had the possibility to influence or change their personal work environment had the highest participation rates. Campaigns regarding the GASAG Group's products and services had significantly lower participation rates.

Exemplary campaigns:

- *Naming the new corporate office building:* When the GASAG Group moved to new headquarters in Berlin, it was necessary to find an adequate name for this building to be used for internal and external communications. In order to find a well-suited name that employees could also identify with, the department for real estate management executed an Internal Crowdsourcing campaign. The campaign was divided into three parts. The first part consisted of a crowdstorming. The GASAG Group employees were asked to brainstorm possible names and submit them to the Internal Crowdsourcing platform. In the second step, the crowdvoting, the employees were asked to go through the final list and mark their favourite names with a 'like'. This resulted in a top-5 ranking of the suggested names most popular with employees. In the last step, the GASAG Group Management Board chose the final name for the company's new headquarters from this list. The entire process, including planning and execution of the campaign, lasted around 4 months. More than 130 employees participated in this campaign.
- *Go-to-market review:* In order to support the GASAG Group's innovation management, the product department used the platform to solve one of the current challenges it is facing. The department conducted an Internal Crowdsourcing campaign to have a go-to-market strategy reviewed and evaluated by the employees. The product and its features were presented to the employees on the crowdsourcing platform along with detailed questions regarding the product features and pricing strategies. The participating employees had the chance to evaluate the product and its pricing models and point out potentials for optimization. The product and its go-to-market strategy were revised afterwards based on the new insights. The planning and execution of this campaign required 3 months' time and 25 employees participated.
- *Future competencies:* The objective to increase the development of employees' competencies by implementing Internal Crowdsourcing was supported by the Human Resources department. As part of strategic staff development, the department conducted an Internal Crowdsourcing campaign with the goal of having a new training module developed by employees. The employees were asked to answer the questions 'Which competencies will be most important in your work environment within the next 5 years?' and 'Which competencies will be most important for you in particular within the next 5 years?'. Each question could be answered based on multiple-choice answers from a predetermined competence catalogue. The results of that campaign were used to revise the GASAG Group's

internal training opportunities. Three months were needed to plan and execute the entire campaign, and it motivated 41 employees to take part in it.

- *Crowdcreation 'learning formats':* In cooperation with the GASAG Group, colleagues from Strategic Personnel Development, the content structure for implementing the crowdsourcing discipline 'crowd creation' was developed, and the corresponding content was created. The staff from the GASAG Group were asked on the crowdsourcing platform to develop concepts for new learning formats that could potentially optimize the GASAG Group's internal training opportunities. In a second step, the employees had the chance to present their concepts on the crowdsourcing platform and pitch them against each other. Event vouchers for the Mercedes-Benz Arena in Berlin to the amount of 250 euros were awarded as a prize for the winners. To ensure that the concepts submitted by the employees were comparable, the participants had to fulfill different requirement criteria in their concept and answer various key questions. For example, describe the target groups, the required working materials, the structure as well as the structure of the learning format or the requirements for the trainer/moderator. After two employees from the GASAG Group submitted their concepts, the project team put them into a uniform structure and published them for the entire workforce with a request for feedback. Following that, the concept owners had the chance to rewrite their concepts based on the feedback submitted. A jury consisting of employees from the Strategic Personnel Development team then had to name the winning concept. Regardless of the feedback from the workforce, the jury team decided to award both of the concepts for new learning formats submitted as winners, as both concepts were of very high quality in terms of their content but were difficult to compare due to their different approaches. The planning and execution of the campaign lasted 4 months. The Strategic Personnel Development team aimed to implement both concepts in 2020.

An important lesson learned regarding the selection of Internal Crowdsourcing campaign topics is that, despite intense promotion and efforts to encourage participation, it was hard to find departments and executives willing to contribute appropriate campaign topics. On the one hand, executives seem to be more likely to choose established and reliable working methods to solve their department's tasks than to try other methods. On the other hand, executives were worried about making what they are working on transparent and did not want to hand over control of the solution process to employees from other departments.

2.4 Works Agreement

When implementing a new working method like Internal Crowdsourcing, to be executed with a new technical application, a lot of questions arise from both employees and management. These include the following: Who is allowed to participate? Is participation permitted during and/or outside of working hours? Is data security ensured? Who can read my content? Is it possible to participate anonymously? A works agreement was developed as part of the project in order to address these questions and to establish a transparent companywide guideline with labour regulations regarding Internal Crowdsourcing.

2.5 Internal Communication and Community Management

As described above, the GASAG Group's employees, executives and works councils were involved in the planning process and took part in workshops and focus interviews.

Within these workshops and interviews, the participants were asked for ideas about what content would be suitable for Internal Crowdsourcing campaigns. The participants also had the chance to outline their personal wishes, goals and concerns regarding the implementation of Internal Crowdsourcing.

In addition, a communication strategy was created with detailed descriptions of stakeholders, target groups, goals, channels and instruments.

To further support the flow of communication, roadshows were executed within the GASAG Group's departments to promote the project, the Internet platform, workflows and advantages of Internal Crowdsourcing.

3 Critical Success Factors

As described above, the ICU Project had an 8-month phase during which it could test platform functionalities and campaign participation mechanisms within the corporate group. During that phase, various data and statistics were gathered and analysed. The resulting, now more specific knowledge on participation rates as well as campaign and platform functionalities were used to review the initial strategies and plans regarding the digital platform as well as to identify critical success factors that seem to have a critical impact on the successful launch of Internal Crowdsourcing solutions.

In order to validate the success factors identified within the GASAG Group, different companies running similar Internal Crowdsourcing platforms were interviewed with the aim of exchanging information about their experiences with these. A comparison of the interview results showed that there were certain factors all interviewed companies had in common with the success factors identified by the GASAG Group. The critical success factors are described below.

3.1 Management Commitment

Internal Crowdsourcing solutions were implemented successfully particularly in companies where the management board actively supported the project. The management commitment was mainly expressed by committing the managerial staff to use the Internal Crowdsourcing solutions to outline their goals. Some of the companies even had target agreements with the managerial staff that demanded the use of Internal Crowdsourcing. By comparison, companies without a clear management commitment regularly struggled to find relevant crowdsourcing topics. Since using new techniques and working methods to solve tasks often entails extra effort in order to familiarize oneself with the new processes, managerial staff sometimes tend to abstain from trying new methods when it is not mandatory for them to use these.

3.2 Clear and Precise Goals

Internal Crowdsourcing solutions are successfully implemented especially in those companies that had clear and precise goals that aligned with the overall strategic direction of the company. For example, some Internal Crowdsourcing solutions aimed to identify revenue or savings potentials. Others had the primary goal of developing new products and business models. Only topics that aimed at these goals could be published on the platforms. As opposed to this, companies without a clearly worded crowdsourcing strategy struggled to find relevant crowdsourcing topics on a regular basis, because internal stakeholders and managerial staff could not identify a clear utility or added value of the new Internal Crowdsourcing solutions with respect to their individual tasks.

3.3 Companywide Agreements

Works agreements containing transparent companywide guidelines and labour regulations regarding Internal Crowdsourcing are a major factor contributing to the successful implementation of this new working method. A clear and transparent works agreement creates trust and clarity on the use options and opportunities for participation.

3.4 Company Culture and Leadership Culture

Companies planning to implement an Internal Crowdsourcing solution should consider that establishing new ways of collaboration and delegation takes some time for familiarization, especially if the company has a more traditional and hierarchical business environment. Managerial staff may not be used to implementing participation instruments in order to solve a task. Employees may not be used to having the freedom to participate in topics beyond their usual range of duties. The readjustment in the leadership and company culture takes a lot of change management efforts, and the features and benefits need to be communicated well. Therefore, companies with a more traditional and hierarchical business environment that plan to implement an Internal Crowdsourcing solution should calculate bigger investments in change management as well as sufficient time for people to become used to this new work feature, until it establishes itself as a work habit within the company.

3.5 *Project Schedule*

The kick-off date for an Internal Crowdsourcing platform should be well-timed. Companies planning to implement Internal Crowdsourcing solutions need to identify a reasonable time slot by overviewing the company's project portfolio concerning competing projects and by monitoring the status quo of the company's strategic goals. Furthermore, the kick-off date for individual participation formats within the scope of Internal Crowdsourcing needs to be chosen wisely. In a fiscal year, companies go through phases that are more or less suitable to start employee participation workflows. Periods like holiday seasons, annual closures or the high season should be examined critically as, during such times, employees possibly won't have time to participate or are simply out of the office. This could lower participation rates and threaten the success of the project.

3.6 *Further Theses*

In addition to the identified success factors, the project has spawned further thoughts and theses that can be examined in further research. For example, one could argue that the use of digital applications for Internal Crowdsourcing is more suitable for larger, more anonymous and complex organizations than for small- and medium-sized companies. The involvement of colleagues from other departments in developing solutions may be more difficult to implement in major corporations than in small- and medium-sized companies, which is why the use of central, digital platforms promises greater added value here. In medium-sized companies such as the GASAG Group, on the other hand, collaboration on topics is more shaped by personal relationships, joint meetings or workshops. Even under the condition of finding interdisciplinary and cross-departmental solutions, non-digital formats of Internal Crowdsourcing have been able to produce faster and higher-quality results than using digital platforms.

4 Conclusion

The focus of the ICU Project was to develop a cross-industry reference model for the implementation of Internal Crowdsourcing in a corporate environment, in order to support companies in mobilizing existing, unused knowledge and skills internally, networking them across divisions and integrating them productively into company processes.

To develop this reference model, case studies were analysed and a theoretical model for Internal Crowdsourcing was developed by the project partners from the Technical University of Berlin. This theoretical Internal Crowdsourcing model was adapted by the GASAG Group for their own application, tested and further developed into a model for 'Good Practice' for Internal Crowdsourcing in the service sector. The project consortium, the implementation partners and the extended project network then formed this model into a cross-sector reference model.

As part of the project, several success factors for the implementation of Internal Crowdsourcing in a corporate environment could be identified. These success factors can be grouped in the categories:

- Management commitment
- Clear and precise goals
- Works agreements
- Company culture and leadership culture
- Project schedule

A detailed checklist including guiding questions for each category can be found at the end of this article.

Even though this list is not intended to be complete, companies planning to implement Internal Crowdsourcing workflows to their business environment may take a more in-depth look into these success factors in order to increase the probability of a successful launch.

When it comes to further research, one question that emerged within the ICU Project was whether the use of digital applications for Internal Crowdsourcing is more suitable for larger, more anonymous major organizations than for small- and medium-sized companies.

4.1 Checklist 'Critical Success Factors for the Implementation of Internal Crowdsourcing'

1. Management Commitment

    - Make sure the management board actively endorses the project.
    - Make sure the management board actively supports the project while it is ongoing.

- Make sure that target agreements with the managerial staff for the use of Internal Crowdsourcing methods are implemented.

2. Clear and Precise Goals

- Make sure the Internal Crowdsourcing approach has clear and precise goals that align with the overall strategic direction of the company.
- Make sure Internal Crowdsourcing supports the company's current strategic goals.
- Make sure that internal stakeholders, employees and managerial staff see a clear utility or added value for their work to be gained by using Internal Crowdsourcing solutions.

3. Works Agreement

- Make sure a works agreement containing transparent companywide guidelines and labour regulations regarding Internal Crowdsourcing is implemented.

4. Company Culture and Leadership Culture

- Make sure bigger investments in change management measures are calculated within the project budget.
- Make sure sufficient time is scheduled in the project for employees and managerial staff to familiarize themselves with it.
- Make sure the management board understands the need for the investments in change management and the familiarization period.

5. Project Schedule

- Make sure no competing projects that endanger the successful implementation of Internal Crowdsourcing are to be launched during the project period.
- Identify a reasonable time slot for the kick-off of Internal Crowdsourcing projects or campaigns by bypassing holiday seasons, annual closures or high seasons.

Florian Porth studied Business Administration in Berlin and works as project manager focusing on digital transformation. At the GASAG Group, he initially started as a member of the project team and later became fully responsible for the introduction of Internal Crowdsourcing in the GASAG Group.

The Living Group Works Council Agreement as Social Innovation: Internal Crowdsourcing in the GASAG Group

Andreas Otte, Welf Schröter, Ingo Breite, Frank Gerth, Sylvia Laur, Volker Ost, Can Sekertekin, Andreas Tabor, Marco Wedel, and Hannah Ulbrich

Abstract Shortly after the formal launch of the ICU project in the summer of 2017, representatives from the group works council of the GASAG group sat down with the trade union network Forum for the Social Forms of Technology, the FST, to start up an independent practical initiative to examine the topic of internal crowdsourcing to be implemented soon after. In 2018, a model works council agreement between the group works council and the management was agreed, henceforth framing the IC procedure in the GASAG group. The agreement is meant to serve as a template for the introduction of internal crowdsourcing in other companies and industries. A special feature of the agreement is the so-called 'living' group works council agreement. The following article analyses its significance and provides a translation by reproducing the agreement in its wording (This text is based on an original version in the German language that was published under the provisions of the Creative Commons at the URL: www.blog-zukunft-der-arbeit.de/betriebsraete-setzen-starken-innovationsimpuls-fuer-digitalen-aufbruch or www.blog-zukunft-der-arbeit.de.).

Keywords Social innovation · Living group works council agreement · Internal crowdsourcing group works council agreement

---

A. Otte · I. Breite · F. Gerth · S. Laur · V. Ost · C. Sekertekin · A. Tabor
GASAG AG, Groups Work Council, Berlin, Germany

W. Schröter
Forum Soziale Technikgestaltung beim DGB, Baden-Württemberg, Mössingen, Germany
e-mail: schroeter@talheimer.de

M. Wedel (✉) · H. Ulbrich
Technische Universität Berlin, Institute for Vocational Education and Work Studies, Berlin, Germany
e-mail: marco.wedel@tu-berlin.de; hannah.ulbrich@tu-berlin.de

H. Ulbrich et al. (eds.), *Internal Crowdsourcing in Companies*, Contributions to Management Science, https://doi.org/10.1007/978-3-030-52881-2_9

1 About the ICU Project

The following piece was written as part of the Federal Ministry of Education and Research project 'Internal Crowdsourcing in Companies: Employee-friendly process innovations through the digital participation of employees', the ICU.

Shortly after the formal launch of the ICU project in the summer of 2017, representatives from the group works council of the GASAG group sat down with the trade union network Forum for the Social Forms of Technology, the FST, to start up an independent practical initiative to examine the topic of internal crowdsourcing to be implemented soon after. The colleagues' aim was to work out and present an own innovation concept, with them taking on the role of initiators and pioneers. This proactive concept aimed to secure employment, not by working against new digital applications but rather by actively using new IT technology. The group works council emphasized here its existing openness towards innovation and its innovation competence. The concept consisted of five action steps:

1. Consultation concerning the significance and impact of internal crowdsourcing
2. Drafting and approving a list of the main points for binding aspects concerning the design
3. Drafting and approving the design of an own draft initiative for a group works council agreement (in German 'KBV')
4. Negotiating a group works council agreement together with the group management
5. Living the 'KBV' in practice

The members of the group works council and the individual company works councils were to implement steps 1–3 in 5 months. The negotiations with the group management concerning the KBV were to take 3 months.

Between September 2017 and April 2018, an unusual agreement came into being in the GASAG group which allowed the group works council and the group management to become joint pioneers in the field of internal crowdsourcing. They signed one of the first legally binding works council agreements in this area in the Federal Republic of Germany.

2 Consulting on and Drawing up the KBV

A participation-oriented, voluntary, company-internal innovation management process was chosen above all as a practical introduction that was accessible via an electronic platform within the GASAG group. Put more simply, a traditional voluntary proposal scheme, which to date had been organized on paper or by posting information on noticeboards, could be modernized using IC. This model was transformed into a digital platform environment. The aim here was to provide the opportunity for a working culture with 'swarm intelligence' to emerge as a way to source knowledge and new ideas from employees (therefore the term 'crowdsourcing') and to promote cross-departmental working.

From the perspective of trade unions and works councils, this gave rise to broader and additional aspects. The discourse between the group works council, the individual company works councils and the FST saw the voluntary, innovative sourcing of ideas as only one of the many faces of internal crowdsourcing.

One of the ways the trade unions looked at it is that we must expect, above all, that in addition to voluntary, innovative crowdsourcing, there will also be order-related crowdsourcing arising from the instruction right of the employer as provided for in labour law—if not immediately, then at some point in the future.

According to the works councils, voluntary IC must be designed in such a way that it takes into consideration the expected order-related and binding form of IC and, as a preventive measure, provides for codetermination (Schröter 2018b).

An approach based only on the voluntary part of IC would undervalue the potentials that IC allows for. Linking both perspectives was key for the group works council, in German 'KBR (Konzernbetriebsrat)', and FST to achieving the intended humanization strategy. This way of looking at things was the first step in the joint conceptual approach shared by the KBR and FST.

In the second action phase, an extensive list of the main points was drawn up. What points were to be developed, how were they to be developed and when? In a comprehensive dialogue, this resulted in a requirements list comprising almost 70 individual tasks. These were divided into the following sections:

- Goals for the company innovation management from the standpoint of the KBR
- Conditions for the company innovation management
- Using the electronic platforms
- Humane work design—humane work organization
- Legal framework conditions for innovation management

The first version of the list of main points was drafted by a working group made up of KBR and FST. This version was dealt with at a special session of the KBR. After adding to it, a regular KBR session approved the document as the basis for the independent draft by the KBR and FST for the initiative towards a socially innovative group works council agreement.

The third action phase of the concept was about coming up with a courageous draft for an own innovation strategy. What did the colleagues want the future of work to look like? What social standards were important? How could people organize their own learning process? The first draft of the initiative towards a group works council agreement placed the idea of a 'living KBV' at the centre of its considerations. Works council representatives and employees did not want to be pushed by the introduction of technology, wanting instead to act on their own initiative and proactively for the future of the company on an equal standing and with an active role in decision-making.

The principles behind this approach included on the one hand the realization that, at the beginning of a complex technology introduction, neither the group management nor the group works council knew exactly whether the goals that had been set would be successfully achieved.

What was needed was a flexible concept for change that allowed learning to take place. In addition to the idea[1] of 'a living KBV' came the concept of "agile cooperative change management of the digital transformation" (Schröter 2017).

The fourth action phase saw the negotiation process begin with the employee side presenting the first draft. In the negotiations, the contractual parties came closer to one another in the core task of assessing the various crowdsourcing tendencies and reached a binding understanding after 3 months of talks (see items 1.7–1.9 in 'Wording'):

With this arrangement, the group management and the group works council created a transparent and calculable entry point into designing innovative platform-based working environments (Schröter 2018a). For the KBR, it was not only important to create new innovative products and services but above all to safeguard jobs as well as forge a path towards good digital work.

Besides the points such as health and safety at work, integration and inclusion, data protection, regulating working hours and availability, etc., the two contract partners reached agreement through the KBR initiative concerning qualification steps (see 5.11. in 'Wording').

The fifth and last action phase paved the way for the new communication and work-design culture to be developed. The aim was that the contract partners come together at regular intervals in order to assess their experiences with the process and to push the further development of the 'living KBV' (see 5.13 a in 'Wording').

This was the beginning of a cooperative learning process. The 'living KBV' as social innovation and the experiences gained during its practical implementation constituted an important building block on the way towards innovative work-design competence (Otte and Schröter 2019). The plan is to pass this competence on to other sectors and companies.

The Wording of the KBV

3 The Group Works Council Agreement (KBV) Internal Crowdsourcing in the GASAG Group ('The Living KBV')

3.1 Definition of Internal Crowdsourcing in the GASAG Group (IC)

1. "As a direct result of the technological developments of the last 10 years, 'internal crowdsourcing' today represents a new form of organizing company-internal

[1] An idea that came from KBR Chairman Andreas Otte.

cooperation and knowledge transfer processes. Through internal crowdsourcing, previously inaccessible knowledge resources, i.e. unutilized specialized and personnel know-how gained from experience by the employees is mobilized in a fast and highly efficient manner and can be sourced in interactive crowdworking in order to develop new ideas and creative solutions to problems. Proposals can then be used in a beneficial way to produce innovative, market-ready products and services, thus contributing towards an increase in the company's efficiency and profit" (Federal Ministry of Education and Research ICU project application, 2017). The GASAG group wants to use this added value from IC to its own benefit.

2. When designing IC in the GASAG group, the following IC components are relevant, among others: innovation management, employee participation and expansion of competence.
3. The goal of IC is—besides employee participation and innovation management—to develop approaches to expand employee competences by using IC. In doing so, collaborative work processes are practised in the crowd and monitored in order to evaluate existing qualification measures at GASAG on the basis of this or to realign these. The employer does not keep a record of individual competences as part of this. At the same time, the employees have the opportunity to discover their own competences and interests themselves and to articulate any further training needs or wishes and to carry out the corresponding measures.
4. From a methodological point of view, IC can be divided up into crowdstorming (making suggestions), crowdvoting, crowdsolving (putting forward concrete solution proposals) and crowdtesting (testing functionalities).
5. The topics placed on the platform to be worked through by the crowd are described as 'IC campaigns' and are named from out of the GASAG group.
6. In IC, the circle of participants is limited to the employees of the participating companies from the GASAG group.
7. External crowdsourcing (the circle of those questioned consists only of people external to the company), just like crowdworking (assigning internal work activities to an external crowd with the aim of having previously internal work activities carried out externally), is not a project goal and therefore also not part of the KBV on internal crowdsourcing in the GASAG group.
8. Order-related internal crowdsourcing (processing customer orders on the platform (also) with internal employees) is not planned at the present time as part of IC.
9. The parties agree that, before introducing crowdworking in the sense of item 1.7 or order-related crowdsourcing in the sense of item 1.8, the living group works council agreement (see item 2) will be added to accordingly or a separate group works council agreement will be concluded.

3.2 The 'Living Group Works Council Agreement' as Social Innovation: A Preamble

1. The group management of the GASAG group and the group works council are treading new ground with this type of 'living group works council agreement' and allowing for new opportunities for social, technical and nontechnical innovations in the group as a whole as well as for the digital transformation of the working environments within the group.
2. The 'living group works council agreement' for platform-based internal crowdsourcing opens up new fields of action for the working culture and IC. The group management and the group works council see the agreement as a point of entry into a holistic process of organizing work with foresight, which is open going forward. Both partners undertake to carry out cooperative change management on an equal footing that is to be organized in a results-oriented manner and that is professionally and methodically agile.
3. The 'living group works council agreement' aims, on the basis of an agile, cooperative change management, to promote mutual learning throughout the group as well as the acquisition of work-design competences. For this purpose, joint assessments, joint evaluations and joint updates of the group works council agreement will take place at regular intervals as well as jointly structured evaluations of their practical implementation. Both partners work together to adapt the group works council agreement to the experience gained and the learning steps in each case.
4. The 'living group works council agreement' is to be developed in connection with the Federal Ministry of Education and Research project 'Internal Crowdsourcing in Companies' (ICU) and with its pilot phases (April 2018 until the end of February 2019) and with its best-practice phases (March 2019 until the end of November 2019).
5. The 'living group works council agreement' is at the same time based on the already existing relevant group works council agreements. Existing group works council agreements and works council agreements will not be replaced by this new additional 'living group works council agreement', and their validity, which is based on earlier decisions, will not be affected. This applies, in particular, to the group works council agreement titled 'Introduction and implementation of information and communications technology' (IuK) from 27 August 2015; for the group works council agreement titled 'Code of conduct in the GASAG companies' from 15 March 2017; or for the group works council agreement titled 'Software for multi-project management' from 8 December 2008. All signed KBVs as well as the works council agreements of the companies of the GASAG group continue to apply without restriction.

3.3 Goals

The group management of the GASAG group and the group works council link the following goals to the introduction of IC:

1. Promoting employee participation, the ability to innovate and the expansion of competences.
2. Creating the prerequisites for the development of new value creation paths, new products and new services.
3. Promoting the safeguarding of local jobs and strengthening the ecologically sustainable profile of the company. The aim is, among other things, to increase the efficiency of the company as a whole through IC.
4. An IC oriented towards the values of humanization of work in line with Annex 6.8—excerpt from the KBV IuK.
5. Protecting the employees from excessive workloads is an essential aspect.
6. Influencing the corporate culture through the mutual respect people have for one another and the respectful way they treat one another.
7. The 'living group works council agreement' is a building block towards a joint future dialogue between the group management of the GASAG group and the group works council.
8. The introduction and implementation of IC does not aim to rationalize and/or cut jobs.

3.4 Area of Application

1. The 'living group works council agreement' applies to all employees of the GASAG group in the sense of Article 5 paragraph 1 of the Works Constitution Act if these companies participate in IC.
2. The participating companies are listed in Annex 1. If required, the Annex can be added to or amended by concluding supplementary agreements.
3. Any deviations from existing local or groupwide regulations refer exclusively to the use of IC. Existing regulations are generally not affected by it.

3.5 Principles and Conditions of IC

1. The participation of the employees of the GASAG group in IC is voluntary.
2. Employees face no disadvantages due to their participation or nonparticipation in IC.
3. The implementation of IC does not lead to changes in company organization.
4. The participation of the employees in IC takes places during working hours. The time spent working on platforms is working time.

5. Specific times apply for employees who are subject to working instructions via workforce systems, or possibilities will be stored in the system pertaining to when they can take part in IC during working hours. The specific local regulations apply in each case.
6. All existing works council agreements concerning working hours as well as the Working Hours Act will be complied with for all types of utilization of IC.
7. To the extent that tasks connected to internal crowdsourcing are suitable for work from home (remote working), the employees have the chance to carry out these tasks at their home office, in line with the respectively applicable works council agreement for remote working.
8. Access to IC will be provided by the company at the workplace, mobile on a laptop (if available) and in an employee's home office. No additional IT accesses or IT workplaces will be provided for. Employees without IT access can place IT initiatives directly via the crowdmanager.
9. Measures to motivate employees to become more involved in IC must be carried out in a data-sensitive manner. Employee participation in points systems or ranking systems that are accessible to the group or to employers is exclusively voluntary. People are free to choose to use either their own name or a pseudonym.
10. Individual employees have a right of initiative, taking into consideration the definition agreed to in item 1 as part of IC, and can place company-related topics on the IC platform on their own (if necessary, via the crowdmanager if there are technical issues). This also applies for all representations of employee interests. If, in the future, it seems it would be make sense to steer the topics, the parties will consult with one another, and this regulation will be adapted accordingly.
11. The group management of the GASAG group and the group works council agree that digitization requires an expansion or improvement of the employees' competences. They therefore assess the requirements for formulating a joint qualification concept and a qualifications programme for IC at regular monitoring meetings (item 5.14) in order to make the introduction of IC easier for the employees. As part of this, the parties will check, in particular, how (a) older and (b) less technically astute employees can be encouraged and motivated to work with the IC platform. That is why, in addition to instruction in IC using eLearning, face-to-face teaching sessions will also be offered. Furthermore, all regulations concerning qualification, training and instruction as outlined in the IuK apply.
12. The rules of the group works council agreement 'Introduction and implementation of information and communications technology' (IuK) from 27 August 2015 apply for the access rights of the group works council to user data.
13. The parties agree to the following regular monitoring meetings:

    (a) The parties will jointly evaluate the implementation of IC on a quarterly basis. When doing so, they will check whether there is a need to train employees, particularly older and less technically proficient employees.

(b) The parties will carry out an annual joint assessment of the effects of IC on the group as a whole. In connection with this, data monitoring with respect to platform use will take place. The structuring and implementation of the data monitoring will be realized in binding coordination with the KBR.
(c) The parties will assess on an annual basis whether there has been an increase in mental illnesses.

3.6 Using an Electronic IC Platform

1. To implement IC, an online platform hosted by crowdees will be used as a white-label solution in the GASAG group. The IC platform is not generally accessible to third parties, with the exception of the administrators.
2. With respect to the internal crowdsourcing with the help of the group-internal platform, the GASAG group undertakes to handle data security and data protection in a particularly sensitive manner that goes beyond the regulations laid down in the Federal Data Protection Act. Any use data generated for the platform will only be made available to the company bodies or departmental heads and supervisors in an aggregated and anonymized form and, if requested, to the research consortium. A person-related breakdown of data does not take place. The aim of this is to strengthen the employees' right to self-determination over their personal data as well as their trust in the company and its mindful corporate culture.
3. The goal is to have an open and transparent exchange among the employees. In order to keep people's inhibitions in using IC as low as possible, the employees will have the individual right to use a pseudonym for their inputs.
4. The data traffic to and from the platform will be encoded (HTTPS).
5. In order to safeguard the employee concerns and rights worthy of protection, reference is made to the group works council agreement 'Introduction and implementation of information and communications technology' (IuK) from 27 August 2015 (cf. the quotations in the Annex).
6. The processing of voluntarily submitted user data requires a separate agreement. The processing of voluntarily submitted user data in gaming contexts requires the explicit consent of the gamer in question. Any profiles created beyond that are not permitted.
7. Following the end of the experimental and best-practice phase, the group management of the GASAG group and the group works council jointly decide what analyses or evaluations should be drawn up. Based on this, the parties agree to use the data available from the IC platform explicitly for this purpose. Data under a pseudonym may not be subsequently transformed into real names and evaluated.
8. The storing of user data is limited to a maximum of 1 year.
9. An evaluation portal will be added to the IC platform thus enabling employees of the GASAG group to assess the platform interface, the platform usability, the

IC moderation and the quality of the communications processes in the same way as school grades are given and, if required, to make comments.
10. Individual access to the platform is provided using registered employee accounts.
11. Disclosing a real name behind a pseudonym requires the dual consent of the group works council and the group management. This is done if persons using a pseudonym insult other people or otherwise do not comply with heedful and respectful conduct or if they violate obligations to maintain secrecy arising from employment contracts or provisions from the informational unbundling. The disclosure takes place with the involvement of a KBR member.
12. The group management will work with the operator to ensure that the platform interface and its architecture meet the requirements of accessibility for the deaf, visually impaired, etc. (reading function, zoom function, etc.). On the other hand, end devices must be retrofitted accordingly if participation in IC is otherwise not possible.

3.7 Humane Work Design: Humane Work Organization

1. With respect to humane work design and work organization, reference is drawn to Annex 6.8—excerpt from the KBV IuK.
2. In order to protect employees, no controls of performance or conduct will take place. Online surveillance of any kind and monitoring of performance and conduct controls is not permitted. Ranking—also in connection with gamification—is not possible without the consent of the group works council. The parties do agree, however, that gamification is a useful instrument for motivating employees to use the platform.
3. IC is to be managed with a culture of mutual respect and appreciative conduct towards one another as well as in accordance with the values of inclusion and diversity.
4. In order to reinforce health and safety at work and to improve forward-looking work design and occupational safety, a risk assessment will be carried out within the group during the pilot phase in accordance with the statutory obligations. Among other things, mental stress is to be assessed. Particular attention must be paid to complexity, work concentration, independent work planning and collaboration that topics remain varied and to employee participation, which are relevant in connection with agile forms of work. After the IC introduction, risk assessments are to be carried out as required.
5. The parties agree that, if it is necessary and sensible to conclude a group works council agreement on 'Good Agile Work' in order to best exploit the advantages of agile organizational models and semiautonomous forms of work in the sense of a humanization of work, such a KBV will be negotiated. This agreement will, in particular, set upper limits for agile work areas and the rights of the employees

concerned. If the group management and the KBR recognize the need for such a KBV, they will seek to conclude said agreement in due time.

3.8 Legal Framework Conditions for IC

1. The group management of the GASAG group and the group works council undertake to conclude an agreement on a bonus regulation for successfully accepted innovation suggestions after the end of the experimental and best-practice phase and based on an evaluation of the motivation steps to increase the number of employees participating. Here, earlier experiences gained from idea management should be taken into consideration. This regulation will be agreed as a supplement to this KBV.
2. Innovation ideas that are brought into IC by company employees of the GASAG group become the legal property of the group. Providers of ideas have the right to an appropriate remuneration. The details are to be agreed in the regulation to be met according to item 8.1.
3. The contents of IC are subject to confidentiality.
4. In the case of unintended misconduct concerning patents or rights of use by the employee, the company is liable.
5. The laws of the Federal Republic of Germany apply to all matters pertaining to copyright, rights of use or patent issues that are communicated concerning IC.

3.9 Entering into Force, Termination and Continued Application

1. This works council agreement enters into force upon signing. After being signed, the document is public.
2. During the pilot phase (April 2018 to the end of March 2019) and the best-practice phase (April 2019 to the end of December 2019), this works council agreement can be terminated in writing under compliance with the statutory period of notice. It continues to be valid, to the extent that the regulations are subject to enforceable codetermination.
3. Following that, if IC is to continue on a long-term basis, the group works council agreement can be terminated by each of the contractual parties with a period of notice of 3 months to the end of the calendar year. Termination requires the written form.
4. The group works council agreement continues to be valid to the extent that the regulations are subject to enforceable codetermination.
5. If this group works council agreement is terminated, irrespective by what party, the parties undertake to start negotiations within 3 months of receiving the

termination concerning a regulation to replace this group works council agreement. This does not apply if the employer does not want to continue IC.

signed GASAG signed KBR

Annex 1 Participating Group Companies

[. . .]

Annex 2 Excerpts from the Group Works Council Agreement 'Introduction and Implementation of Information and Communications Technology' (IuK) from 27 August 2015

Excerpt Concerning 5.11

Qualifying the Users, Training Courses and Instruction

- The qualifications necessary for using the applications, as well as follow-up and advanced training courses for the employees are to be carried out at the cost of the employer. The respective contracting party is responsible for the execution of such measures. The project management or division can be assigned to do this. The divisions are generally responsible for follow-up training courses.
- The time at which qualification measures are carried out is to be chosen, if possible, so that these have been completed by the time the new system is launched and working with the new system can begin as soon as possible following completion of the qualification. Qualification measures generally take place during working hours or are set off against working hours.
- The training and further training measures must enable the employee to carry out their work using the IuK technologies to be introduced.
- In line with the Works Constitution Act, the responsible works council representatives will be involved in any training concept.
- Participation in training measures is to be confirmed by issuing a certificate or confirmation of participation.
- Training or further training measures are assessed immediately following completion of the measure in order to take into consideration possible improvements.

Excerpt Concerning 6.5

Main Features of the Application of the IuK

1. Decisions concerning the introduction of IuK technologies require an analysis of the work organization, a needs analysis and a tasks analysis as well as a feasibility study. These initial planning steps must also include a concept for personnel development and analysis of the qualification needs.
2. In IuK projects, the affected employees must be involved at an early stage. This requires IuK projects to be transparent; the employees also need to be qualified for the project work and, if necessary, released from their normal work duties.
3. The following principles are to be agreed as a framework for orientation and as a guideline both for the introduction of new systems and the further development of existing ones:
   Humane work design:
   - Humane work design covers the three areas technology, work organization and employee qualification. When change happens in one of the three areas, the consequences for the other areas must be taken into consideration at the same time and with the same priority, and the corresponding measures for their design must be taken and/or taken into consideration in planning for the future.

   Holism:
   - The work tasks must be designed holistically. They include planning, steering, executing and monitoring activities. The work tasks must be organized in such a way that the employees concentrate on the scope they have to make decisions and take action in line with the responsibility and work tasks assigned to them. When working with computer monitors, the work content should be such that working on the monitors is alternated with other work.

Protection from Controls of Performance or Conduct

1. Personal data pertaining to conduct and performance are only evaluated as part of the intended purpose of the employment relationship and to fulfil the legal, collective-agreement-related or other contractually agreed duties (e.g. violation against group directives, guidelines or organizational guidelines) and in each individual case only with the prior consent of the works council and with the involvement of the responsible data protection officer. The regulations concerning the collection, processing and use as well as correction, deletion and blocking of data in the employment relationship pursuant to the Federal Data Protection Act (BDSG)—in particular sections 32 and 35—must be observed. In the case of abuse proceedings (fraud), the following prerequisites apply and must basically justify such proceedings:

- Concrete suspicion against a specific employee that a crime has been committed.
- Actual indications that justify the suspicion.
- An obligation to document these indications.
- The control measures must be reasonable.

This assessment also requires the prior consent of the works council.

2. Pseudonyms or usernames may be saved and displayed in application programmes in order to identify a responsible, competent or contactable person in individual cases and to comply with legal regulations.

   The protection of personal data by external service providers as part of the contracted-out processing of data is carried out in accordance with the provisions of the German Data Protection Act and the DSHB.

   Personnel measures based on information obtained in violation of this agreement are invalid and must be reversed.

References

Otte A, Schröter W (2019) Zusammenarbeit mit Ingo Breite, Frank Gerth, Sylvia Laur, Volker Ost, Can Sekertekin, Andreas Tabor: Lebende Konzernbetriebsvereinbarung als soziale Innovation. Internes Crowdsourcing in der GASAG-Gruppe. Bedeutung – Bewertung – Wortlaut. In: Schröter W (ed) Der mitbestimmte Algorithmus. Gestaltungskompetenz für den Wandel der Arbeit. Talheimer Sammlung kritisches Wissen, vol 85. Technologien, Mössingen, pp 185–212

Schröter W (2017) Selbstbestimmung zwischen "nachholender Digitalisierung" und "autonomen Software-Systemen". Wenn Betriebsräte "vorausschauende Arbeitsgestaltung" erproben. In: Schröter W (ed) Autonomie des Menschen – Autonomie der Systeme. Humanisierungspotenziale und Grenzen moderner Technologien. Sammlung kritisches Wissen, vol 71. Technologien, Mössingen, pp 187–256

Schröter W (2018a) Identität in der Virtualität. Arbeit als Identitätsarbeit. In: Beutin H, Beutin W, Bleicher-Nagelsmann H (eds) "Reich der Notwendigkeit – Reich der Freiheit". Arbeitswelten in und Literatur und Kunst. Talheimer Sammlung kritisches Wissen, vol 80. Talheimer, Mössingen, pp 257–267

Schröter W (2018b) Plädoyer für einen Perspektivwechsel im gewerkschaftlichen Gestaltungsdiskurs. WSI-Mitteilungen 71(3):247–248

Andreas Otte is Chairman of the group works council of GASAG AG. **Welf Schröter** is head of the personnel network 'Forum Soziale Technikgestaltung' (in German 'FST') at DGB Baden-Württemberg and acts as a partner in the Federal Ministry of Education and Research project 'Internes Crowdsourcing in Unternehmen: Arbeitnehmergerechte Prozessinnovationen durch digitale Beteiligung von Mitarbeiter/innen' (Internal Crowdsourcing in Companies: Employee-friendly process innovations through the digital participation of employees; in German 'ICU'). **Andreas Tabor** is Deputy Chairman of the group works council. **Ingo Breite**, **Frank Gerth**, **Volker Ost**, **Can Sekertekin** and **Andreas Tabor** as works council representatives, together with the Representative of Employees with Disabilities **Sylvia Laur**, as well as Andreas Otte and Welf Schröter, formed the negotiating delegation for the employee side. The ICU project is run by the Institute of Vocational Education and Work Studies (IBBA) at the Technical University Berlin. Overall management is in the hands of sociologist (Dipl. Soz.).

Dr. Marco Wedel is a Political Scientist (Dipl.rer.pol., Dr. phil.) and Senior Researcher at the Department of Vocational Education, Technology and Participation at the Technical University of Berlin. In addition to study visits to Boston, Constance and Berlin, he has worked in the Energy Sector (BASF) and in Science Management (Falling Walls Foundation), among other things. His current research activities focus on the topics future of work, entrepreneurship, digitalization and media competence. His long-term research focuses on European integration, democratic competence and sustainable development. Marco Wedel is co-editor of the science journal 'Innovation—The European Journal of Social Science Research'.

Hannah Ulbrich holds a Degree in Sociology (Dipl. Soz.—Bielefeld/Berlin) and is a Senior Researcher at the Department of Vocational Education, Technology and Participation at the Technical University of Berlin. There, she is the project leader of the BMBF- and ESF-funded research project 'ICU—Internal Crowdsourcing in Companies'. In addition to her work as a project manager, she is a scholarship holder of the Berlin Professional School of Economics and Law where she is currently completing a part-time MBA programme. Her research focus is on entrepreneurship and innovation, new work and agility and digital transformation and leadership.

The Use of Internal Crowdsourcing for Qualification and Competence Development in Organizations

André Uhl and Edgar Göll

Abstract This article deals with the question of how internal crowdsourcing can be used as a tool to support employee qualification measures and help develop their competencies in organizations. The first chapter examines the current state of the competence research. A paradigm shift from 'qualification and professional development' towards 'competencies' and the implications for the concept are described. Chapter "An Introduction to Internal Crowdsourcing" deals with the analyses and work on the subject of competence acquisition and development, including considering the results of two interview series and two workshops. In chapter "Managing the Crowd: A Literature Review of Empirical Studies on Internal Crowdsourcing", the authors present a combined and practical approach to support competence development through internal crowdsourcing in organizations. Finally, the last chapter sums up main results and perspectives for competence development through a combination of virtual and face-to-face working processes.

Keywords Qualification and competence development · Professional development · New learning culture · Virtual and face-to-face working processes

1 Introduction

The authors of this article try to find answers to the questions concerning how to design an approach for competence development through internal crowdsourcing in order to create value for the employees as well as for the organization as a whole. In order to find these answers, the authors developed an application-oriented concept for qualification, further education, qualification and competence development through the use of internal crowdsourcing as part of the research project 'Internes Crowdsourcing in Unternehmen—ICU' (internal crowdsourcing in companies).

A. Uhl (✉) · E. Göll
IZT – Institut für Zukunftsstudien und Technologiebewertung, Berlin, Germany
e-mail: a.uhl@izt.de; e.goell@izt.de

H. Ulbrich et al. (eds.), *Internal Crowdsourcing in Companies*, Contributions to Management Science, https://doi.org/10.1007/978-3-030-52881-2_10

The search for a suitable approach and the concept development were mainly based on two sources: Firstly, the current situation in the theoretical and empirical research work on the subject of qualification and competence development was examined, taking into consideration the corresponding preconditions, framework conditions and examples. Secondly, this research was processed together with an empirical part consisting of different collaborative elements that were developed together with the industry partner, the utility company GASAG. These empirical elements included interviews with employees and managers from that company, workshops with their employees and with employees of other companies who are responsible for personnel development and experienced in the topic.

Measures for competence development through internal crowdsourcing do not intend to replace current training measures for employee qualification but are designed to complement them and provide starting points for reviewing the previous qualification efforts and education programmes. The establishment of an internal company network, the transfer of knowledge as well as an exchange between employees from different departments and areas are central elements in the concept which first had to be put in place. The intention was to create an application-oriented concept for qualification, further education, for developing qualification measures and competencies through the use of internal crowdsourcing. By applying the concept, the aim was that employees be given opportunities to discover their individual competencies and interests, to develop them further and to articulate their existing qualifications. Furthermore, the development of digital skills, especially using digital application software, should play a special role in the development of measures and concepts.

Taking into consideration these framework conditions underlying an application-oriented concept for qualification and competence development, three approaches are suggested, each of which involves processing in the digital crowdsourcing application:

1. Crowdvoting for a collaborative assessment and prioritization of competencies
2. A multiple choice test for assessing existing knowledge and expertise as well as knowledge transfer
3. The use of crowdcreation processes for competence development and as a starting point for the promotion of a knowledge transfer and an internal company network

These three approaches, which are further elaborated on in chapter “Managing the Crowd: A Literature Review of Empirical Studies on Internal Crowdsourcing” of this article, intend to enable employees as well as the management to develop a self-reflective learning process close to everyday working conditions and tasks. This article describes a possible application of these three approaches, which together form the basis for the application-oriented concept for qualification, further education and competence development through the use of internal crowdsourcing.

2 Paradigm Shift: From 'Qualification and Professional Development' Towards 'Competences'

A paradigm shift has been observed in the last two decades both in the specialist debates in German-speaking countries and in the human resources development departments of many companies. A shift is taking place from the classical forms of employee qualification to a concentration on the competencies of employees—and with it a shift from classical training and further education activities in companies to competence development approaches. The following section describes how the concept of competence is defined, against background of which the focus has shifted from qualification to competence, and how this shift is interpreted and evaluated in the specialist debate—particularly in German-speaking countries—and used in this research project.

The concept of competence has been discussed in detail in specialist literature since the 1990s and has been further differentiated and specified by Erpenbeck, among others. Accordingly, competence generally encompasses all skills, knowledge and approaches that a person has acquired and also applies in the course of his or her life (Erpenbeck and Heyse 1996, pp. 9–13; Baitsch 1996, pp. 102–112).

In a detailed description of the concept of competence and in addition to earlier remarks, competencies are described as 'self-organization dispositions' (Erpenbeck and Rosenstiel 2007, p. 489), in contrast to other aspects and constructs such as skills, knowledge or qualifications. While these can be tested directly, competencies can only be developed from the realization of existing and developed dispositions, i.e. only retrospectively from the actions or performance of a person. This applies in particular to creative solutions to nonroutine tasks and new challenges. 'Competencies can contain experiences, abilities, will components, knowledge and values—but they cannot be reduced to these, but include them in relationships relevant to disposition and action. Competencies are founded by knowledge, constituted by values, disposed as abilities, consolidated by experience, realized on the basis of will. Self-organized ability to act is the goal of every competence development' (Erpenbeck and Rosenstiel 2007, p. 489, see also Lichtenberger 1999, p. 257). Competencies require different types of knowledge, such as specialist or methodological knowledge. What is decisive, however, is the fact that and how this knowledge is combined with individual experience, skills and behaviour and applied in everyday work.

In its definition of competence, the OECD also emphasizes the interplay of different knowledge stocks, skills, attitudes and behaviours, highlighting communication competence as an example: 'A competence is more than just knowledge and cognitive abilities. It is about the ability to cope with complex demands by using psychosocial resources [...] in a certain context. For example, the ability to communicate is a competence that can be based on a person's language skills, practical IT skills and attitudes towards the communication partner' (OECD 2005, p. 6). From a socio-educational perspective, Veith sheds light on the concept of competence and stresses the need for children, young people and adults to acquire 'intelligent knowledge' in order to deal with complexity and insecurity in various areas of life. In connection with competencies, it also points to the development of individual strategies for action in order to be able to act autonomously (as a 'subject' in the sense of the term) in concrete cases of application. An overview of further definitions and classifications of the concept of competence can be found in Stark (Stark 2009, p. 6).

2.1 The Societal-Cultural Context of Competence

A shift in focus from classical qualification to competence development would seem to make sense taking into consideration the challenges that are emerging within the framework of a complex modern and accelerating working world. The increasing examination of competence in the specialist literature in comparison to qualification also points towards a change of focus from input orientation towards outcome orientation. This lends greater importance to a person's individual abilities, skills and knowledge than to what has been learned in vocational training or studies (Erpenbeck and Rosenstiel 2007, p. XIV; Münchhausen and Schröder 2009, p. 19). As such, classical training and further education programmes are changing to take on new approaches to individual competence development, which presupposes vocational qualification and the corresponding knowledge as a basis.

Through targeted competence development based on individual learning and development processes and different forms of learning in training and work, competencies are to be developed and deepened. According to Borner, this also requires a new learning culture in which the focus of learning shifts "... away from the teachers to the learners, towards individual learning needs, development biographies and constructions of meaning. New learning culture is [...] facilitation-oriented, emancipative-self-organizational and competence-centred and contains and thematizes real social and communicative requirements'" (Borner 2008, p. 6). In a similar way, Sprafke emphasizes the importance of individual employee competencies for the dynamics and adaptability of companies and goes in greater depth into the function of empowerment, i.e. the empowerment of employees to act in a self-determined or self-responsible manner when developing competencies (Sprafke 2016). This also includes designing work processes in such a way that they activate and promote competencies and continuously support independent learning processes. 'Furthermore, the working environment should be designed in such a way that existing competencies are exploited to the full for the benefit of employees and companies. [...] However, individual experiences and interests should be increasingly taken into account in order to make it possible to build on competencies already acquired' (Richter M et al. 2005, p. 8).

In addition to supporters of concentrating competencies in the learning and working world, however, critical voices can also be heard within the specialist debate, where this development is questioned and regarded as problematic. Bolder and Dobischat, for example, point out that with an increasing concentration on the development of competencies, which takes the place of company and institutionalized qualification and further training measures and should also be as self-organized and self-responsible as possible, responsibility is transferred to the individual, as are the monetary costs and the time required (Bolder and Dobischat 2009, p. 7). Veith warns of a 'competence trap', i.e. the danger of burnout and self-exploitation, which can arise from continuous performance optimization and the tireless pursuit of maintaining and improving one's own competitiveness (Veith 2014, p. 63). Lederer, on the other hand, complains in this context that competence orientation tends to be instrumental and that it is too strongly oriented towards market-economy behaviour (Lederer 2014, p. 263).

Erpenbeck and Sauter also deal with this criticism in detail but come to a completely different conclusion. They take up the debate about the pros and cons of a shift from qualifications to competencies and argue in favour of an even stronger orientation towards competence in order to prevent the 'disappearance of knowledge' (Erpenbeck and Sauter 2016, p. 25). The reality has to be acknowledged that companies will increasingly shift their focus to a demand-oriented development of skills, abilities and expertise. This tendency will determine future competence development measures and 'stock learning' will be replaced by 'learning on demand' (Erpenbeck and Sauter 2016, p. 129). The authors classify the competence society as a 'social megatrend' in which competence development is the 'education of the future' (Erpenbeck and Sauter 2016, p. 242). Therefore an 'education revolution' is to be demanded (Erpenbeck and Sauter 2016, p. 250).

2.2 *Capacity Assessment and Competence Development*

The concept of competence thus encompasses different abilities, skills, experiences and areas of knowledge as well as their combination in specific contexts and under specific situational conditions and challenges. Due to the complex interplay of different influencing factors, special requirements are associated with both the recording and the development of competencies.

The acquisition of competencies by employees is the necessary basis to render them able to consciously and creatively participate in a company and to be able to further develop in a targeted manner. Accordingly, the demand for concrete methods and measuring procedures—beyond the more traditional procedures for checking knowledge and certifying qualifications—has increased in recent years. The intention behind using such procedures is to identify competencies that are relevant for a company in order to find suitable personnel, deploy them optimally and organize targeted further training measures (Münk and Reglin 2009, p. 7). Against this background of the increasing importance of a 'learning enterprise' that continuously adapts to dynamic conditions, the relevance of competence recording and competence development based on it also becomes clear (Richter M et al. 2005, p. 15).

Of fundamental importance for any consideration and application of competence assessment is also the situational relevance of competencies. A specific (work) situation determines both the activation of competencies and their degree of development. This means, on the one hand, that the situation sets the framework for which competencies can be regarded as relevant and which are visible and thus ascertainable. To be able to make reliable and comprehensive statements regarding a person's competence, the situation must therefore be taken into account in the development and use of competence assessment procedures. It should be described as precisely as possible in order to place the competence recorded in context and assess it accordingly and to serve as a starting point for further competence development (Kaufhold 2006, p. 24). The actions of a person in a certain situation are therefore ideally the category in which competence is recorded. Conversely, a competence assessment must always be viewed in the concrete and realistic context of action (Kaufhold 2006, p. 96). On the other hand, the connection between situation and competence means that a competence assessment is more meaningful in different situations than in only one situation. For the most far-reaching and meaningful possible recording of existing competencies, it is therefore advisable to conduct a survey of these in different situations (Kaufhold 2006, p. 24).

One way of recording competence as a way of capacity assessment in the context of a particular situation is to use case-oriented tests to achieve a realistic representation of a situation, i.e. a direct reference to the situation. Such tests include possible conditions for action, courses of action and actors involved. The application of such procedures can provide insights into a person's performance, which in turn can be used to draw conclusions about their competencies and their further development (Kaiser 1998, p. 199). In addition to case-oriented tests, surveys can also be used to record or assess competencies as long as the prerequisite for classification in a situational context is fulfilled. Such surveys can be found, for example, in multiple choice tests as part of assessment centres or related assessment procedures (Schuhmacher 2009; Obermann 2018).

In addition to these theoretical assumptions, a number of practical framework conditions must also be taken into account when identifying and developing competencies in a company. In principle, such measures should always be considered in conjunction with the underlying explicit and implicit objectives, the corresponding actors and groups of actors and their interests. This is used to decide which procedure or combination of different procedures is appropriate. The following questions are associated with this: Which general goals are to be achieved with the measurement, i.e. which statement is it trying to make? And: What concrete entrepreneurial goals are associated with competence assessment and development? Individual methods for competence assessment are '... depending on the research objectives and purposes as well as the underlying understanding of competence, each of them differently suitable' (Kaufhold 2006, p. 31). On the basis of a chosen strategy, the objectives are further defined, as well as the period in which a measure is carried out, the method(s) used, the indicators to be collected and the person(s) involved. Further factors for a successful competence assessment include a high degree of "... participation through the involvement of all participants, credibility through inclusion in the overall strategy, transparency through broad information and disclosure of objectives and purposes and the exploitation of results, reliability through compliance with quality criteria in implementation, legitimacy through the exclusion of use for selection, professionalism through appropriate preparation, implementation and follow-up of competence measurement, sustainability through the combination of competence measurement and competence enhancement" (Richter M et al. 2005, p. 14).

2.3 Competence Models, Competence Classes, 'Action Anchors' and Measurement Methods

Proceeding from a concept of competence as described above, which is widely accepted in German-speaking companies, i.e. the concept of competence as the ability to self-organize and creatively act in new tasks and challenges, the competence models are also based on the principle of self-organization and on the ability to '... act in a self-organized manner in open, complex and dynamic situations' (Sauter and Staudt 2016b, p. 14).

The main competence areas provide a starting point from which competencies can be categorized in a competence model—thus providing an estimation of what competencies exist. Some of these are also referred to in the literature as 'partial competencies' (Bunk 1994), 'basic types of competence' (Richter M et al. 2005), 'basic dimensions of competence' (Sauter and Staudt 2016b), 'basic competencies' (Erpenbeck and Sauter 2016), 'competence classes' or 'key competencies' (both Erpenbeck and Rosenstiel 2007).

We will continue to use the term 'competence classes' and initially orient ourselves towards the classification logic of Erpenbeck and Rosenstiel, which is widely recognized in the literature:

1. Personal competencies: The dispositions of a person to act in a reflexive, self-organized manner, i.e. to assess themselves, to develop productive attitudes, values, motives and self-images, to develop their own talents, motivations, performance and proposals and to develop and learn creatively within the framework of work and outside.
2. Activity- and implementation-oriented competencies: The disposition of a person to act actively and holistically in an organized manner and to direct this action towards the implementation of intentions, projects and plans—either for oneself or also for others and with others, in a team, in the company and in the organization. These dispositions thus include the ability to integrate one's own emotions, motivations, abilities and experiences and all other competences—personal, technical-methodical and social-communicative—into one's own desire to perform and to successfully implement actions.
3. Technical-methodical competencies: The disposition of a person to act in a self-organized manner, both mentally and physically, when solving objective problems, i.e. to solve problems creatively with technical and instrumental knowledge, skills and abilities, to classify and to evaluate knowledge in a

meaningful way; this includes the disposition to organize activities, tasks and solutions in a methodically self-organized manner and to develop the methods creatively.
4. Social-communicative competencies: The dispositions to act in a communicative and cooperative way, i.e. to engage creatively with others, to build relationships, to behave in a group and relationship-oriented way and to develop new plans, tasks and goals.

These four competence classes are used in many companies as a basis for competence models, which in turn can be used for competence assessment. As a rule, they are supplemented by additional information such as fields of competence (e.g. 'leadership competence'), the competencies themselves (e.g. 'delegation ability') and so-called anchors for action (e.g. 'delegation of demanding tasks and competencies') and thus further concretized. Sauter and Staudt propose a description of the individual competencies with up to six action anchors, as well as an expression of the individual competencies on a scale from 'hardly available' to 'extraordinarily strong' (partly also 'abundantly available') (Sauter and Staudt 2016b, p. 16).

The approach of the action anchors has a kind of 'bridge function' both in the development of competence models and in the recording or assessment of competencies. The term 'action anchor' (e.g. Erpenbeck and Sauter 2016, p. 23) refers to concrete actions or behaviours through which competencies can be made visible and finally ascertainable. They thus represent a formulation of competencies as behaviours. This principle is also used in the evaluation of answers and solutions within the framework of assessment centres. There, this formulation of competencies is partly called 'behavioural anchor' but pursues the same goal (Obermann 2018, p. 95; Schuhmacher 2009, p. 76). Conversely, action and behaviour anchors also offer good starting points for formulating questions on competence recording in advance in such a way that plausible and comprehensible conclusions can be drawn about competencies (Fig. 1).

There are many different approaches and procedures for competence assessment that are used in practice. There is no such thing as a 'standard procedure' as there is no such thing as the 'best' procedure. Rather, the choice of a certain procedure depends on the objective pursued with the competence recording, the company's orientation and the job profiles of the employees (Richter M et al. 2005, p. 8). As a rule, competence assessment procedures are derived from different aptitude diagnosis procedures or form a hybrid of these. These include biographical methods, activity analysis, interviews, personality procedures, assessment centre procedures, self-description and external description (or combinations of these two approaches), work samples, case studies, test procedures or simulations and scenarios (Sauter and Staudt 2016a, p. 7). In addition to complex and time-consuming methods for recording competencies, there are also simple methods that are specially designed for high user-friendliness. The latter include, for example, multiple choice surveys, which are similar to an assessment centre procedure and are aimed both at the pure query of knowledge and at the acquisition of specialist and methodological competencies.

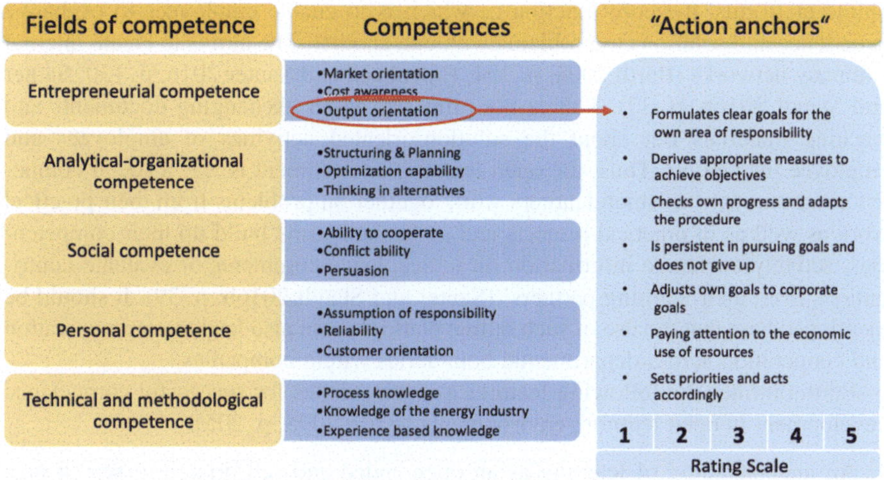

Fig. 1 Competence model with operationalization example (modified from Sauter and Staudt 2016b)

2.4 *Competence Development and a New Learning Culture*

In this study, the term 'competence development' is used synonymously with the terms 'competence promotion' or 'competence extension'. It thus refers to the development or expansion of competencies among the employees of a company. These are competencies which are classified by the management as decisive against the background of the strategic orientation of the company, as well as those which are regarded by the employees as particularly relevant for their own work.

A concept for qualification and further training through internal crowdsourcing with a focus on competence development can include classic elements of knowledge transfer (such as training courses, seminars or workshops) but should go much further. Internal crowdsourcing—and specifically the crowdsourcing application software—should represent a platform to enable, promote and consolidate competence development as a process. In this way, internal crowdsourcing can ideally function as a vehicle for a 'new learning culture': 'The new learning culture attaches great importance to informal learning outside of continuing educational institutions and specified certifications and makes it possible in a systematic manner. It assumes the dominant role of self-organized learning over forms of externally controlled or externally organized learning. [. . .] The new learning culture is thus oriented towards enabling, self-organising and is competence-centred. It is thus directed towards comprehensive competence development—comprehensive competence development requires the new learning culture; both are inseparable' (Erpenbeck and Rosenstiel 2007, p. XX).

Open learning environments are a promising way of developing competencies in the light of a new learning culture of this kind. These are generally provided via online platforms, the core function of which is to enable employees to exchange experience and solutions to problems with one another. The aim is to create internal company networks (Barth 2008, p. 204; Erpenbeck and Sauter 2016, p. 130; Sauter and Staudt 2016b, p. 37). This is not primarily about exchanging documents and teaching materials but about the solution-oriented activities of employees and employee interaction. Thus, the open learning environment is '... a social competence community, in which learners work together on problems from their practical work as well as in practical projects and at the same time build up their competencies, actively exchange information on topics, leave comments or evaluate contributions from their learning partners' (Sauter and Staudt 2016b, p. 39). It should be mentioned here that the use of such online platforms can also lead to communication and cooperation across departmental boundaries within companies.

Barth outlines the following features as prerequisites for successful competence development in open learning environments (Barth 2008, p. 205):

1. An understanding of learning as an open-ended and self-organized search process, which strengthens the individual's initiative and responsibility
2. An ability to solve problems based on participation, empathy and collaboration
3. Dealing with complex and authentic problems from different perspectives

Since employees in most companies are more accustomed to classical learning and further training formats, Erpenbeck and Sauter propose that self-organized forms of learning be introduced gradually. In this way, employees are given the opportunity to gradually get used to this new form of collaborative learning (Erpenbeck and Sauter 2016, p. 130). For example, along the lines of a blended learning concept, a didactically meaningful combination of conventional face-to-face courses and new e-learning formats can take place, in which the staff members drive forward their further training on their own initiative and responsibility, but this is embedded in a framework of given contents and binding learning objectives and possibly accompanied by tutors. Beyond such knowledge transfer, in a further step, competence development could take place within the framework of a social blended learning arrangement in which the employees work collaboratively within an open learning environment on a real or realistic case study. This also seems very advisable or necessary in order to involve employees who are not very technically proficient and to be able to support them in their competence development.

3 Analyses and Work on the Subject of Competence Acquisition and Development

By examining the usability of intranet approaches[1] to improve innovation processes and to develop competencies, the ICU Project is breaking new ground. In addition to the elaboration and derivation of theoretical and conceptual foundations, it was essential to obtain concrete and authentic experiences and assessments on this topic directly from the company of the industry partner. Therefore, several guideline-supported interviews with a coordinated selection of high-level personnel as well as co-workers were accomplished. This is described below.

3.1 Interviews: Perspectives for GASAG Executives

As part of the ICU Project, five guideline interviews were conducted in September 2017 with members of GASAG's senior management. The aim of these interviews was to find out more about the attitudes and perspectives of the interviewees on the topics of qualification, further training and competencies. People from several different divisions of management were interviewed.

The survey was conducted using a structured interview guideline, with the questions being clustered into two areas: on the one hand, questions were asked about previous measures in the company, as well as about personal experiences and the corresponding assessments of these measures. On the other hand, questions tended to be asked about the future, relating to understanding, expectations and possible goals associated with qualification and competence expansion within the framework of ICU.

3.2 Summary of the Core Statements

From the interview results, the following core statements can be made about the needs and expectations for successful qualification, further training and competence expansion:

- The measures for imparting specialist knowledge should be improved.
- A common and interdisciplinary search for solutions to problems and a shared accomplishment of tasks should be promoted.
- More flexible forms of cooperation within the company should be developed and implemented.

[1]In the ICU project, this was a separate Crowdsourcing Platform ('GASAG IDEENlabor').

- It would be desirable to create an overview of the competencies available in the company.
- Digital and entrepreneurial competencies should be strengthened.
- A networking of employees with multipliers from different areas of the company is to be aimed at.
- A more open corporate culture, more flexible work organization and more employee participation are desired in order to facilitate competence development.
- Possible worries by employees about there being increased employee control should be taken seriously and allayed.

The answers from the interviews were taken into consideration when developing the application-oriented concept for qualification and competence development. Some of the core statements (e.g. the implementation of more flexible forms of cooperation, the desire for an internal employee network or the desire to strengthen digital and entrepreneurial competencies) were directly implemented into the development of the third approach 'crowdsolving/crowdcreation' (see section "Synthesis of the Literature").

3.3 *Interviews: Perspectives of GASAG Employees*

Interviews were conducted with employees of GASAG Group companies. These were six interviews with people from different divisions of the company.

Just like the interviews with members of GASAG's management, the employee interviews were also conducted with the aim of finding out more about the perspectives of the discussion partners on the topics of qualification, further training and competencies. As before, this survey was conducted according to a structured interview guideline, whereby the questions were clustered into three areas: questions about experiences with qualification and further training (reference to the past), questions about the perception and understanding of competencies, as well as questions about needs, ideas and expectations regarding qualification, further training and competence expansion within the framework of the ICU Project (reference to the future).

3.4 *Summary of the Core Statements*

From the interview results, the following core statements were identified, which express the needs and expectations of a successful qualification, further training and competence extension:

- Qualification and further training measures should be geared closely to the working reality of the employees and contain practical tasks.

- An exchange among employees should be encouraged, and an internal company network should be established to facilitate knowledge transfer.
- Employees should be able to contribute their own questions, interests and ideas.
- Competencies such as teamwork, independence, flexibility, openness and the ability to change perspectives are seen as particularly important for future work.
- The way digital application programs are handled should be improved.
- Certificates can be a useful incentive to participate in qualification measures.
- It would be interesting to have a cross-functional combination of employees in the sense of competence-based teams for special topics.
- There could be 'mentors' for different topics who could help with the realization of projects.

Like the answers from the previous interviews with GASAG executives, the perspectives of the employees were taken into consideration when developing the approaches for the application-oriented concept for qualification and competence management. This is particularly reflected in the third approach 'crowdsolving/ crowdcreation' (see section "Synthesis of the Literature"), where answers are given to some of the employees' needs and wishes (e.g. fostering exchange among employees, building of competence-based teams for special topics based on a cross-functional combination of employees or a more direct combination of qualification and further training measures based on the employee's working reality).

3.5 *Findings from the IC-Forum*

In order to collect and discuss the findings from current experiments and expertise with the use of internal crowdsourcing in corporations, an 'IC Forum' was conducted in the premises of BMBF. Experts from various corporations, scientists, the labour union and NGOs came together and created an overview of the state of the art of IC in corporations in Germany. The IC Forum was a specific form of workshop which enabled participants to bring in their experiences and to get an overview of the early stages and of the different forms of using IC in corporations. The Forum was structured into three phases of intense communication, starting with presentations of the project. During the central second phase, small groups of two or three experts were selected to discuss several aspects of their activities and their experiences. This kind of setting was well suited to creating an atmosphere of open exchange and debate. It is not common for representatives of corporations and other institutions to talk openly about new inventions and new procedures, especially not when this means talking about problems in their work. A broad variety of the existing strategies and procedures for conceptualising, introducing and managing IC in corporations was reported and discussed and finally presented with all experts in the Forum.

It became obvious that practical experiences focused on employee participation, campaign design and competence development. Communication was identified as a key element of internal crowdsourcing and as a success factor. The possibility of personal exchange creates a pleasant comfort zone on the one hand and provides incentives for participation by regularly presenting rewards for good comments on the other. Employee involvement is also an essential point for promoting identification with the company, and it is also important to make the performance and ideas of employees public so that intrinsic and extrinsic motivation come together. These practical activities have positive effects for competence development, mainly because discussing new ideas and approaches strengthens the ability to self-reflect in each employee individually as well as in whole teams. The Forum stressed the fact that the integration and early involvement of stakeholders (works councils, shop stewards, staff councils) are crucial to create trust and transparency. Such involvement is often an additional element and impulse for competence development.

Corporate culture is another important success factor for establishing and developing IC in corporations. Key figures can help to evaluate how many employees are reached and how actively they participate. If there are few employees, it must be asked why this is so, which ultimately leads to the question of culture. Participating in such activities increases the opportunities for employees to detect and utilize their capabilities and their competencies. At the same time, it can also be a step that encourages them to ask management for more specific qualification opportunities (i.e. specific qualification courses).

For a corporation or team to be more competitive, a cultural change in the sense of new work attitudes and requirements is necessary, and this also includes overcoming classic modes of management thinking in the sense of less control, more self-determination, availability of leeway and flat hierarchies, i.e. ('away from push to pull'). Leadership structures must create trust and joy in work through meaningful and inspiring tasks, and they must enable participation and co-determination. In the sense of efficiency as a success factor, participants also concluded that less control and leadership are not meaningful and possible in all areas and also not for all types of employees. Boundaries and middle ways must be found, and traditional and new leadership strategies must be linked.

The most important factors for successful work processes and ICU are appropriate communication and the early involvement of all employees. Depending on the company and its structure as well as the problem, those instruments and communication channels must be chosen which are able to involve all areas and employees of a company and that allow access for all. Internal crowdsourcing ultimately leads to the democratization of corporate processes and redistributes responsibility within companies. This, however, requires a suitable framework and appropriate support as well as leadership skills that focus on the cost-benefit from an entrepreneurial point of view and can intervene if necessary.

3.6 First Conclusions and Approaches to Qualification, Further Training and Competence Development

The results from the previous interviews provide important insights into the perspectives of the employees and members of GASAG's management surveyed. The statements regarding previous experience with qualification and further training measures as well as expectations and wishes for future qualification, further training and competence development are particularly relevant. They are to be used in addition to the theoretical findings described in chapter "Introduction to 'Internal Crowdsourcing: Theoretical Foundations and Practical Applications'".

From the combination of the elaborated theory and empiricism, framework conditions can now be derived which are to be taken into account in the development of an application-oriented concept. The following aspects are therefore part of the framework conditions:

- An introduction to the topic of competence development through internal crowdsourcing as well as employee participation should take place at an early stage and at low thresholds in order to arouse interest and achieve long-term support.
- Measures for qualification, further training and competence development through internal crowdsourcing should not replace current further training measures but complement them and offer starting points for reviewing the previous further training programme.
- The approaches should be closely geared to the working reality of GASAG employees and aim to create practical added value for day-to-day work.
- The expansion of digital skills, especially the use of digital application software, should play a special role in the design of measures.
- The establishment of an internal company network, a transfer of knowledge and an exchange between employees from different departments and areas are central elements of the application-oriented concept.
- Findings from competence research and open learning environments are also taken into account, as is criticism of a too rigid orientation towards the competence concept.
- Participation in measures for qualification, further training and competence expansion through internal crowdsourcing are basically voluntary and take place anonymously or pseudonymously.
- There is no internal 'employee ranking' on the basis of competence by the company management, but an overview of existing competencies in the company should be facilitated.
- Employees should be given the opportunity to discover their individual competencies and interests, to develop them further and to articulate existing qualification, further training and competence development needs and to make use of appropriate measures.

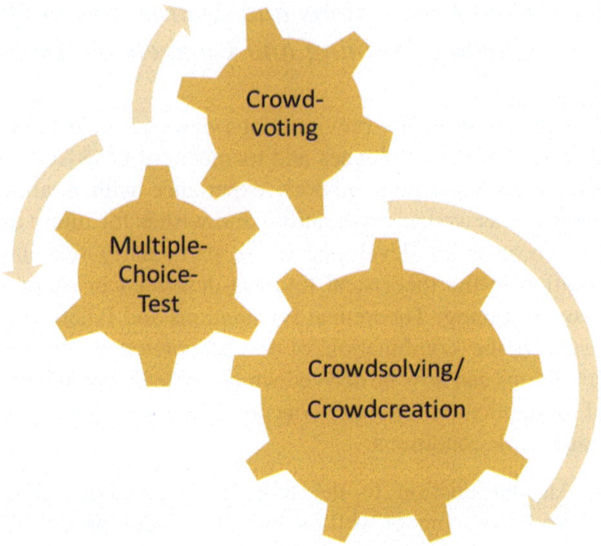

Fig. 2 Approaches for an application-oriented concept for qualification, further education and competence development through internal crowdsourcing

4 A New Concept for Qualification, Further Education and Competence Development through IC: Results and Options for Action

Considering the needs, interests and framework conditions listed in section "The Crowdsourcing Process" for an application-oriented concept for qualification, further training and competence development, three approaches are proposed below, each of which involves working on a task in the digital crowdsourcing application:

1. An employee crowdvoting to collaboratively assess and prioritize competencies
2. A multiple choice test to assess existing knowledge and skills and to impart knowledge
3. The use of crowdsolving/crowdcreation processes for competence development and as a starting point for promoting knowledge transfer and an internal company network

Approaches 1 and 3 are based on general types of crowdsourcing tasks already defined for the project. Approach 2 deviates from these task types but makes use of the technical possibilities already offered by the Crowdee platform provided by the Institute for Software Engineering and Theoretical Computer Science/FG Quality and Usability Lab (QUL) and serves as a useful addition to a company's traditional continuing education programme. The following is a possible application of these three approaches, which together form the basis for the application-oriented concept of qualification, further training and competence development through the use of internal crowdsourcing (Fig. 2).

4.1 Crowdvoting

In order to provide an initial introduction to the topic of competence development through internal crowdsourcing, an anonymous employee survey based on a crowdvoting process is proposed. Participants are given the opportunity to provide their assessment of the relevance of different competencies. A list of competencies is derived from the existing competence model of the company. From this list, the employees can select five competencies which they consider to be particularly relevant for their own work within the next 5 years. It is also possible to make further suggestions, leave comments or ask questions by freely entering text. Subsequently, the results are evaluated by the crowdmanager, and the resulting need for action or qualification is derived and communicated. The employees are given the opportunity to comment on and discuss these results and proposals for action again in the crowd.

This approach serves as an introduction to the area of competence development and internal crowdsourcing and allows employees a low threshold introduction to dealing with a new digital application. Crowdvoting gives employees the opportunity to participate in a common prioritization of competencies and thus to participate in the process of identifying focal competency aspects within the scope of later competency development measures. The results of crowdvoting, i.e. both the ticking behaviour and the comments in the free text input, will be used to check GASAG's current range of qualification and further training courses and, if necessary, to adapt or add to them. Together with the results from the interviews, the crowdvoting results provide indications for aspects which need special consideration in the development of a multiple choice test (see section "Methodology") as well as in the development of the approach for crowdsolving/crowdcreation (see section "Synthesis of the Literature").

They provide information as to which competencies should be given special consideration from the point of view of the participants. Finally, this approach supports transparency and strengthens an open corporate culture and a 'sense of unity'.

The crowdvoting process consists of two phases: one is the survey phase, i.e. the actual 'voting' by the employees. This phase should extend over a period of at least 2 weeks in order to give the employees sufficient time to answer the questions. Afterwards, the crowdmanager evaluates and prepares the results, which is followed by a second participation phase, i.e. the possibility to submit queries, further comments or ideas on the results. This should, in turn, extend over a period of at least 2 weeks. Alternatively, an unlimited commenting function is also conceivable, whereby the crowdmanager should regularly check any comments and, if necessary, answer and use them (Fig. 3).

A further clarification of the procedure also depends on the specific structures in the organization in which the IC campaign is to be carried out. These include questions such as the time period in which the survey is to take place, how comprehensively the results are to be processed, on which further communication

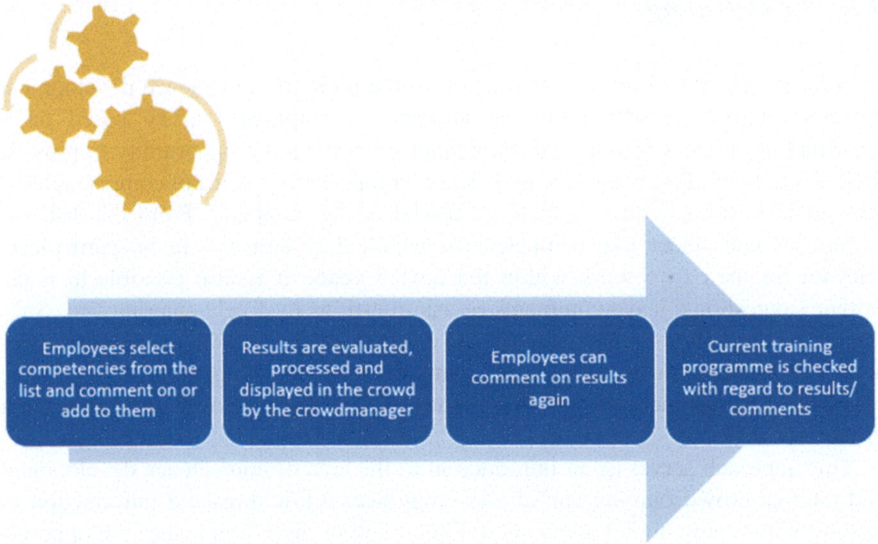

Fig. 3 Crowdvoting process on the topic of 'competence development'

channels (i.e. beyond the crowdsourcing platform) the results are to be communicated, how crowd management is to be organized and which person(s) is/are responsible for it, etc. In what timeframe is the IC campaign is to be carried out? A possible variant can be illustrated on the basis of a first implementation of such a crowdvoting with the focus on the topic 'competencies' by the industry partner GASAG within the framework of the ICU Project.

4.2 *Multiple Choice Test*

This approach gives employees the opportunity to take part in a standardized multiple choice test via the crowdsourcing platform. On the one hand, employees' basic knowledge on a previously defined topic is tested, on the other hand decisions concerning alternatives for action in certain work situations weighed up, while the way that solutions are selected and justified is evaluated. In preparation for the multiple choice test, in-depth information material can be made available via online links and compiled according to the focus of the subject. Following participation, the employees receive a certificate which proves their knowledge and skills in the respective field (Fig. 4).

A multiple choice test includes questions on how to use digital application software, on facts and areas of work in the respective industry (here: energy industry) or on other topics relevant to the majority of employees. With the answer to the last question in the test, the participants receive a test evaluation and the option of

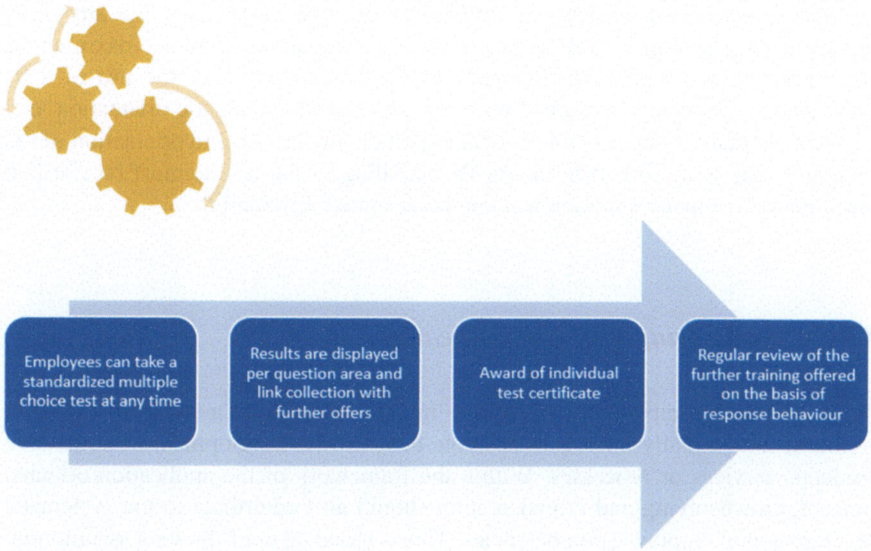

Fig. 4 Process for a multiple choice test

receiving a certificate, which identifies them as one of four different role types (high potentials, team workers, experts and consultants). The evaluation of the individual response behaviour shows which questions were answered correctly, which were answered incorrectly or incompletely, and contains links via which employees can directly access teaching materials on the relevant topics.

Irrespective of the respective content, a multiple choice test like this always aims to assess and expand specialist knowledge as well as technical and methodological skills. Participation in the survey is an independent further training measure, which is certified by awarding a certificate. Employees can take the initiative to participate in the survey at any time and thus check their own development and progress in the respective subject areas. If they identify a need for further development, they can contact their superiors and discuss opportunities for further training. Awarding a certificate offers direct and visible added value for employees.

In addition, the collective response behaviour provides conclusions on the strengths, potentials or needs of the workforce, which can be used to regularly review the company's further training programme and adjust it if necessary. It is also conceivable that 'high performers' in this test be networked with employees who have personally identified a need for further training. Such persons could provide support and help with questions and problems.

The effort required to develop such an approach is manageable, and the effort required on the part of the company is also limited, since the evaluation of the multiple choice test is largely automated after implementation. Time and effort are required above all when designing the survey, when providing follow-up support in the event of a possible need for further training and (if desired) when developing of appropriate teaching materials. All employees are free to participate at any time. However, it is also conceivable, for example, to limit participation to a maximum of one employee per month. With regard to the amount of time, the use of self-developed or externally developed teaching materials, the thematic orientation, etc. different alternatives are possible depending on the preference and orientation of the company. The issue of certificates or the handling of the results must be clarified based on the company situation and can be designed differently.

4.3 Crowdsolving and Crowdcreation

The voluntary participation of employees in the processing of a task over a defined period of time initially intends to promote the (further) development of innovative products, services or processes. Within the framework of the application-oriented concept, crowdsolving and crowdcreation should also contribute to the systematic development of employee competencies. This is based on our following assumption:

> *Crowdsolving and crowdcreation processes provide information on existing competencies of the participating employees as well as on possible competence requirements on the part of the company.*

A case study would require either participation in the solution of a problem (crowdsolving) or the development of ideas for an innovation (crowdcreation). In order to create access to the area of competence development via the processing process, different competencies are to be defined which are necessary for the successful processing of the case study. Thus, it is possible to identify employees with particularly pronounced competencies, as long as they are interested and willing to take part.

Just like the other two approaches, voting and multiple choice, this approach also offers points of reference for reviewing current continuing education activities within the corporation and supplementing them with explicit learning activities. Every employee has the opportunity to discuss individual qualification options with their superiors. The decisive question now, however, is how exactly or on what basis (further) development of employee competencies can take place and what conditions must be met. The key to this lies in networking the employees, transferring know-how and, above all, in cross-departmental cooperation in heterogeneous project teams assembled according to specific characteristics. These areas should therefore be at the centre of the competence development strategy (Fig. 5).

Against this background, competence development can be realized on at least two levels: on the one hand, on the digital level, by playing solution paths back into the crowd and incorporating several feedback loops in order to initiate a process of dialogue or reflection concerning joint work. In addition, the employees gain a better systemic understanding of the company and can position themselves more consciously in it. On the other hand, on the face-to-face level, the crowdsolving/crowdcreation tasks are further processed in 'real' and cross-departmental project

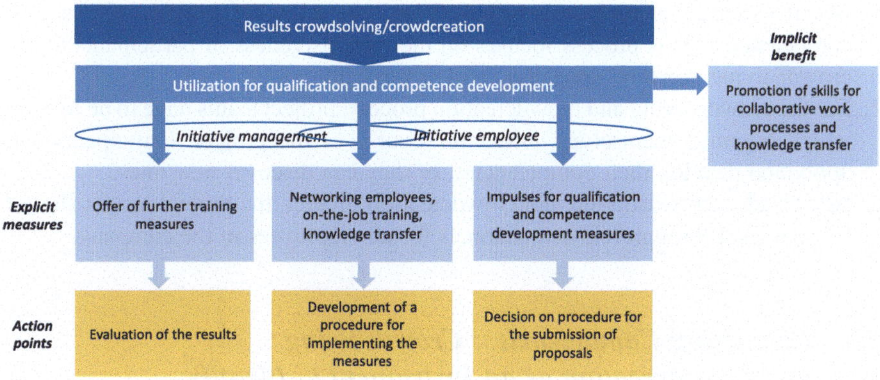

Fig. 5 Process for crowdsolving/crowdcreation and competence development

teams. As explained in section "GASAG Group", a promising further development of competencies should take place 'on the job', i.e. under real working conditions—not least because of the importance of the meaningfulness of such an activity. In such a context, not only the mere application of (specialist) knowledge is required but rather a combination of this knowledge with personal experience, skills and abilities and further individual characteristics with regard to a specific question or problem.

This approach is similar to the action learning approach, in which employees learn a realistic task by participating in a solution to be worked out together and reflect on this work and learning process at the same time (Revans 2012). Against the background of a desired competence development, an expansion of the joint work on concrete questions in project teams therefore appears to be a format that makes particular sense.

The topics that are dealt with in the context of crowdsolving and crowdcreation serve as a content resource for the project teams, where they can be dealt with more intensively and systematically, using and continuously developing the competencies of individual team members. The response and dialogue behaviour of the participants in crowdsolving and crowdcreation tasks can be used to obtain information on the development of competencies. This information can in turn help when putting together the team to further process the task.

In order to promote an internal transfer of knowledge within the company and to stimulate possible impulses and provide employees with food for thought outside of the project teams and outside of the participants in the crowd tasks, the results of the project work should again be made available to all employees of the company in an appropriate form. Systematically documenting the work performed in the project teams and—with the consent of the participants—providing an overview of the participating team members and their roles also provides a valuable resource for the work of strategic personnel development.

In summary, this strategy results in a three-step process to enable qualification and competence development through crowdsolving/crowdcreation:

1. In a first step, a searching process has to be conducted to gather evidence of strong competencies. This process focuses on the responsiveness of participants in the crowdsolving and crowdcreation tasks or projects.
2. For the crowdsolving and crowdcreation process, project teams have to be formed which organize themselves during the course of the project. Participants can apply and develop their competencies, or they can discover new ones.
3. After such a crowdsolving and crowdcreation project, the project results should be published through relevant channels for all employees in the company.

4.4 Identifying Competencies: Crowdsolving and Crowdcreation as an Instrument to Identify Competencies

In terms of competence theory, crowdsolving and crowdcreation tasks are also characterized by the fact that they do not simply involve querying knowledge but rather initiate a discussion and work process for a real or realistic task. The solution of such a task profits from the cooperation of the participants and the mutual picking up on and discussing of discussion contributions. Within the spectrum of conceivable crowd tasks, crowdsolving and crowdcreation processes are therefore particularly suitable when searching for hints pointing towards competencies and their characteristics.

The first step will therefore be to gain information on the development of certain competencies based on the participants' response behaviour. This is because it is generally difficult to make unambiguous statements about the undoubted development of certain competencies. Nevertheless, the response and solution behaviour of the participants allows conclusions to be drawn as to which of the competencies sought could be strongly developed or which of the participants have promising potential to develop the competencies sought. Such assessments tend to be subjective in nature but can be limited by taking into account previously defined criteria.

With every crowdsolving/crowdcreation task, the first question that arises is: Which competencies are required to successfully complete this task? Therefore, the competencies that appear necessary to solve a task should be defined in advance. This usually includes competencies or areas of competence that are generally helpful in dialogue-oriented processes, such as collaborative and communicative competence or the ability to put oneself in other perspectives. In addition, competencies should be defined that are necessary for solving this specific task, such as technical or methodological competencies for a specific manufacturing process, process-oriented competencies for specific work processes or entrepreneurial competencies.

In order to gain suitable clues for an assessment of when or under what conditions a competence could be particularly pronounced, criteria must be formulated that can be applied when searching for hints pointing towards the existence of the previously defined competencies. For this purpose, the concept of action anchors (also known as 'behaviour anchors') is used, which is described by Erpenbeck and Sauter,

Obermann and others (see section "GASAG Group"). Such action anchors describe certain perceptible behaviour patterns, which in turn allow conclusions to be drawn about competencies. For example, for the competence 'result orientation', action-related statements such as 'sets own priorities and acts accordingly' or 'derives suitable measures for own goals' can be derived. For the assessment of the competence 'ability to work in a team', on the other hand, statements such as 'also works together with others in competitive situations and helps them' or 'balances differences in the group and contributes to a common solution' help. Such statements are formulated for each of the competencies that were previously identified as necessary for solving the respective task.

After a crowdsolving/crowdcreation campaign has been completed and all participants have submitted their contributions and participated in the work process, the response and solution behaviour of the participants can be evaluated on the basis of the assessments of personnel managers with the help of the action anchors. The contributions are examined in terms of both content and interaction with other participants according to their respective competence. At Sauter and Staudt, the assessment of competencies with regard to the anchors for action is carried out on a scale with values from 1 to 5, whereby 1 is awarded for very weakly developed and 5 for very strongly developed competencies (Sauter and Staudt 2016b, p. 16).

Against the background of the debate about an internal 'employee ranking' and with regard to the statements from the interviews with members of GASAG's management and the negotiated group works agreement, however, an assessment of competence levels below an average can be regarded as critical. Such an individual assessment could, despite the use of pseudonyms, trigger concerns among employees. Such an individual assessment could, despite the use of pseudonyms, raise concerns/fear among employees and ultimately lead to little or no participation in crowdsolving and crowdcreation tasks. In any case, the main aim of this approach is to identify those employees who have a distinct need in specific areas in order to specifically support them in developing their competencies. In order to prevent corresponding concerns about negative evaluations, an evaluation should only be carried out (and also documented) by those participants who are suspected of possessing a strong development of the competencies in question or who are prepared to disclose and promote these.

However, the employee contributions do not only provide information on the characteristics of possible competencies. They also offer the opportunity for further insights, especially into the areas of interest and the aptitudes of employees for certain topics and questions. Such findings are valuable both for the personnel managers and for the employees themselves, who may not have had the opportunity before to deal with such topics and questions. The presumed level to which certain competencies are developed is therefore only one indicator to be thought about when considering employees for the later composition of project team, for example. Interest, understanding and commitment can also be important conditions for this.

A possible alternative to take even greater account of the commitment and interest of the employees when putting together the team, and at the same time to further reduce concerns about an internal employee ranking, is to open an internal application procedure. After the crowd process, the participating employees are given the opportunity to apply for participation in a topic-specific project team. Only after the application has been received would the individual response behaviour be evaluated and, for example, an interview with the project team leader offered. If there is mutual agreement on the development potential and possible development goals with regard to competencies, the candidate can be included in a pool for a project team to be formed at a later date.

Irrespective of the concrete design of the process, the ultimate goal of this first step is to consider those employees who are assumed to have strongly developed the competencies in question and those who show a particular aptitude and commitment in the context of crowdsolving and crowdcreation for inclusion in a respective employee pool. In the next step, the project teams can be put together from this pool after consulting the HR managers, crowd managers and topic experts.

4.5 *Developing Competencies: Formation of Topic- and Project-Specific Teams*

In a next step, project teams can be formed that systematically deal with the previously set crowdsolving/crowdcreation task over a certain period of time. Regular cooperation in such teams promotes an exchange of knowledge and enables employees to use and develop their skills in a targeted manner. Teamwork is accompanied by the use of teaching materials and appropriate further training measures for the team members. Joint teamwork thus represents a form of learning integrated into the process, with knowledge acquisition and competence development taking place on the basis of concrete work processes.

In order to put together a team that has both the potential to work efficiently on the respective topic or concrete task and sufficient flexibility to organize itself to a large extent, the size of the team should be manageable and range from a minimum of five to a maximum of ten members. The team is composed of employees who can, if possible, be assigned to the following four types, among others: high potentials, team workers, experts and consultants. While members of the first two categories are identified from the group of participants in crowdsolving and crowdcreation tasks, members of the last two categories can also be those who have not yet participated in internal crowdsourcing. The four role types in work teams can be described as follows:

1. High potentials: Participants in the crowdsourcing task whose technical or methodological competence level was assessed as strong to very strong, i.e. who showed a special understanding of the task at hand and made high-quality and solution-oriented contributions.
2. Team workers: Participants of the crowd task whose social competence level was assessed as strong to very strong, who, e.g. respond in a special way to the

contributions of others and develop them further, who have an integrative and constructive effect or who have special communicative strengths.

3. Experts: Employees who, due to their work in the company, have special specialist skills and whose department is usually responsible for the content of the corresponding task. The team's project leader should also be appointed from this group, and this person should at the same time serve as a coach or mentor. In addition to a balanced distribution of work and adherence to project goals, the project management must also ensure smooth communication, motivation and the involvement of all team members.
4. Consultant: Employees who have many years of professional experience and are particularly familiar with certain processes and earlier project phases but who have not yet participated in the ICU process.

Such a heterogeneous team composition, in which the individual team members contribute their respective strengths, promises great solution potential with regard to both the development of innovative solution approaches and the further development of employee competencies. All team members should take on active roles in the team and be responsible for handling concrete tasks. The combination of experts, crowdworkers and consultants already results in different roles within the team. The distribution of tasks can result in an organic process during the first meetings, but it is ultimately the responsibility of the project management.

In addition to the question of which participants from the crowdsolving/crowdcreation process and which other employees from the company should be integrated into a team, there are a number of other questions that should be clarified during the project planning phase. These include:

- What is the aim of the project, both in terms of the task to be completed and in terms of the development of employee skills?
- How long is the project expected to last?
- Which time capacities must be planned for the project team and can be realized with the selected project members?
- Which departments are affected by the composition of the team and with which areas of responsibility must this be clarified?
- Are there tasks in the project that cannot be solved by the team but have to be solved externally?
- How often should (or can) there be joint project meetings considering everyday tasks?
- What is the relationship between individual team members?
- How should the project work and the results achieved be documented, made accessible or published in the company?

The answers to such and similar questions depend to a great extent on the structures and organizational culture in the respective company. A general clarification of these questions—and thus the creation of appropriate framework conditions—is always necessary in order to facilitate smooth, constructive and trusting cooperation. However, the work in the project team should not be 'overregulated' under any circumstances. Particularly against the background of the desired competence development and the creative and intellectual development, a high degree of organizational freedom is indispensable.

In this context, the idea of a self-organising team, as described by Klein (2010), seems to provide an interesting reference. Such teams independently plan, review and improve their work processes, set their own goals and create their own work plans. They also assess their performance in group discussions, coordinate cooperation with other departments and take care of the professional training of their members. The principle of a self-organising team would seem to make sense in this context of innovation and competence development—and under the premise that the framework conditions mentioned above are created.

4.6 Disseminate Knowledge: Documentation of the Project Work and Internal Publication of the Results

The results achieved in the project teams are not only relevant for company management. The knowledge produced can also offer exciting insights into new areas for the other employees of the company or provide an impulse for new ideas—or at best even contain important information for one's own work. In addition, it makes sense to make the team members and their tasks known to other employees as well, since they can develop into 'experts' for the respective topic and serve as possible contact persons—and thus gain recognition. Last but not least, the transparency lived in the company also suggests that every employee in the company should have the opportunity to access the results and be given an overview of the team members involved. This should also improve the corporate culture.

In order to enable the results to be disseminated within the company, various questions have to be clarified. First of all, project work has to be documented: Who should take the minutes? What exactly should be documented in what frequency and with what level of detail? Which system and which medium should be used? Answers to these questions depend on the respective project as well as on the documentation methods normally used in the company. Decisions between alternatives should be made by the team leader.

The central questions are 'How' and 'Where': How should the results be prepared so that they are informative, useful and understandable for all employees? And where, i.e. on which platform or using which medium, should the results be published? A clear text in three sections is recommended for the type of preparation. First, the project background, the relevance for the company, and the respective topic should be explained as well as the question and the underlying crowdsolving or crowdcreation task. Then the results (possibly supplemented by visualizations) should be summarized, and finally a concise explanation should be given of what the results are used for in the company and what the next steps will be. In addition to

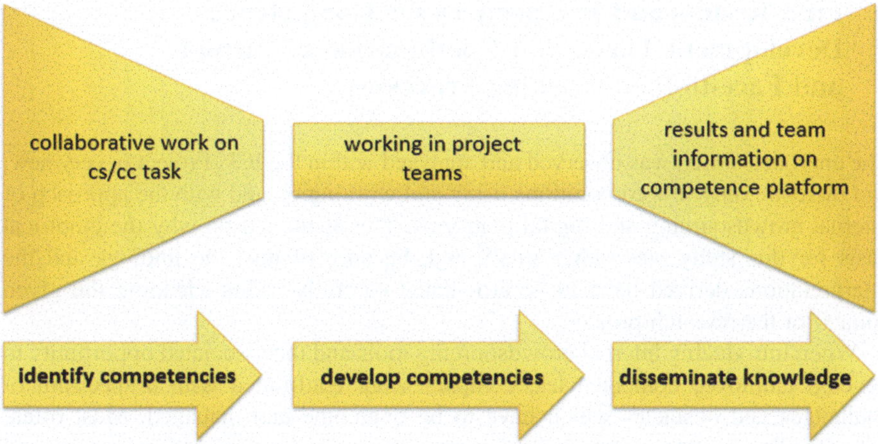

Fig. 6 Process approach to competence development through internal crowdsourcing

a clear presentation of results, it is also important to clearly and comprehensibly embed the use of results in the company context.

An advanced and more complex variant would be to develop a knowledge and competence platform that would also access the intranet and use it as a framework architecture but with its own system and extended functions. In addition to a more detailed presentation of project work, the platform could also include a glossary explaining key terms and an overview of employees who have worked in project teams or are designated as contact persons for specific topics. In addition, it is possible to tag contributions (= keywords) and link terms. Such a knowledge and competence platform would thus correspond in its structure and logic to a company wiki, i.e. an open knowledge environment that could be continually expanded over time and whose benefits would increase with increasing input. However, the detailed conception, development and continuous maintenance of such a platform require extensive time capacities and a corresponding budget.

In addition, other internal communication channels should also be used to draw attention to the project results or their publication or significant progress, especially to employees who have not (yet) participated in crowd activities. These include articles in a newsletter, in the company magazine or information via the internal email distribution list (Fig. 6).

5 First Results and Perspectives for Competence Development Through a Combination of Virtual and Face-to-face Working Processes

The approach which was observed and analysed within the ICU Project is very new, and there are only few corporations using and working on and with the approach of internal crowdsourcing and digital platforms. This is the reason why the empirical basis for this study was rather small, and, because of this, the findings and the interpretations derived have to be articulated carefully, acknowledging the given context of the research project.

When introducing internal crowdsourcing tools and the associated opportunity to develop employee competencies, companies are confronted with a spectrum of challenges and obstacles which have to be overcome and managed. Most often, long-standing routines, communication procedures, decision-making processes and working patterns have to be changed and transformed.

One basic challenge is related to a kind of contradiction. When establishing internal crowdsourcing tools and grasping the associated opportunity to develop employee competencies, companies and specifically their management find themselves in an arena of conflict between control and democratization, hierarchy and participation, top-down culture and motivated-active employees. Therefore, the early involvement of shop stewards and employee representatives (works council, staff council) is extremely important. Such innovations have to be institutionalized and defined in the contracts.

In order to achieve effective competence development, (virtual) work using digital collaboration tools should be combined with face-to-face teamwork process. This is to some extent relevant because some personnel may not be trained or equipped to handle and manage the intranet and other platforms. Digital collaboration must also be embedded in the already existing and established organizational structures of the company in order to find resonance and effective utilization by a majority of employees.

The organization of certain work processes in self-organising project teams requires a high degree of self-discipline from the employees and a fundamental openness of the management towards flexible work structures as well as regarding roles, hierarchies and responsibilities. This should be supported by the management adequately, for instance, though routine staff meetings or staff appraisals. This is an additional contribution towards competence development.

The use of internal crowdsourcing and digital collaboration tools for competence development is particularly suitable for larger companies with a large number of employees. There is, in particular, potential to reveal and consequently promote previously hidden competencies of employees if this is in their own interest and if they ask for such courses or training.

The specific process approach to competence development through internal crowdsourcing enables both the promotion of employee competencies on an individual level and an internal networking of employees and knowledge transfer on a broad collective level. Taking all this together can lead to an advanced and improved corporate culture and more job satisfaction—and to a better overall performance of the corporation.

Based on the tentative impressions and analysis of the examples of digital collaboration in corporations, it can be expected that such approaches will be used much more often in the near future, especially in corporations with young and open-minded employees and management. However, the experience described and discussed here shows that certain lessons learned should be taken to heart in order to bypass obstacles and conflicts. Additional research in this field is necessary to help understand and reflect on the rapid introduction of digital collaboration approaches in corporations and other institutions for the competence development of employees, which is much more necessary than it already has been in the past.

References

Baitsch C (1996) Kompetenz von Individuen, Gruppen und Organisationen. Psychologische Überlegungen zu einem Analyse- und Bewertungskonzept. In: Denisow K, Fricke W, Stieler-Lorenz B (eds) Partizipation und Produktivität. Zu einigen kulturellen Aspekten der Ökonomie. Friedrich Ebert Stiftung, Bonn, pp 102–112

Barth M (2008) Das Lernen mit neuen Medien als Ansatz zur Vermittlung von Gestaltungskompetenz. In: Bormann I, de Haan G (eds) Kompetenzen der Bildung für nachhaltige Entwicklung Operationalisierung, Messung, Rahmenbedingungen, Befunde. VS Verlag für Sozialwissenschaften, Wiesbaden, pp 199–213

Bolder A, Dobischat R (2009) Objekt oder Subjekt von Wissensmanagement? Was bringt uns die Publizierung der 'heimlichen' Qualifikationen? In: Bolder A, Dobischat R (eds) Eigen-Sinn und Widerstand. Kritische Beiträge zum Kompetenzentwicklungsdiskurs. Springer, Wiesbaden, pp 7–18

Borner J (2008) Die Entwicklung und Strukturierung des Kompetenzbegriffes – Von der Qualifikation zur Kompetenz. Kolleg für Management und Gestaltung nachhaltiger Entwicklung, Berlin, pp 1–8

Bunk G (1994) Kompetenzvermittlung in der beruflichen Aus- und Weiterbildung in Deutschland. In: Europäische Zeitschrift für Berufsbildung, vol 1. Begriff und Fakten, Kompetenzen, pp 9–15

Erpenbeck J, Heyse V (1996) Berufliche Weiterbildung und berufliche Kompetenzentwicklung. In: Arbeitsgemeinschaft Qualifikation-Entwicklung-Management (ed) Kompetenzentwicklung 96: Strukturwandel und Trends in der betrieblichen Weiterbildung. Waxmann, Münster, pp 15–152

Erpenbeck J, Rosenstiel v L (2007) Handbuch Kompetenzmessung. Schäffer- Poeschel, Stuttgart

Erpenbeck J, Sauter W (2016) Stoppt die Kompetenzkatastrophe! Wege in eine neue Bildungswelt. Springer, Berlin

Kaiser A (1998) Carte de competence: Wie lassen sich Kompetenzen feststellen? In GdWZ 5:199–201

Kaufhold M (2006) Kompetenz und Kompetenzerfassung. Analyse und Beurteilung von Verfahren der Kompetenzerfassung. VS Verlag, Wiesbaden

Klein A (2010) Projektmanagement für Kulturmanager. Springer, Wiesbaden

Lederer B (2014) Kompetenz oder Bildung. Eine Analyse jüngerer Konnotationsverschiebungen des Bildungsbegriffs und Plädoyer für eine Rück- und Neubesinnung auf ein transinstrumentelles Bildungsverständnis. IUP, Innsbruck

Lichtenberger Y (1999) Von der Qualifikation zur Kompetenz. Die Herausforderungen der Arbeitsorganisation in Frankreich. In: Arbeitsgemeinschaft Qualifikations-Entwicklungs-

Management (ed) Kompetenzentwicklung. Aspekte einer neuen Lernkultur. Argumente, Erfahrungen, Konsequenzen. Waxmann, Münster, pp 275–307

Münchhausen G, Schröder U (2009) Erfassung von informell erworbenen Kompetenzen. Impulse aus europäischen Projekten nutzen. Berufsbildung in Wissenschaft und Praxis (BWP) 6:19–23

Münk D, Reglin T (2009) Theorie und Praxis der Kompetenzfeststellung im Betrieb – Status quo und Entwicklungsbedarf. In: Münk D, Reglin T (eds) Theorie und Praxis der Kompetenzfeststellung im Betrieb – Status quo und Entwicklungsbedarf. Schriften zur Berufsbildungsforschung der Arbeitsgemeinschaft Berufsbildungsforschungsnetz. BIBB, Bonn, pp 5–15

Obermann C (2018) Assessment Center. Entwicklung, Durchführung, Trends. Mit neuen originalen AC-Übungen. Springer Gabler, Wiesbaden

Revans R (2012) ABC of action learning. Überarbeitete Neuauflage. Gower, Farnham

Richter M, et al (2005) Kompetenzermittlung bei Führungskräften: eine praktische Anleitung zur Messung der beruflichen Handlungskompetenz. LASA-Praxishilfe Nr. 14, Landesagentur für Struktur und Arbeit Brandenburg, LASA

Sauter W, Staudt F-P (2016a) Kompetenzmessung in der Praxis Mitarbeiterpotenziale erfassen und analysieren. Springer Gabler, Wiesbaden

Sauter W, Staudt F-P (2016b) Strategisches Kompetenzmanagement 2.0. Potenziale nutzen – Performance steigern. Springer Gabler, Wiesbaden

Schuhmacher F (2009) Mythos Assessment Center. Risikomanagement bei Personalentscheidungen und Leitfaden zur Anwendung. Springer Gabler, Wiesbaden

Sprafke N (2016) Kompetente Mitarbeiter und wandlungsfähige Organisationen. Zum Zusammenhang von Dynamic Capabilities, individueller Kompetenz und Empowerment. Springer Gabler, Wiesbaden

Stark G (2009) Kompetenzermittlung im Rahmen der betrieblichen Weiterbildung. Expertise im Auftrag des zbw Zentrum für betriebliches Weiterbildungsmanagement, Nürnberg

Veith H (2014) Kompetenz – Anmerkungen zu einem bildungstheoretischen Paradigmenwechsel. In: Faas S et al (eds) Kompetenz, Performanz, soziale Teilhabe. Sozialpädagogische Perspektiven auf ein bildungstheoretisches Konstrukt. Springer, Wiesbaden, pp 51–65

André Uhl is a futurologist and researcher at the IZT (Institute for Future Studies and Technology Assessment). His work focuses on theories and methods of futurology and technology assessment, the combination of qualitative and quantitative research, discourse and media analyses and the emergence and development of visions of the future. He has worked on research projects for the European Commission, the Federal Ministry of Education and Research and the German Bundestag.

Dr. Edgar Göll is a social scientist and has been working at the IZT (Institute for Future Studies and Technology Assessment) since 1995, now head of research of the cluster 'Future Studies and Participation'. Main areas of work: futures studies, sustainable development, governance and participation. He is a lecturer in the master's degree course 'futures studies' at the Institut Futur at the Free University of Berlin and board member of the supranational network 'Zukunftsforschung'.

Power to the Network: The Concept of Social Business and Its Relevance for IC

Christian Zinke-Wehlmann, Julia Friedrich, and Vanita Römer

Abstract The concept of IC puts the employee, in its potential role as crowdsource, Campaign Owner or initiator into focus. This reflects the emancipatory and participatory principle that goes hand in hand with the concept of Social Business. The basic idea of Social Business is not to link the business success of a company exclusively to its management capabilities or the business plan, but to understand and value the individual stakeholder as part of a successful enterprise network. For Social Business, value is not exclusively understood as business value; rather, the perspective is expanded to include social added value, in the sense that the value of the work for the employee, society or the environment is considered as an indirect corporate goal. Thus, Social Business is defined as a framework or strategy that uses digital social networks (enterprise social networks) with the primary goal of generating social, ecological and economic benefits. This article introduces the Social Business reference model, which supports the adoption and implementation of the outlined strategy and contrasts it to the ICU Model in order to identify the strengths as well as weaknesses of both models.

Keywords Social Business · Enterprise social network · Collaboration · Business transformation · Internal crowdsourcing

1 Introduction

"Ultimately everything that can be social will be social" (Hinchcliffe and Kim 2012, p. 55). This quote from Dion Hinchcliffe and Peter Kim illustrates a trend that is becoming obvious in almost all facets of businesses. The rise of Web 2.0 transformed the World Wide Web from a static information source into an interactive space. Web 2.0 brought "new technologies (like web services, AJAX, RSS,

C. Zinke-Wehlmann (✉) · J. Friedrich · V. Römer
Institut für Angewandte Informatik e. V., Leipzig, Germany
e-mail: zinke@infai.org; friedrich@infai.org; vanita.roemer@infai.org

H. Ulbrich et al. (eds.), *Internal Crowdsourcing in Companies*, Contributions to Management Science, https://doi.org/10.1007/978-3-030-52881-2_11

mashups), new types of applications (i.e. social software, like wikis, blogs, social networking), new patterns of interaction, and new principles of organisation (e.g. participation, wisdom of crowds) as well as new business models (such as long tail, webtop, etc.)" (Fuchs-Kittowski et al. 2009, p. 372). Today, social networks and social media platforms such as Facebook, Instagram, wikis and blogs are ubiquitous. They are used in daily communication and provide for an instant exchange of information. Their impact on opinion-forming and communication processes has been progressively growing in the last decade. According to the Global Digital Report, 45% of the worldwide population actively uses social media in their daily lives (We are social and Hootsuite 2019). The rapid development of innovative digital solutions has sustainably transformed how people communicate and exchange knowledge. With the rise of social media, the perception of social presence is determined by the degree of immediacy (Kaplan and Haenlein 2010). This popularity also has a clear effect on the expectations of employees regarding the processes at their workplace (Cook 2017, p. 15). Within the context of business communication, both in B2C and B2B, latencies are more and more perceived as unnecessary and unpleasant delays. This means that organizations are expected to respond quickly in order to satisfy their customers' needs. Likewise, the fast and permanent availability of information in the sense of knowledge management is of high relevance for employees.

The described changes have created a demand for organizational requirements (Haiba et al. 2014, p. 111; Shirish et al. 2016, p. 1121) and a novel understanding of work approaches, e.g., for flexibility and digital skills. Innovative approaches like the results-only work environment (ROWE) approach (Kelly and Moen 2007, p. 496), the New Work movement (Hackl et al. 2017) or enterprise gamification practices (Rauch 2013) are tackling these demands and stand in contrast to the traditional culture of doing business and work. Accordingly, it is not exaggerated to say that Web 2.0 has revolutionized the world of business. Internal Crowdsourcing (IC), as a community (crowd)-driven process that promotes the creation of improved products and processes, is only one example for new collaboration processes within companies that are supported by social technologies like enterprise social networks (Turban et al. 2011, pp. 205) and illustrate their transformative power. Moreover, enterprise social networks (ESN) support:

- Communication (e.g. information dissemination or feedback or support)
- Management (e.g. recruitment or agile team building)
- Innovation (e.g. crowdsourcing, bulletin boards or social bots as problem-solving services)
- Knowledge management (e.g. acquisition of specialist knowledge, knowledge exchange or crowdstorming)
- Training and learning (e.g. training exercises or technical support)
- Democratization of work (e.g. open discussion or empowerment of employees)
- Collaboration (e.g. parallel editing of documents and project plans)

The concept of Social Business basically describes the idea of implementing social technology within the enterprise to pursue a holistic business strategy for

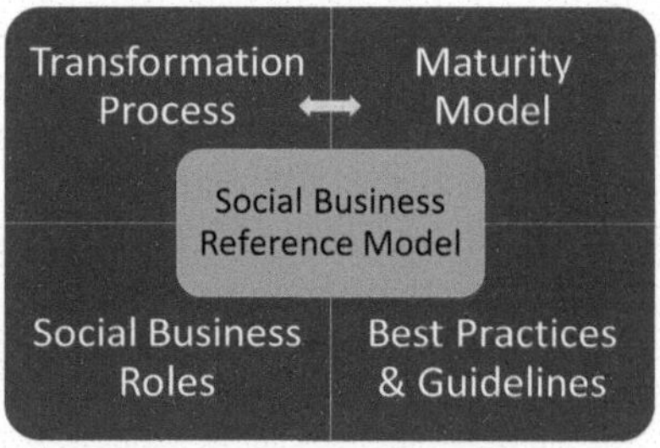

Fig. 1 The Social Business reference model

optimization with the aim of creating value from using network effects and removing "unnecessary boundaries between experts inside the company and experts in the marketplace" (Enache and Sbughea 2015, p. 11). In a broader sense, Social Business is a framework or strategy that is applied with the primary goal to generate a social, ecological and economic benefit.

To develop a broader scientific foundations and demonstrate the benefits of Social Business, the research project SB:Digital aims at providing support to companies that strive to proactively design internal corporate processes and networks by using social technology. The developed framework, which we refer to as the Social Business reference model (Fig. 1), includes a process model that guides enterprises through the transformation process, a maturity model that allows an analysis of a company's status quo in regard to Social Business, a Social Business role model as well as a collection of best practices. Within this paper, this framework will be compared to the presented ICU Process and role model in chapter "Systematization Approach for the Development and Description of an Internal Crowdsourcing System" to enhance the knowledge about the general question concerning how digital social applications can be applied successfully.

The guiding research questions of this paper are:

- How can processes and roles of IC be interpreted in the context of Social Business?
- Can the roles and processes defined in the ICU Model for the concrete ESN application area of internal crowdsourcing also be transferred to the (meta-)level of Social Business?
- What are the strengths and weaknesses of each perspective and how can they benefit each other?

2 The ICU Model

In order to build a basis for a comparative analysis of the ICU Model and the concept of Social Business, we will give a brief summary of the basic principles that have been presented in detail in chapter "Systematization Approach for the Development and Description of an Internal Crowdsourcing System" of this book.

Following the literature, we define IC as "an (a) IT-enabled (b) group activity based on an (c) open call for participation (d) in an enterprise" (Zuchowski et al. 2016). In order to understand the processes that constitute the ICU Model, we need to distinguish the different levels on which communication and decision-making regarding the process are taking place. In accordance with Ulbrich and Wedel (see chapter "Systematization Approach for the Development and Description of an Internal Crowdsourcing System"), three levels of communication can be distinguished:

- Macro Level: Overall Process

  On this level, the IC Process and its added value need to be justified and communicated at the decision level. It is important that the overall process can be aligned with the framework conditions of IC in the company as well as with the company's short-term and long-term goals. The communication target group here is the organization's management.
- Meso-Level: Campaign

  This is where the core piece of the IC Process takes place: The topic and the strategy are defined and communicated to the relevant sections of the organization. These processes are described as "invisible" as they are not open to the whole community.
- Micro Level" Community/Crowd

  On the micro level, the process phases happen in the community, which means among the employees. These are described as "visible" phases, as they include marketing and promotion processes as well as communication about the ongoing progress of the crowd activities.

2.1 Process and Roles of ICU

Within the ICU Model, a specification of the process phases, the process levels and the roles are given. With reference to the process model of Gassmann et al. (2013, 2017), Ulbrich and Wedel design a process sequence that can be applied to the specific ICU context. For them, seven steps are necessary in order to complete a cycle of ICU application. These are defined as follows:

1. Impetus
2. Decision
3. Conceptualization
4. Execution
5. Assessment
6. Exploitation
7. Feedback

First of all, an IC Process needs to start with an (1) impetus, which can be induced by any person working at any level of the organization. Ideas are addressed to the

Crowd Team (as described below), which then decides whether or not to consider the proposal as a following step. This (2) decision is made regarding the necessities within the organization and the availability, to take responsibility for the content ownership of the outcomes. If a proposal is accepted, a campaign is initiated, and, as a following and third step, a (3) campaign concept is designed. Within the concept, it is necessary to first define the aims and objectives, in order for the campaign to lead to a meaningful and useable outcome. Depending on the defined goals, the strategy is concretized, which includes a timetable, marketing strategy and the various implementation steps. Next, the planned process is (4) executed, which means that after the marketing strategy, the campaign itself is carried out under the supervision of a Campaign Team. Critical in that phase is IT management and content management. What is more, communication with the crowd/community is a crucial part in this phase. After implementation, the collected content needs (5) assessment, which means a proof of relevancy regarding the initially set goals. The output needs to be sorted and (6) exploited in regard to the initially set campaign aims. The outcome can also be taken as a starting point for a following campaign. Ultimately, in order to ensure the ongoing success of the campaign and of IC in general, a continuous and transparent communication throughout the whole campaign is a decisive aspect.

Crucial for a successful implementation of IC is a division and assignation of roles. In the ICU Research Project, an ICU Role Model was created, which is based on the *Scrum* procedure model but ultimately contains a bigger variety of roles. They can be divided into primary roles, the ones that are crucial for a successful implementation of an IC Process and secondary roles, which fulfil more supportive tasks. All representatives together make the so-called Campaign Team.

1. Crowd Master: Working on the macro level and meso-level, the Crowd Master is responsible for the general progress as well as the realization of the aims of the IC within the organization. Other functions are process monitoring and supporting the Campaign Owner in their task. The Crowd Master also has a connective key role as a representative of IC and promotes its implementation.
2. Campaign Owner: The Campaign Owner works at the meso-level and micro level and has a central function within the design and implementation of IC campaigns, connecting different perspectives and working closely with many others: Content Owner, Crowd-Technology Manager and the "Crowd". They have the responsibility for the overall design and execution, developing a campaign timetable, coordinating all activities and monitoring the entire process. Another central function of the Campaign Owner is to be disposable to the Crowd in case there are any questions or doubts. After ending the campaign, the Campaign Owner and the Crowd Master together make a preselection of the results.
3. Crowd-Technology Manager: As the Campaign Owner, the Crowd-Technology Manager works at the meso-level and micro level. They are responsible for the technological implementation of the campaign, as well as for designing and implementing the IT process and its various working phases (publishing the campaign, Crowdvoting, Crowdstorming, etc.). If there are any technological issues, the Crowd-Technology Manager can be contacted.

The secondary roles are crucial for the execution of the campaign, yet they do not have any directing functions. The Content Owner has the necessary expertise for the campaign topic and supports the Campaign Owner in developing the campaign design. Usually, but not necessarily, they are the one who initially proposed the campaign topic. Apart from the Content Owner, there are other supportive functions, called Secondary Counterparts. These roles are not fixed and can be represented by any expert that supports the Campaign Owner (e.g. the marketing department) or the Crowd-Technology Manager (e.g. the IT department) in the completion of their tasks. Finally, the role model describes the Crowd as the role that carries out the campaign tasks and brings in the content on which the results are based.

3 The Social Business Reference Model

In contrast to the ICU Model, as a process-oriented approach that supports a communication and innovation strategy within an enterprise, Social Business is a concept with a broader scope. As we defined earlier, the term "Social Business" basically describes the idea of implementing any kind of social technology within the enterprise to pursue a holistic business strategy for optimization with the aim of creating value in the meaning of social, ecological or economic benefit, from using network effects and removing collaboration barriers. While most of the enterprises nowadays use social technologies in their daily processes, the decision to use the technology with a strategic purpose requires a reflexion process. The Social Business reference model supports enterprises in the process of strategic reorganization.

3.1 Social Business Transformation Process

The first and major part of the Social Business reference model is the transformation process, illustrated in Fig. 2. It includes the Social Business maturity model. Overall, the process consists of four steps, which are outlined below.

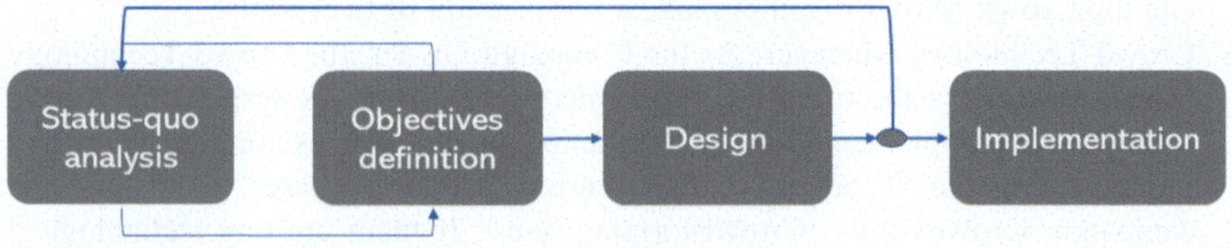

Fig. 2 Transformation process towards Social Business

3.1.1 Step 1: The Status Quo Analysis—Maturity Model

Unlike IC, which can be understood as an encapsulated innovation process, Social Business is a holistic corporate strategy. In the case of Social Business, it is therefore necessary to broaden the view when considering prerequisites and framework conditions. Thus, the starting point for the Social Business transformation is a comprehensive status quo analysis. For this comprehensive analysis, we refer to the Human-Technology-Organization concept (Ulrich 2013; Strohm and Ulrich 1997), which is commonly used to examine sociotechnical operating systems. All three levels of an enterprise have to be examined in terms of their maturity. The levels are reflected in the five dimensions of the maturity model.

In the first place, the degree to which social technologies, e.g. ESN or enterprise blogs, and Web 2.0 functionalities, like media sharing or bookmarking, fit in the Social Business infrastructure of a company and are integrated, e.g. by creating interfaces for existing software systems, is reflected in the dimension of Social Business Technology. But the mere existence of technologies does not make a Social Business. Hence, the extent to which the applied technologies are used for collaborative processes within the enterprise (and beyond) is another indicator for the maturity and, thus, another dimension of the model. Furthermore, the (non-) existence of roles, which may be informal, due to a bottom-up evolutionary process, or ultimately a determined relevant factor of a Social Business strategy, is also a maturity indicator. Next to these technical and organizational aspects, the empowerment of the individual, a key element of the Social Business concept, has to be regarded. Thus, the individual's awareness in regard to enterprise collaboration, their ability to understand the effectiveness and benefits of Social Business and also their competence to identify challenges for Social Business are of high relevance. The last dimension of the maturity model looks at skills employees need to acquire to work in a self-determined network and collaborative environment. A lack of individual awareness and skills may result in a need for corporate trainings or campaigns. A summarizing overview of the dimension and the defined levels of the Social Business maturity model is given in Table 1.

An analysis of the maturity reveals weak points that stand in the way of a successful transformation and impede the adoption of the Social Business strategy.

Table 1 Social Business maturity model

Dimension	Maturity level			
Awareness	Lacking	Problem awareness	Process awareness	Responsibility
Skills	No SB skills	Understanding	Participating	Networking
Roles	No SB roles	Marketing-driven	Informal	Dedicated
Collaboration	Ad hoc	Team-wide	Company-wide	Network
Social Business infrastructure	No social technology	External services	ESN	Social software integration

As an example, an enterprise may have put a lot of effort into developing a technological architecture that integrates all types of social software. A lack of awareness on the part of the employees, who are the key elements of network-based communication processes, can nevertheless stand in the way of successful collaboration and thus achievement of the company's goals.

3.1.2 Step 2: Objective Definition

Based on the status quo analysis, it is necessary to define objectives that take into account the overcoming of any identified weaknesses. The objective definition is essential in order to initiate the right processes like awareness campaigns but also to choose the right technological instruments and indicators to measure the success of the approach. It is not necessary to limit the number of objectives. Of course, an enterprise might want to achieve higher efficiency in regard to knowledge management and information dissemination between its employees and, at the same time, establish a sustainability culture within the business park by using network technology to support commuting and change the mobility behaviour of their employees (Zinke-Wehlmann and Friedrich 2019). Whatever the objectives of an enterprise might be, it must be understood that the transformation towards Social Business is not a linear process, but an iterative one. This means that the objectives might not be achieved in total in the first attempt. Also, it might be necessary to adopt or completely change single objectives due to changing framework conditions. Basically, three different types of objectives should be distinguished. These are:

- Optimization of the existing
  The existing or current status has a considerable potential and can be further optimized.
- Extension of the existing
  Progress can be built on existing solutions and can therefore be connected to functioning solutions.
- New solution:
  Something new has to be developed as previous solutions do not meet the new or existing target requirements.

3.1.3 Step 3: Design and Transformation Process

While the first two steps, status quo analysis and objective, can be understood as the theoretical foundation or initial phase, the design work begins in the third step. In the design phase, again, the three levels of individual, organization and technology should be considered.

From a technological point of view, it is crucial to design the network or social technology according to the formulated objectives and requirements. The elaboration of required technologies moreover includes an individualization of solutions (branding, CI, adaptation of technical workflows to processes in the organization). And Social Business design on a technological level also includes other relevant points, such as:

- Determination of adaptability and distribution of rights of the solution for the employees
- Definition and regular check of data protection guidelines, compliance and deletion rules
- Planning feedback channels and linking to corresponding responsibilities
- Examination of integration possibilities and evaluation of their suitability
- Determination of an implementation strategy

In addition, on the organizational level, certain framework conditions, such as work design (Koch 2008, p. 423) or an empowerment culture (Turban et al. 2016, p. 183; Winkler and Schulman 2012, p. 3), support the successful implementation of Social Business. In general, the employee is to be understood as a central element in Social Business, keeping the collaboration process running and carrying it with their actions. For this reason, organizations should establish an empowerment culture which, for example, involves the transfer of responsibility. Likewise, an open leadership style that does not restrict employees through hierarchical structures is supportive for Social Business (Schönbohm 2016, pp. 264). Further relevant aspects on the organizational level are:

- Development of roles, participation mechanisms and transparency
- Identification of actors and responsibilities
- Definition of new processes
- Formulation of communication strategy and guidelines
- Identification of knowledge flows
- Planning success control, development of key figures and parameters

On the individual level, it needs to be clear that the more networking and social interaction takes place, the more work becomes flexible, and the higher the level of self-determination is. It is therefore necessary to enable employees to act in a self-determined manner and freely within the social network in order to see themselves as the relevant stakeholders they are. This brings new requirements to the corporate culture but, at the same time, new chances for motivation and growth. Training or communication campaigns within the company may be necessary to sensitize employees to this new way of working. Next to these measures, Social Business design on the level of the individual means:

- Identification of competencies and establishment of training mechanisms
- Creation of incentives for active participation (e.g. feedback channels)
- Positive framing of employees and work groups
- Demonstration of advantages and benefits

This shows that the design and transformation process must not be limited to the technological perspective but has to take framework conditions and individual needs and requirements into consideration.

3.1.4 Step 4: Implementation

The final implementation is the operationalization of the Social Business concept that has been developed. At the same time, it can be the starting point for another iteration of the design process that might be initiated by another status quo analysis and an adaption or reformulation of objectives. The regular evaluation of the chosen approach, both from a management and stakeholder perspective, makes it possible to ensure the success of Social Business. The collection of feedback also makes it possible to identify undesirable developments at an early stage and to initiate suitable countermeasures.

3.2 *Social Business Roles*

Within the Social Business reference model, a Social Business role model was developed, as it became clear that, for a successful transformation, (new) roles and responsibilities need to be defined and assigned. The model is built on an empirical study that was run during the project and which included an analysis of job advertisements, expert interviews as well as a large-scale survey. It is important to point out that a role is not equivalent to a person or a job position. There were six roles included in this model:

- Social Business Manager
- Content Manager
- Developer
- Communication Manager
- Community Stakeholder
- Executive

These roles were defined more clearly by assigning responsibilities and functions which already had been specified at an earlier stage of the research:

The role with the most extensive responsibility is the *Social Business Manager's* role. The responsibilities are located in many different sections of the organization. First, they are responsible for creating a Social Business concept and strategy as well as channels for collaboration. Apart from that, a Social Business Manager is responsible for designing and carrying out trainings that are needed in the transformation. During the entire process, another task is to analyse and report on the progress as well as to take care of the ongoing supervision and optimization of the social network.

The *Content Manager* is, as the name says, responsible for the research of information in order to provide a continuous creation of new and interesting content. They also develop new digital formats to present this content.

In Social Business, the *Developer* role contains the development of a suitable infrastructure (system integration, direct communication) as well as the development and supervision of chat applications.

Another central role is represented by the *Communication Manager*, who is essential for the direct and overall communication regarding Social Business within the organization or company. They act as a contact point to where questions and doubts of the community can be directed. By doing that, and with the creation and supervision of feedback channels, the Communication Manager collects and reports the employees' needs. Generally, they plan and carry out communication campaigns and issue guidelines and best-practice reports for internal communication.

The *Community Stakeholder* role is not further defined. Community members have no directly assigned responsibilities. Instead they are allocated supportive duties when it comes to reporting their needs, promoting a supportive corporate culture, attending and collaborating in trainings and developing the employees' autonomy.

Finally, the *Executive's* role works more on the basis of the transformation. This person is responsible for promoting a supportive company culture as well as promoting and supporting the employees' autonomy. They also need to facilitate employee participation.

3.3 Guidelines and Good Practice

The piloting within the research project created the opportunity to collect a number of examples of good practice for Social Business. Some of these were:

- The early involvement of works councils in order to create transparency and gather broad requirements at an early stage.
- Consider the data protection requirements of all stakeholders (business internal and external) right from the start.
- Define dos and don'ts for the network communication.
- Set incentives for the users (work facilitation, mechanisms of peer recognition).
- Failure is part of the (iterative) process.
- Create an infrastructure for digital collaboration that really meets the stakeholders' needs (create feedback channels).
- Strengthen the self-organization of employees.
- Give employees space and allow self-determination.
- Defining goals at all levels.
- Think and execute processes more flexibly.
- Neglect instructions and provide support and structure.

Moreover, we strongly recommend the tenets of Hinchcliffe and Kim (2012) as well as the recommendations given by Haiba et al. (2014).

4 The Relationship Between the ICU Model and Social Business

If we consider the levels of the two concepts, we can see that IC can be understood as one iteration in the transformation process towards Social Business. If IC is a concrete setting for Social Business, then a Social Business reference model could represent a metamodel for the ICU Model. The present article will, in the following, describe a comparative analysis of both models presented to point out the strengths and weaknesses of both models and suggest how both can be improved by complementing each other.

First of all, the paper will start with a small classification of IC within Social Business. For this purpose, the following framework (Table 2) is suggested. Aspects that are affected by Internal Crowdsourcing are marked green.

Due to the width of their scopes, both concepts set a different focus. The ICU Model is a precise and process-oriented model that supports the strategic conceptualization and realization of various topics relevant to the company. The strength of ICU lies in its precisely defined process model, which guides enterprises through the whole crowdsourcing process. Moreover, the description of dedicated roles helps to quickly assign responsibilities and, thus, get the process rolling. However, precisely at this point, i.e. the start of the process, a weakness of the model becomes apparent. Other than the reference model for Social Business, the ICU Model does not define any prerequisites. The presented state-of-the-art ICU Model is a campaign-based process; it starts with an impulse targeted at a specific (existing) team. There are some preconditions for this process:

1. First of all, to generate any IC impulses, previously a critical mass of employees/managers has to be aware of the potentials of IC and handle the IC-IT.
2. Some kind of a technical basis has to be set to realize this process.
3. Thirdly, there needs to be a community structure (roles and responsibilities) that can be addressed by the crowd.
4. In order to assure a successful implementation, there has to be an existing management strategy for IC.

Thus, the proposed ICU Model does not focus on the strategic development of IC; it is about the practical implementation and change processes of IC. That might be one reason why the analysis of the conditions does not have a prominent place within the model. However, the very detailed development process for each campaign and the general role model is one of the strengths of the ICU Model. Obviously, the model is highly content-driven and goal-oriented—which means that not the foundation for IC is addressed, but rather the IC design and implementation. Accordingly, the process ends with the campaign.

While the ICU Model proposes a detailed design and implementation process, the SB concept mainly focuses on an analytical part and comes with general guidelines for design and implementation. The proposed process is a strategy to apply a high variation of Social Business applications within organizations. Thus, the main focus

Table 2 IC in the context of SB

<table>
<tr><td colspan="7">Social Business</td></tr>
<tr><td>Main business function</td><td>Innovation</td><td>Collaboration</td><td>Management</td><td>Knowledge management</td><td colspan="2">Training and learning</td></tr>
<tr><td>Effects on</td><td>Idea and content creation</td><td>Communication activities</td><td>Work organization</td><td>Knowledge exchange</td><td>Learning activities</td><td>Democratization of work</td></tr>
<tr><td>Process</td><td colspan="3">Campaign-based processes</td><td colspan="3">Continuous transformation processes</td></tr>
<tr><td>User</td><td colspan="2">Intra-organizational</td><td colspan="2">Customer-oriented</td><td colspan="2">Cross-organizational</td></tr>
<tr><td>Roles</td><td colspan="3">Determined (top-down)</td><td colspan="3">Evolved (bottom-up)</td></tr>
</table>

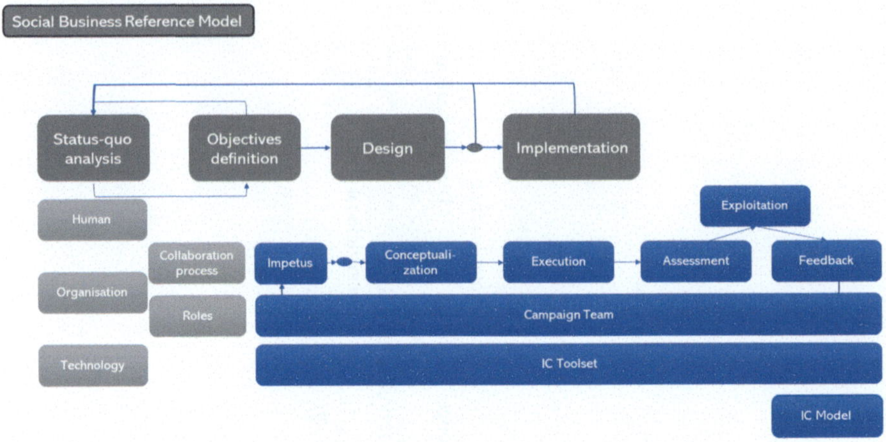

Fig. 3 Analytical comparison of Social Business reference model and ICU Model

of the SB concept lies in the development of enabling factors for digital collaborative processes based on specific starting conditions and strategic objectives (as well as operative objectives). The definition of objectives as well as the design of the transformative process mainly targets the three dimensions of the maturity model: human, organization and technology.

Obviously, both models meet at the design and implementation phase but on different levels. While the ICU Process is content-driven and seeks to define goals and practices for the concrete campaign, Social Business aims to design and implement the transformation to enable such processes like IC. Thus, the Social Business reference model builds the framework in which concrete steps on different application areas can be initiated and realized. Thus, it creates an environment for IC in general and the ICU Model in particular. The relationship between both models is illustrated in Fig. 3.

What can be seen is that the Social Business transformation process sets the preconditions to start a collaboration process—for example, the IC Process – and supports a structured processing by defining responsibilities and associated roles. In addition, by evaluating the human and technology dimension, the Social Business reference model enables organizations to define measures to develop required IC tools as well as create awareness and skills to finally get the ICU Process started.

4.1 Benefits for the ICU Model

The Social Business reference model propagates the idea that you never start a digital collaborative process on the greenfield and that it is also never enough to develop and implement an IT tool in order to be successful. Being successful always includes considering all affected levels: human, organization and technology. Within this view, an ICU Model is a resulting collaborative model—as an output of the design phase. And the implementation of such processes and roles means a successful implementation of Social Business. Thus, Social Business can support processes that enable IC within a company—creating awareness, skills and the technological basis and applying processes, like the ICU Reference Model.

4.2 Benefits for Social Business

The ICU Model impressively demonstrates the needs for defined collaboration processes and role models within the organization for the design and transformation process and validates the presented SB concept. Moreover, it also shows the importance of content-driven processes, besides the required transformation processes. Keeping the transformation also on content level and engaging the users is important, as well as to develop a communication strategy for all organizational and process levels, like the ICU Model does.

4.3 Roles and Processes

The design of new processes for novel digital collaboration depends on the character and goals of the aspired Social Business application—that is the reason why the Social Business transformation process does not give any further advice for reference processes. The question is whether the ICU Reference Model also provides a generic process for a campaign-based Social Business application. The ICU Process starts with an impulse or a crowd-based trigger. For campaign-based scenarios, this is not always the case. There are existing campaign-based applications that allow a campaign to be launched based on a time consideration (such as monthly campaigns for changing situations) or a certain event (e.g. social-learning activities). Thus, an impulse or a crowd-based trigger is not a strictly necessary but rather an optional process component. Nevertheless, it is clear that every campaign has to be designed—to set goals, communication measures as well as various implementation steps. These campaigns are mostly analysed but on different levels. It is not always good to measure and analyse all activities at management level, because this can create mistrust and feelings of surveillance. Much more productive might be feedback mechanisms for the users (and only for the users) – which can be part of the analysis. This is also valid for debriefings/feedback and exploitation. Even if the crowd or the community is very productive, it is very important to include the stakeholders in the activities, especially for analysis, exploitation and the debriefing.

Furthermore, the ICU Model indicates a communication strategy for different levels of stakeholders. While the Social Business reference model up to now has only referred to the formulation of a communication strategy and provides some guidelines (or principles), the IC Model can enhance this recommendation.

Table 3 Synergetic functions of ICU and SB roles

ICU	Synergetic function	Social Business
Crowd Master	• Representative of the Social Business activities • Develops the overall concept, including transformation activities • Supervises the community • Supports the Community Manager • Sets goals and realizes benchmarking	Social Business Manager
Campaign Owner	• Develops and implements content-driven processes • Has to design, carry, foster and coordinate the Social Business communication activities and projects • Monitors compliance with communication guidelines • Collects and reports community needs	Communication Manager
Technology Manager	• Is responsible for development of a suitable infrastructure	Developer
Content manager	• Creates and maintains contents • Fosters and maintains community-driven content creation • Integrates and distributes content	Content Manager
Crowd	• Brings in needs and information	Community Stakeholder

Communication and promotion are very important success factors; thus, the communication strategy is important on different levels (micro, meso, macro). However, digital collaboration and enterprise social networks also foster the democratization. This also involves the opportunity to soften hierarchies within the collaboration process because a crowd includes all actors within an organization on every level and each idea needs to be appreciated, whether it comes from the CEO or from a random employee. Even more, management and team or group leaders need to be active—it is also a success factor for cross-cutting collaborative activities (Schiller and Zinke-Wehlmann 2019, p. 49).

The third important insight of the presented comprehensive analysis results from the comparison of the developed role models. While, from the perspective of Social Business, a general distinction is made between community-driven roles and organizational roles, the ICU Model concentrates on formal roles by adapting agile schemas. This makes sense, because it seems to be very clear that IC is an agile process. However, the importance of informal roles needs to be considered, because of the digital power of influencers as well as trolls to affect the success or failure of the campaign. To enrich both models, the following fundamental functions of the developed roles will be described in detail (see Table 3).

5 Summary

To finalize the work, we will give a brief answer to our introduced research questions.

Table 4 Strengths and weaknesses of the compared models

	Social Business	ICU
Strength	• Generalized approach suitable for a lot of social applications • Highly focused on analysis and enabling of social application • Gives a framework	• Detailed processes and implementation advices for IC campaigns • Focused on holistic communication activities • Gives practical advices
Weakness	• High-level model, with high efforts to specify (not content-driven)	• Has some prerequisites

- How can processes and roles of ICU be interpreted in the context of Social Business?

  As described, both models work on different levels and prerequisites. From the authors' view, the ICU Model is one instance of Social Business, with the condition that the presented ICU roles, processes as well as some kind of technical infrastructure and a basic understanding (awareness and skills) are given within the organization applying ICU. Thus, with an assumed medium to high Social Business maturity, the ICU Model is a perfect reference to implement IC campaigns successfully.
- Can the roles and processes defined in the ICU Model for the concrete ESN application area of internal crowdsourcing also be transferred to the (meta-)level of Social Business?

  With the help of a small framework, parts of the ICU Process Model can be integrated into the Social Business context. One of the key results is the synergetic role understanding for both, the ICU and the Social Business model, presented above.
- What are the strengths and weaknesses of each perspective and how can they benefit each other (Table 4)?

6 Outlook

The work finally shows the strong connection between Internal Crowdsourcing and Social Business. Both are growing approaches in organizations—triggered by the New Work movement, democratic demands of the employees and the forces for organizations to win the war for talents as well as the economic benefits of digital collaborations. However, there is a need for organizations to develop and implement IC as well as general Social Business applications within their specific organizations, with specific goals. Mostly, these models imply a top-down approach, where management actively develops such digital collaboration schemas. In contrast to these approaches, a lot of initiatives develop from the bottom up. Most impressively, the Working Out Loud[1] scene demonstrates how to boost a democratic culture within an organization. Researchers need to be very aware of these movements, as well as the social impact these tools bring into an organization. The integration of Social Media into business processes is a double-edged sword, and all stakeholders need to be aware of these two edges. On the one edge, you have the principle of equality and that every voice matters, which strengthens the democratic character of work. On the other side, the possibility of bullying and novel forms of discrimination are also very relevant.

Acknowledgement The work leading to this publication was funded by the German Federal Ministry of Education and Research under grant number 02L15A070 (Project: SB:Digital). The authors would like to express their thanks for this funding.

References

Cook N (2017) Enterprise 2.0. Routledge, London

Enache MC, Sbughea C (2015) Social business models. arthra.ugal.ro

Fuchs-Kittowski F, Klassen N, Faust D, Einhaus J (2009) A comparative study on the use of Web 2.0 in enterprises. researchgate.net

Gassmann O, Friesike S, Häuselmann C (2013) Crowdsourcing: Eine kurze Einführung. In: Gassmann O (ed) Crowdsourcing.: Innovationsmanagement mit Schwarmintelligenz: interaktiv Ideen finden, kollektives Wissen effektiv nutzen, 2nd edn. Hanser, München

Gassmann O, Friesike S, Daiber M (2017) Crowdsourcing Methode und Prozess. In: Crowd Entrepreneurship (ed) Harald Pechlaner and Xenia-Isabel Poppe. Springer Fachmedien Wiesbaden, Wiesbaden, pp 23–39

Hackl B, Wagner M, Attmer L, Baumann D (2017) Große Veränderungen und Ansätze für eine Neue Welt der Arbeit. In: Hackl B, Wagner M, Attmer L, Baumann D (eds) New Work: Auf dem Weg zur neuen Arbeitswelt. Springer Fachmedien Wiesbaden, Wiesbaden, pp 1–46

Haiba M, El Bassiti L, Ajhoun R (2014) Toward enterprise 2.0: Opportunities, weaknesses and best practices. Int J Bus Manage Study (IJBMS) 1(3):108–113

Hinchcliffe D, Kim P (2012) Social business by design: transformative social media strategies for the connected company. John Wiley & Sons, Hoboken

Kaplan AM, Haenlein M (2010) Users of the world, unite! The challenges and opportunities of social media. Bus Horiz 53(1):59–68. https://doi.org/10.1016/j.bushor.2009.09.003

Kelly EL, Moen P (2007) Rethinking the clockwork of work: why schedule control may pay off at work and at home. Adv Dev Hum Resour 9(4):487–506. https://doi.org/10.1177/1523422307305489

Koch M (2008) CSCW and enterprise 2.0: towards an integrated perspective. BLED 2008 proceedings

Rauch M (2013) Best practices for using enterprise gamification to engage employees and customers. In: Hutchison D, Kanade T, Kittler J, Kleinberg JM, Mattern F, Mitchell JC, Naor M, Nierstrasz O, Rangan CP, Steffen B, Sudan M, Terzopoulos D, Tygar D, Vardi MY, Weikum G, Kurosu M (eds) *Human-computer interaction. Applications and services*. Springer, Berlin, pp 276–283

[1] https://workingoutloud.com/blog//a-recipe-for-changing-your-corporate-culture

Schiller C, Zinke-Wehlmann C (eds) (2019) Social Business: Studie über den Einsatz interner sozialer Netzwerke in Unternehmen. Fraunhofer Verlag, Stuttgart

Schönbohm R (2016) Enterprise Social Networks (ESN): Keimzelle agiler Unternehmen. In: Rossmann A, Stei G, Besch M (eds) Enterprise social networks. Springer Fachmedien Wiesbaden, Wiesbaden, pp 247–275

Shirish A, Boughzala I, Srivastava SC (2016) Adaptive use of social networking applications in contemporary organizations: Examining the motivations of Gen Y cohorts. Int J Inf Manage 36 (6):1111–1123. https://doi.org/10.1016/j.ijinfomgt.2016.04.002

Strohm O, Ulrich E (1997) Unternehmen arbeitspsychologisch bewerten. vdf, Hochschulverl. an der ETH Zürich, Zürich

Turban E, Bolloju N, Liang T-P (2011) Enterprise social networking: opportunities, adoption, and risk mitigation. J Organ Comput Electron Commer 21(3):202–220. https://doi.org/10.1080/10919392.2011.590109

Turban E, Strauss J, Lai L (2016) The social enterprise: from recruiting to problem solving and collaboration. In: Commerce S (ed) Efraim Turban, Judy Strauss and Linda Lai. Springer, Cham, pp 181–203

Ulrich E (2013) Arbeitssysteme als Soziotechnische Systeme – eine Erinnerung. J Psychologie des Alltagshandelns 6(1):4–12

We are social, and Hootsuite (2019) Global digital report 2019. https://wearesocial.com/global-digital-report-2019. Accessed 29 February 2020

Winkler C, Schulman SA (2012) Social business: an emerging Entrepreneurship research focus. Entrep Res J 2(4). https://doi.org/10.1515/2157-5665.1089

Zinke-Wehlmann C, Friedrich J (2019) Commute green! The potential of Enterprise social networks for ecological mobility concepts. In: Camarinha-Matos LM, Afsarmanesh H, Antonelli D (eds) Collaborative networks and digital transformation. Springer, Cham, pp 128–139

Zuchowski O, Posegga O, Schlagwein D, Fischbach K (2016) Internal crowdsourcing: conceptual framework, structured review, and research agenda. J Inf Technol 31(2):166–184. https://doi.org/10.1057/jit.2016.14

Dr. Christian Zinke-Wehlmann is the Leader of the Service and Knowledge Management group at the Institut für Angewandte Informatik (InfAI). He works in the field of sociotechnical support systems at the interface of work, technology and service systems and focuses on design-oriented research, human-technology interaction, digital collaboration platforms, empirical social research and the development of complex service systems.

Julia Friedrich holds a Master's Degree in the Study of Religions and Indology. She is a Research Associate at the InfAI's Service and Knowledge Management research group. Her primary research focus is the field of human-computer interaction. The results of her research which, besides Social Business, are mainly concerned with knowledge management and gamification, have been published in international journals and at conferences.

Vanita Römer is a Student Assistant at the Service and Knowledge Management group at InfAI. She brings first-hand experience in the implementation of social networks in enterprises and combines this with her expertise in the field of cultural studies.

The manufacturer's authorised representative in the EU is Springer Nature Customer Service Centre GmbH, Europaplatz 3, 69115 Heidelberg, Germany. If you have any concerns regarding our products, please contact ProductSafety@springernature.com

Printed and bound by CPI Group (UK) Ltd, Croydon, CR0 4YY
30/09/2026
02225452-0005